The Handbook of Urban Morphology

The Handbook of Urban Morphology

Karl Kropf

WILEY

ISBN 978-1-118-74769-8 (pbk)
ISBN 978-1-118-74773-5 (pdf)
ISBN 978-1-118-74782-7 (epub)
ISBN 978-1-118-74771-1 (O-bk)

A catalogue record for this book is available from the British Library.

Executive Commissioning Editor: Helen Castle
Project Editor: David Sassian
Assistant Editor: Calver Lezama

Page design by Artmedia
Cover design and page layouts by Artmedia
Printed in Italy by Printer Trento Srl
Cover photograph: gettyimages/richgreentea

To Emma

ACKNOWLEDGEMENTS

This book is the result of a long process of fermentation involving research and practice that has built on the work of many people. It started with the perception of a resemblance between the work of MRG Conzen on the one hand, and Gianfranco Caniggia and Gian Luigi Maffei on the other. The aim and hope has been to work through that resemblance and show that both were early expressions of a larger, coherent body of ideas, principles and logic. Any such body of knowledge is the product of a large group of people and there are many to whom this book owes a significant debt of both substance and gratitude. People on whose work I have drawn and whom I have also had the privilege and good fortune to meet and discuss their ideas include: MRG Conzen, Gianfranco Caniggia, Gian Luigi Maffei, Jeremy Whitehand, Anne Vernez Moudon, Sylvain Malfroy, Terry Slater, Jean Castex, Attilio Petruccioli, Giuseppe Strappa, Michael Conzen, Brenda Case Scheer, Nicola Marzot, Marco Maretto, Stephen Marshall, Philip Steadman and Alan Wilson. To these people the book owes its strengths, while I must take responsibility for any weaknesses.

If any book is the product of wider learning and experience I would also like to acknowledge and thank a number of people who have provided support and direction along the way. These include: Randy Hester and Paul Groth from the University of California at Berkeley for early inspiration, thoughtful discussions and promoting an open-minded and inquiring view of our surroundings; Mario Violich for stretching and expansive conversations, work and java; Joe Geller of Geller Associates and Josefina Yanguas Perez of Café Pamplona for support and insights into the balance between the practical and the aesthetic; the Joint Centre for Urban Design at Oxford Polytechnic (now Brookes University), in particular Ivor Samuels and Brian Goodey for their introduction to urban morphology and early advice, and Richard Hayward for instilling an intelligent political consciousness; John Kriken, Kathrin Moore and Steve Townsend and the rest of the Urban Design Team at Skidmore, Owings & Merrill, San Francisco, for an understanding of design quality and professionalism as well as a positive sense of teamwork; Ann and Alan Gore for unswerving loyalty, deep knowledge and aesthetic sense; Jeremy Whitehand for innumerable forms of support and encouragement combined with learning, experience and standards of scholarship; Mark Griffiths for countless discussions and fertile analogical thinking; Sylvain Malfroy for encouraging conceptual breadth and rigour as well as intellectual and linguistic nuance; Anne Vernez Moudon for bringing people together, supporting exchange and synthesis, and agreeing to disagree and carry on a very fruitful debate about plots and lots; Attilio Petruccioli for providing opportunities to air and explore ideas and for imparting diverse knowledge and pragmatic grace; John Marshall for his standards, learning and generosity of spirit; Brenda Case Scheer for vigorous, intelligent debate and getting things done; Michael Conzen for consistent encouragement and thoroughgoing, substantive discussions.

Particular recognition and thanks must go to Jeremy Whitehand, who supervised the PhD thesis that took forward the initial perception of similarity between the works of Conzen, Caniggia and Maffei. Over many years he has continued to show infinite patience while providing encouraging questions, input and advice.

Similarly, thanks to Ivor Samuels, who supervised the Master's dissertation that was the germ of this book and who also provided constructive critiques and irreplaceable opportunities for testing ideas and putting them into practice – along with Paul Lassus and the Asnières team.

I would also like to thank Michelle Thomas and Georgia Butina Watson of Oxford Brookes University for providing an environment that has allowed the ideas in the book to mature – fostering the fermentation process.

I am extremely grateful to Stephen George of Bath and North East Somerset Council for his enlightened approach and focused determination in commissioning the City of Bath Morphological Study. Needless to say, the study has made a significant contribution to the book both in terms of illustrations and testing.

Thanks are also due to Elin Børrud and Marius Grønning along with Gordana Marjanovic of the Department of Landscape Architecture and Spatial Planning at the Norwegian University of Life Sciences, for helping to further test the ideas in the book by providing the opportunity to present them to PhD students.

The book clearly benefits from the inclusion of the case studies and the significant thought, energy and expertise that went into them. I am therefore very grateful to the authors of the work for their kind permission to include the material and their cooperation and efforts in providing it.

Nigel Baker
Amy Burbidge
Yones Changalvaiee
Jon Cooper
Staël de Alvarenga Pereira Costa
Peter Ferguson
Eline Hanson
Christian Keim
Marco Maretto
Mei-Lin Su
Karin Schwabe Meneguetti
Vitor Oliveira
Paul Osmond
Marc Planard
The Municipality of Porto
The Municipality of Rennes
Philipp Rode
Brenda Case Scheer
Taz
Gil Thompson
Tolga Ünlü
Benjamin Vis

I owe an enormous debt of gratitude to Helen Castle of John Wiley for her efforts, perseverance and patience in commissioning the book and to Calver Lezama, Paul Sayer, Kirsten Nasdeo, David Sassian and rest of the Hoboken team for seeing it through.

Lastly, many, many thanks to my wife Emma and two daughters Imogen and Flavia for infinite patience and support.

Contents

Introduction

Slowing down the normative impulse

Cities exert an enormous pull on our imagination. We invest in them in innumerable ways, mentally, physically and financially. We expend great energy on them, and they are part of us as a species, essential to our very survival. Yet they also seem to grow and change by themselves, 'out of our control'. One way or another, we tend to demonstrate a strong sense of territory and drive to create places for our own needs. This is revealed in the rich diversity of places that reflect the different ways people choose to create environments conducive to life (figures 0.1–0.4).

One of the consequences of the deep-rooted connection we have with the places where we live is a **normative impulse** in our perceptions and interpretations of buildings and cities. When we talk about places, we tend to start with preferences and social judgements: beautiful, ugly, fascinating, good neighbourhood, bad neighbourhood, 'not the sort of place you'd want to live'.[1] Professionals are paid to have preferences, to say what is good or bad and whether or not it is worth investing in building.

Figure 0.1
The Atago district,
Minato, Tokyo

Figure 0.2
The Gros-Caillou
quartier, Paris

Figure 0.3
A typical street in the
Yanaka district, Tokyo

At a broader level, the normative impulse is an expression of the fundamentally political nature of creating and changing the built environment and is rooted in our territoriality. Occupying land and putting up buildings (and tearing them down) are political acts, whether by an external power or an internal group (figures 0.5 and 0.6). The preferences of those in control are the ones that are acted upon and expressed.

So if there is this almost irresistible, headlong rush toward the normative, how do we deal with the sense that cities appear out of our control, as if they have a mind of 'their' own? How do we work out who is in control if some things emerge not because of deliberate choice, but as a consequence of a number of individuals' choices about something else?

At the heart of this book is a desire to understand this apparent paradox. Underlying the desire to understand is the conviction that the normative impulse, while ultimately irresistible, can at least be slowed down. We can, with effort and the right tools, temporarily suspend the impulse long enough to examine what is really going on in the built environment. Yes, it is political, but it is not only political.

Figure 0.4
View down Rue Budé, Île Saint-Louis, Paris

Figure 0.5
Ruins of a Roman
villa in Carthage, the
Phoenician city destroyed
and then reoccupied by
the Romans only to be
destroyed again in the
Umayyad conquest. The
site of Carthage is now a
wealthy suburb of Tunis.

Figure 0.6
Aerial view of the
West End of Boston,
Massachusetts, after
demolitions in 1958–9
as part of the city-led
redevelopment project.
Redevelopment of this
kind in the US prompted
Jane Jacobs to write *The
Death and Life of Great
American Cities*.

There are three general sets of tools that provide the basis for suspending the impulse. The first is really just a simple single principle: all places are worthy of our attention. To fully understand what is going on, we have to remain open-minded (figures 0.7 and 0.8). If we exercise our preferences first, we preclude the opportunity to learn, and it is often the places that look the least promising that have the most to offer. We never know what problem we may face in the future and where we might find the most effective solutions.

The second set of tools is the sequence: analysis, comparison, synthesis. Comparison is fundamental to the way the brain works and overcomes the limitations of our isolation behind the veil of our senses. The strength of the methods of morphology that lie at the heart of this book is to make deliberate use of the comparative nature of our cognitive capacities to arrive at a richer understanding. That is, analysis on its own is not enough. We need to compare the results and collate them from different points of view.

The third set of tools is the sequence: description, evaluation, design. These represent a continuum between 'looking' and 'making'. Looking is not entirely passive but infused with values. A start, as a designer working with the built environment, is to see it as a 'material' or 'medium' for design with technical characteristics. We should be able to investigate and speak about the characteristics of different places in a non-normative way and then move on to why we think the places do or do not work – for particular purposes in particular circumstances. The question of whether or not you like a place should not determine your ability to understand how it is put together and works. Even if our interest is prompted initially by a qualitative judgement, however vague, we should be capable of taking a step back to work out what is going on and why the place generates that reaction in us. Once we understand how a place works and why we like it, we are then in a better position to use that knowledge and experience in design, and get better results.

The aim of the material set out in the three parts of this book is to show how to put these tools into practice. Part one of the book explores the core principles that define urban morphology as a field

Figure 0.7
A view of the city of
Bath from the south on
Beechen Cliff

and the different approaches taken in developing and applying those principles. It breaks down the phenomenon of urban form into different aspects for the purposes of investigation – a precursor to comparison and synthesis.

Part two brings together and explains the range of different specific methods used in urban morphological investigations. While the emphasis is on the practical techniques of desktop analysis, field survey and synthesis, these are necessarily tied back into the theoretical considerations that inform the methods and techniques.

Part three gives a survey of different applications of urban morphology, both to illustrate the ways it can be put to use and to shed further light on the ideas and techniques. Applications range from theoretical explorations of possible form and investigation of environmental performance to formulation of planning policy, development control and generation of designs.

Together the three parts can help in slowing down the normative impulse so that we can not only learn from our experience but learn to improve the way that we learn.

DEFINITION OF URBAN MORPHOLOGY AND AIM OF THIS BOOK

Urban morphology is the study of human settlements, their structure and the process of their formation and transformation. It is a specialist but wide-ranging interdisciplinary field contributing to both academic research and professional practice in the built environment. It is concerned with the form and structure of cities, towns and villages, the way that they grow and change and their characteristics as our habitat. Urban morphology provides a range of concepts and tools that articulate the different aspects and elements of urban form, the relations between them and our role as the agents who create, use and transform them. The aim of urban morphological research is to contribute to our understanding of the built environment as a complex physical object, a cultural artefact and quasi-natural phenomenon similar to language.

This book is intended as a practical manual of urban morphological analysis. It provides a guide to methods and techniques of analysis, working definitions, terms and concepts, and approaches to interpretation. It also sets out a number of brief case studies of specific applications to illustrate how urban morphology is used in practice.

At its most basic, urban morphology provides a consistent and rigorous descriptive language of the built environment. It is a set of tools that helps us to 'read' urban form and in turn to tell the story of individual cities, towns and villages. It helps us to understand what makes every city unique and sheds light on the diversity of human culture as expressed through the specific local forms of different human environments, both across the globe and historically. At the same time, urban morphology facilitates rigorous comparison of different places in order to see what they have in common and identify the regularities in the processes by which they emerge and evolve as human habitat and human creations. The information accumulated through morphological analysis lays the foundation for identifying and understanding the common features and regularities of the built environment.

In combination with a range of associated methods and techniques, urban morphology provides tools for investigating and assessing the performance of urban environments as a habitat and the suitability of different forms for different purposes and conditions. Urban morphological concepts provide a rigorous frame of reference for studies into aspects such as energy use, microclimate, acoustics, movement, land use and land value. The clear emphasis on human agency and the activities the built environment is intended to accommodate also mean that urban morphology offers a rigorous frame of reference for investigating cultural habits and undertaking social and cultural critique.

For the urban designer and planner, urban morphology provides basic background knowledge and understanding of the structure and developmental regularities of urban form. Morphological investigations provide significant insight into urban form as a medium for planning and design, and a deeper understanding of the relationships between different aspects such as physical form, use and control, the fine structure of urban form and the ways in which forms can be combined and configured to suit particular aims and purposes. They also provide a means for using the built environment as a design resource by seeing all forms – whether the product of top-down or bottom-up activity – as potential solutions for the future. Because of its focus on the **process** of formation and transformation, urban morphological

analysis gives the designer a rich understanding of the historical roots and significance of places and the potential to make positive use of the regularities and patterns of formation when planning new environments and settlements. For the same reasons, urban morphology is also a crucial tool for historic conservation and heritage protection.

Urban morphology is used within the following fields of study and professional practice, in no particular order:

- Geography
- Urban design
- City/town planning
- Architecture
- Heritage and building conservation
- Landscape architecture
- Archaeology
- Anthropology
- Urban history

Specific applications include:

- General description and explanation
  - Identifying the distinct parts of settlements and their historical origins to explain the settlements' character, diversity and complexity
  - Identifying the generative processes and developmental regularities of human settlements
- Environmental and operational performance
  - Investigating the physical composition of settlements and their characteristics in use for general explanatory purposes
  - Evaluating the environmental performance of urban form and identifying ways to improve performance
- Strategic planning and policy-making
  - Contributing to the evidence base for strategic growth of settlements, devising and supporting planning policy
- Design codes and guidance
  - Undertaking a detailed descriptive account of settlements and typological analysis for the purposes of development control and design guidance
- Character assessments and heritage management
  - Giving a detailed descriptive account of settlements, their historical character and significance for the purposes of heritage protection

- Urban design and masterplanning research and generation of proposals
  - Providing a comprehensive description of the context of a particular site as a foundation for design
  - Identifying potential design solutions within the existing built environment, in particular as produced by informal processes of production
- Historical/archaeological research and reconstruction
  - Reconstructing the state of settlements in different historical periods
- Social and cultural investigation and critique
  - Investigating the social and cultural origins and performance of urban form
  - Exploring the cultural differences of societies
  - Recording ethno-diversity
  - Interpreting social and cultural patterns
- Development and evolution of human settlements
  - Telling the story of the historical development of individual settlements
  - Investigating the evolution of ideas and diversification of urban form
  - Investigating the built environment as a complex adaptive system underpinned by quasi-natural generative and evolutionary processes

While all of these applications ultimately involve the exercise of judgement and preference along the continuum from 'looking' to 'making' – and so involve the operation of the normative impulse – they all benefit from the three sets of tools we can use to slow the impulse down.

They benefit from an openness to investigating all forms of settlement and from working through the steps of analysis-comparison-synthesis and description-evaluation-design. And while this in itself may be seen as a preference, it is built on the conviction that improving our understanding of phenomena in the built environment in an open way with methods that are open to scrutiny and improvement is the best way to deal with the political process of creating and transforming the built environment.

References
1   The tendency toward judgements is encapsulated and amplified in 'Judgmental Maps' <http://judgmentalmaps.com> started by American comedian Trent Gillaspie with an obvious play on Kevin Lynch's principle of the mental map. The alternative place names applied to the maps pick up on social biases and stereotypes that are at once and variously light-hearted, incisive and profane.

Figure 0.8
The Périphérique, the
multi-lane ring road
around the centre of Paris

PART 1

Principles

Core Concepts

As a distinct approach to describing, investigating, planning and creating the built environment, urban morphology is characterised by a number of core concepts. It starts with the recognition that the built environment, like language, has its roots in prehistory. Both language and the built environment have co-evolved with humans as a species. Both can therefore be characterised as quasi-natural. The concepts and methods used to probe and investigate the built environment are therefore not sensibly limited to those from only one or the other of the natural or cultural spheres. This is underlined by the often quoted point made by Jane Jacobs, that 'the city is a problem of organized complexity'.[1] There are regular patterns and an evident order to cities, but they are not simple. The source of the patterns is human action, but not necessarily the deliberate act of creating the pattern. Some patterns emerge as a consequence of a number of individuals acting semi-independently, seeking to achieve other aims.

The notion of **pattern** is itself one of the most central to urban morphology. In a number of ways, morphology is encapsulated in the idea of **patterns of relationship**. Whether the product of deliberate, individual design or the semi-coordinated actions of many people over time, the built environment displays a rich array of repeating arrangements or configurations of particular elements: networks of streets, patchworks of plots and combinations of rooms in a building. These repeating patterns are generally recognised as types of form. If the repeating patterns represent one of the principal ways in which the built environment is organised, one of the principal ways in which it is complex is that the types are themselves connected in a pattern: streets incorporate plots, which incorporate buildings. There is a pattern of patterns that extends into a **hierarchy** of interrelated forms. The patterns also extend in time. Forms are not given but are generated by a **process**: a sequence or pattern of events. There are thus three main concepts in addition to the general notion of pattern that distinguish the morphological approach to the built environment: process, type and hierarchy.

PROCESS

Forms in the built environment are the product of a sequence of more or less deliberate acts of building undertaken by groups and individual people. The act of building is fundamentally a **social and cultural process** involving an interaction between individuals or groups of people and their physical environment. The 'built environment' can be defined in very broad terms as the transformation of the environment through the application of human energy in the process of building.

Because the process involves humans both responding to and modifying their environment, the interacting parts in the process are interdependent and so most usefully seen not as independent, autonomous entities but distinct aspects of the same 'thing'. We co-evolve with the environment we create.

CONFIGURATION AND TYPE

The social process of formation is a kind of **cultural habit** that results in the replication or reproduction of artefacts. Examples are weaving, writing and software development. Artefacts are devised in response to the needs of the group at any given time and reproduced in sufficient numbers to meet those needs. The result is the reproduction of many examples of the same *kind* of thing. Thus we have many different kinds of fabric, stories and computer applications. The thing that makes any particular object recognisable – and also constitutes the basis for reproduction – is the way it is put together: the weave or pattern of a fabric, the narrative structure and style of the writing; the language, syntax and structure of the application. **The reproduction of artefacts using the same pattern or configuration of elements creates a type**. To draw a distinction, a configuration is an arrangement of parts and a type is a configuration that has a degree of **modularity** and **integration** as a cultural habit. The type is a configuration that is or has been actively reproduced. While each example of a type might be slightly different, the configuration remains the same. The configuration is the **set of relationships** between the parts that is reproduced and remains consistent irrespective of differences or changes in the specific nature of the individual parts of a particular artefact. A central principle that follows on from recognising types is the concept of **homology**, which in its most basic form is similarity of configuration and the attendant ability to distinguish similar kinds of part in different examples by their relation to other parts within the configuration. Parts in the same relative position are the same 'type of part'.

HIERARCHY

The social processes and cultural habits that generate the built environment have been operating for millennia. Over that time, simple elements have been combined to make complex artefacts that have in turn been combined to form still more complex artefacts. Single space shelters have been combined or subdivided to create complex buildings; buildings and enclosures have been combined to form plots; and plots and routes have come together to form streets. The result is not a chaotic lumping together of parts but the emergence of a composite artefact with distinct **levels of complexity**. The link between the levels is the relationship of part-to-whole, which forms a compositional hierarchy. In simple form the hierarchy includes:

• Streets
• Plots
• Buildings

The result is in effect a pattern of patterns that lies at the heart of the built environment as a form of organised complexity.

URBAN TISSUE

The combination of streets, plots and buildings seen as a composite, multi-level form is commonly and usefully referred to as **urban tissue**. Urban tissue is the principal constituent or unit of urban growth and transformation. It is the element that is combined to form the larger-scale structure of whole settlements and is composed of the smaller-scale elements that create places and local identity. Urban tissue is an embodiment of the cultural habits that produce it and serves as a reference for coordinating the full range of aspects that constitute urban form.

As will become clear throughout the book, urban tissue and the related concepts of the **plan unit** and **urban character area** are a principal focus of analysis. One of the main tasks of urban morphological analysis is to identify the distinct urban tissues that make up a settlement. Already this suggests that settlements are themselves composite forms but at a higher level of complexity than the constituent tissues. In essence, urban morphology seeks to take account of and understand that complexity using the conceptual tools of types, hierarchies and generative and transformative processes.

COMPARISON, SYNTHESIS AND THE COMPOSITE VIEW

A fundamental tool in identifying the patterns, types and processes of urban form is comparison. To a large extent, comparison is at the core of perception and operates at a subconscious level. To find repeating patterns within the plan drawing of a town, for example, we scan it with our eyes and compare one part with another. In essence, we set patterns 'side by side' and look for similarities and differences. When we recognise a pattern as an existing type we compare it with the examples we recall from previous experience.

The purpose of the analysis is not, however, simply to compile an exhaustive table of deracinated parts. To go beyond a mindless disassembly, comparison is also used as a basis for synthesis. A distinguishing feature of morphology is that it brings our intuitive comparative faculties into conscious application and takes advantage of the brain's capacity for parallel processing. The act of synthesis involves comparing one form with another, comparing the different component parts of a form and the relationships between parts, comparing the different stages in the development, growth and transformation of the forms as well as overlaying and comparing the information about different aspects of the form provided by different fields and disciplines. What emerges from the process is a fundamentally composite view that is conceptually more integrated and articulated as a whole than the view provided by any single perspective. The composite view is not a reductive abstraction but a synthesis based on experience that is developed through cycles of hypothesis, deduction and induction.

Urban morphology goes beyond a thematic analysis by recombining the aspects and elements identified in analysis in order to find characteristic patterns of relationship between the aspects and elements. The three basic steps in a morphological study are: **analysis**, **comparison** and **synthesis**. It is not just a matter of asking, what is the pattern of tissues or where are the nodes, but where are the nodes in relation to routes, landmarks and tissues and what are the relationships between structural characteristics and quantitative measures, say between route structure, areas and densities?

References

1   Jane Jacobs, *The Death and Life of Great American Cities*, Random House (New York), 1961. Print.

Origins and Approaches

In order to establish a broader sense of the core concepts, it is worth taking a brief look at their origin as a complementary set of ideas. The study of *form*, making use of the concepts of pattern, process, type and hierarchy, was initiated and referred to explicitly as *morphology* by Johann Wolfgang von Goethe, a writer, natural philosopher and artist working in the late 18th and early 19th centuries. The focus of Goethe's interest was the growth and metamorphosis of plants and animals, as well as works of art. Discontent with the classification of living forms as static entities, he wanted to understand the diversity of forms in terms of the underlying generative principles. Goethe saw everything as in a state of flux, in a process of becoming, making use of the German word 'Bildung', which translates variously as 'education', 'formation', 'creation', 'shape' and 'image'.[1] The underlying process of *learning* is therefore seen as a fundamental mechanism at play.

In terms of method, Goethe's approach to the objects of morphological investigation is:

> to understand their outwardly visible and tangible parts in relation to one another, to lay hold of them as indicia of the inner parts, and thus, in contemplation, to acquire a degree of mastery over the whole.[2]

'The morphological method is thus a combination of careful empirical observation and a deeper intuition into the idea that guides the pattern of changes over time as an organism interacts with its environment.'[3]

The core principles of morphology are thus the notions of a formative/transformative process and the relative positions or configuration of the parts making up the whole form as it grows and changes. One of Goethe's significant contributions to plant morphology was to see the diverse parts of plants as transformations of the rudimentary leaf and to distinguish and define the different parts by their relative position within the whole plant.

This principle was carried over into Goethe's work on colour theory,[4] in which he recognised the importance of context in our interpretation of particular colours. A given colour (that is, a fixed frequency of light) can appear to an observer as different colours depending on the colours that surround it. Similarly, a form is in part defined by its position within a larger whole and a given object might be classified in different ways depending on its position.

From its roots in Goethe's initial investigations, morphology is now an established sub-discipline in a number of different fields including biology, geology and linguistics. In all these fields, morphology is broadly concerned with identifying and classifying the objects of study in terms of their shape, form and internal structure, as well as seeking to understand how and why the objects take the form they do – whether organisms, geological formations or verbal forms of expression. Again, the common core concepts are pattern and structure, process of formation, type and hierarchy.

APPROACHES TO *URBAN* MORPHOLOGY

While the seminal work of Goethe provides a distinct origin for *morphology* as used in different fields, the subject of *urban* morphology as it stands today does not have a single source. Rather, it not only draws on Goethe's original conception and its application in different fields, but urban morphology has itself emerged independently in different academic and professional disciplines, in particular the fields of geography, architecture and urbanism. Because this book is intended as an operational manual, the aim here is not to provide an exhaustive account of the origins of urban morphology, but to point out its roots in order to characterise it as a way of thinking about, investigating and working with the built environment as a medium of planning and design. In the same way that we seek to understand built form in terms of its process of formation, we can seek to understand urban morphology in terms of the way it has developed as a discipline or field of study.

Today there are four broad approaches to urban morphology, each focusing on slightly different aspects of urban form and using different methods and tools.

- Typo-morphological
- Configurational
- Historico-geographical
- Spatial analytical

The typo-morphological and configurational approaches have origins in the fields of architecture and urbanism and the historico-geographical and spatial analytical have come out of the field of geography.

There are three important associated approaches to the study of urban form that are not explicitly morphological but similar to and complement morphological approaches. These are:

- Townscape
- City image analysis
- Overlay analysis and geographic information systems

Another area of research in which morphological principles are being applied and developed is the field of urban ecology.

The following sketch summaries seek to characterise the approaches mainly as a guide or signpost pointing in the direction of further reading and exploration rather than any kind of critical assessment or analysis. The summaries are necessarily simplified and put together different sources on the basis of their main core common features without highlighting what may be significant differences. The sources are best explored in the original works. Lists of sources for further reading can be found at the end of the book.

THE TYPO-MORPHOLOGICAL APPROACH

The typo-morphological approach to urban morphology, sometimes referred to as *process typology,* developed within the context of architectural practice and education starting in the first half of the 20th century, predominantly in Italy and France.[5] The approach seeks to inform architectural and urban proposals with a critical understanding of the built environment as a context for development by examining its detailed structure and the historical process of its formation. It also seeks to use an understanding of the formative processes and evolution of building types to inform specific design proposals.

Fundamental to the approach are the concepts of the multi-level hierarchical structure of built form and the typological process. The generic typological process is characterised broadly as 'derivation', an essentially cultural evolutionary process. All forms are derived from the experience and interpretation of previous forms in a recursive process. Types are identified as cultural entities at each of the levels in the hierarchy in all three dimensions. Diversification

occurs because different local processes lead to distinct local forms. The core ideas of the approach as developed in the early stages have been taken in a number of different directions and applied to a range of specific issues from archaeological investigations to contemporary social critique. The typo-morphological approach is widely diffused in architectural education and practice in Europe and Latin America.

THE CONFIGURATIONAL APPROACH

The ideas that define the configurational approach emerged out of the mathematical and quantitative investigations of architectural and urban form in the 1960s, principally in the UK. Inspired by the allometric studies of D'Arcy Thompson,[6] the analytical potential of Euler's graph theory[7] and topology, among many other sources, the common feature is the focus on the geometric and topological attributes of built form with the aim of understanding the interrelationships between different attributes and measures, the ways in which different spatial configurations affect the use of urban environments and buildings, as well as seeking to predict and improve function and performance. In addition to topological and quantitative methods, the approach also uses combinatorial analysis and the idea of possible forms to understand the association of factors that lead to the selection of configurations realised on the ground.

The deeper underlying morphological principles that bind the approach together are the notion of configuration itself, rooted in the gestalt principle that elements can be defined by their position within a whole; the interdependence of geometric parameters that is exposed by the exploration of different possible forms and configurations and in the process of growth; the idea that spatial configurations emerge as the result of a generative process; and that global structure arises from the operation of local generative rules.

THE HISTORICO-GEOGRAPHICAL APPROACH

The historico-geographical approach to urban morphology seeks to explain the geographical structure, patterns and character of human settlements through a systematic analysis of their constituent elements and development through time. The approach has its roots in the early-19th-century efforts to identify and explain the diversity of places across the globe, such as von Humboldt's holistic approach to geography[8] and the subsequent development of the ideas of the *cultural landscape* and urban geography. One of the principal methods of the approach is a detailed analysis of the chronological sequence of town plans with the systematic distinction of a hierarchy of plan element complexes including the street pattern, plot pattern and building pattern. In essence, changes are traced through time to effectively animate the development process.

The aim of the analysis is to explain the complex, composite nature of settlements in terms of the underlying long-term, short-term and repeating morphogenetic processes at different levels in the hierarchy of elements. In addition to identifying the various processes, this involves regionalisation of the town plan and association of the morphogenetic changes with the social and economic processes that drive them.

THE SPATIAL ANALYTICAL APPROACH

Growing out of initial analytical ideas such as von Thünen's economic geography[9] and the dynamic models of urban structure of Burgess and Hoyt,[10] the spatial analytical approach to urban morphology focuses primarily on human activity as sets of spatial interactions. The approach makes use of a range of primarily quantitative methods such as mathematical models, in particular entropy-based, fractal and other non-linear forms, agent-based models, cellular automata, graph theory and network analysis.

Central to the spatial analytical approach is the view that cities are complex adaptive systems involving a dynamic, iterative and reciprocal relationship between social and economic interactions and the physical form of settlements. Thus while there is a focus on patterns of interaction and networks such as transport, social and economic exchange and material, energy and information flows, those patterns are seen as both giving rise to and being fundamentally affected by the physical form of cities.

The aim of the approach is to uncover the principles and relationships underlying the dynamics of the system, such as the scaling laws of growth, and begin to identify the relationships between the principles to generate a more comprehensive picture. As with the other approaches, the core morphological principles are the definition and differentiation of elements by their position within a larger structure or configuration and the conception of form and structure being the product of a generative process of formation and transformation.

CITY IMAGE, TOWNSCAPE, PATTERNS AND LAYERS

The terms city image, townscape, patterns and layers identify a more heterogeneous group of approaches to the investigation, interpretation and design of urban form that individually complement the more specifically urban morphological methods. They are important to include because they address in more detail some of the aspects identified in the next section and so provide additional depth to the composite image of human settlements.

A common thread running through these approaches is that for the most part they emerged in response to the physical and social results of early to mid-20th-century planning and urbanism. Though prompted by the specific issues of their time, the methods that were developed remain valid and robust when applied to a very wide range of forms and circumstances and are of great general value.

The ideas of city image and townscape complement the other approaches by incorporating our perception of the built environment as directly experienced from the ground. The idea of a pattern language provides a framework for translating the direct experience of the patterns of relationship that constitute a place into design solutions. Similarly, the overlay method can be used as both a planning and design tool and to build up the composite image and facilitate identification of correlations, associations and patterns of interaction.

URBAN ECOLOGY

Urban ecology is a field that emerged in the 1970s and has become more active over the last 20 to 25 years. As its name suggests, the discipline investigates the urban environment and all its inhabitants as an ecological system. Urban morphology serves as an ancillary discipline to urban ecology, providing principles and methods that aid in distinguishing different 'ecological patches' within the urban environment. At the same time, the work done in the field has contributed to urban morphological thinking, enriching the conception of interactions within cities and in particular highlighting the role of vegetation in the urban environment.

THE RELATIONSHIP BETWEEN THE APPROACHES

As this very brief summary suggests, the different approaches share the basic morphological principles of seeing form in terms of configurations, and seeing those configurations as the product of a generative process involving interactions between humans and their environment. Further common points are the distinction of a compositional hierarchy and distinct levels of complexity in the structure of built form, and distinguishing parts in terms of their position within a configuration. As will be explored further, the hierarchical structure provides a means of at least beginning to see how the different approaches fit together in more specific and formal terms. Identifying those relationships will help to show that far from being in any way mutually exclusive, the different approaches are complementary.

To paraphrase and adapt Goethe's characterisation of morphology generally,[11] urban morphology may be regarded both as an independent and as an auxiliary discipline. It has developed its own concepts and methods and at the same time it draws on urban geography, urban and architectural history, archaeology and anthropology as well as architecture, urbanism, typology, configurational and topological analysis from which it extracts phenomena for its own purposes. Urban morphology necessarily draws on the work of allied fields and disciplines and contributes to them.

THE FOCUS OF THIS HANDBOOK

Having set out the range of approaches that fall within the remit of urban morphology, it is important immediately to make clear that this handbook openly aims to treat only a small part of the activities entailed by those approaches. There are, for example, many sources that provide detailed treatments of the principles and methods of configurational and spatial analysis. The same is not true for the typo-morphological and historico-geographical methods. A principal motivation for compiling this handbook was to fill that void by drawing together in a single source the methods that have been developed by many authors over a number of years and in different places. A further motivation is to begin to establish a basis for integrating the range of different approaches as a set of distinct but complementary methods to help us develop a richer, more broadly based understanding of the diversity and complexity of urban form.

Most fundamentally, the aim of this book is to show how the basic concepts can be put into **practice** in a range of different applications. It is a how-to manual for urban morphological analysis

focused on the central concept of **urban tissue**. The reach of the book is deliberately limited to the core methods of analysis of tissue that can provide the foundation for more extended and detailed techniques and applications. The aim is not to provide wide, exhaustive coverage but to consolidate the central, common methods.

References

1   Johann Wolfgang von Goethe, *Goethe's Botanical Writings*, trans Bertha Mueller, University of Hawaii Press (Honolulu), 1952, p 23. Print.

2   Ibid.

3   Anthony K Jensen, 'Johann Wolfgang von Goethe | Internet Encyclopedia of Philosophy', http://www.iep.utm.edu/goethe/, accessed 25 March 2016.

4   Johann Wolfgang von Goethe, *Theory of Colours*, Courier Corporation (North Chelmsford, MA), 2012. Print.

5   Key initial works are those of Gustavo Giovannoni and Pierre Lavedan: Gustavo Giovannoni, 'Il "Diradamento Edilizio" dei Vecchi Centri', *Nuova Antologia* 997 (1913): 53–76. Print.

-   Pierre Lavedan, *Qu'est-ce que l'Urbanisme?*, Henri Laurens (Paris), 1926. Print.

6   D'Arcy Wentworth Thompson, *On Growth and Form*, Cambridge University Press (Cambridge), 1917. Print.

7   Leonhard Euler, 'Solutio Problematis ad Geometriam Situs Pertinentis or The Seven Bridges of Königsberg', *Graph Theory 1736–1936*, NL Biggs, EK Lloyd and RJ Wilson (eds), Oxford University Press (Oxford), 1976. Print.

8   Alexander von Humboldt, *Aspects of Nature in Different Lands and Different Climates*, Lea and Blanchard (Philadelphia), 1850. Print.

9   Johann Heinrich von Thünen, *Von Thünen's Isolated State*, Peter Hall (ed), trans Carla M Wartenberg, Pergamon Press (Oxford), 1966. Print.

10 Homer Hoyt, *The Structure and Growth of Residential Neighborhoods in American Cities*, Federal Housing Administration (Washington, DC), 1939. Print.

-   Robert E Park and Ernest W Burgess, *The City*, University of Chicago Press (Chicago), 1925. Print.

11 Goethe, *Goethe's Botanical Writings*.

Aspects of Urban Form

Human settlements, from farmsteads and villages, to towns, cities and metropolitan regions, present a density and richness of subjects for investigation hard to find in any other human production. That richness is evident not only in terms of the huge diversity of different settlements and the depth of their individual complexity, but also in terms of the different aspects that they present.

We have co-evolved with our settlements. They are therefore intricately connected with our daily lives and the lives and livelihoods of whole populations. Settlements are a physical manifestation of the social structures and relationships that are necessary for their creation in the first place, and the complementary and sometimes conflicting activities that they support. By the same token, settlements are a manifestation of our interaction with the environment and the ongoing transformation of the environment that supports our life on the planet. We therefore routinely distinguish the social, economic and environmental dimensions of towns and cities in an effort to understand how they come about and how they work. And if we acknowledge that human settlements are diverse and multi-faceted, we should not be seduced by the superficial attractions of a single perspective. Rather, the acknowledgement should place us at the crossroads where many routes radiate out to different points of view.

The composite view of morphology is both a product of the multi-faceted nature of the built environment and a deliberate effort to take account of that nature, coordinating information about the different aspects of settlements around the unifying aspect of physical form. Kevin Lynch took a similar view when he likened theories of city form to the branches of a tree, but qualified the analogy, stating that, 'unlike the branches of trees we know, they should not diverge. They should interconnect and support each other at many points. A comprehensive theory of cities would be a mat of vegetation, and some day the branches will no longer exist in separate form'.[1]

In brief, urban form has many different interrelated aspects.

The core aspects are rooted in the definition of the built environment: the transformation of natural features by the deliberate application of human energy to suit human needs and purposes.

The core aspects are thus:

- The natural environment
- Human activities, including movement and occupation of land
- The physical products of transformation, including both built and planted features

Kevin Lynch usefully extends the definition of urban form to include:[2]

- The spatial arrangement of persons doing things
- The resulting spatial flows of persons, goods and information
- The physical features which modify space in a way significant to those actions
  - enclosures
  - surfaces
  - channels
  - ambiences
  - objects
- Cyclical and secular changes in those spatial distributions
- The control of space
- The perception of all these elements

The aspects identified by Lynch can be defined on a more formal basis in terms of the spatial relations of physical form, the relations between humans and built form and the temporal relations that make up the processes of formation and transformation.

The fundamental aspects based on the spatial relations between physical objects include:

- Natural environment
- Built environment

The aspects defined in terms of the relationships between humans and built form include:

- Use or activities, including movement
- Control (for example, ownership, governmental authority)
- Social and economic drivers
- Intention and design
- Construction
- Perception

Aspects defined in terms of temporal relations include:

- Natural flows of resources
- Human-induced flows of resources
- Change, historical development and evolution

The aspects are essentially broad headings that aid the systematic investigation of a place. Usefully, they also correspond to elements and steps in the process of formation and transformation. The aspects can also be seen as the features or attributes we can use to describe and distinguish different places. Each place is a distinct and unique combination of the different aspects. For any particular application it may be that only some of the aspects will be relevant. Most frequently, the core aspects of natural environment, built form and use are supplemented by social and economic drivers, historical development and perception. In all cases, principally for reasons of time and budgetary constraints, the information about the aspects will be a partial selection of what might be collected.

The following sketch definitions are intended to highlight only the most relevant attributes of the aspects for applications of urban morphological analysis. They are set out here in a sequence that helps to build up a picture of their interrelationships in the process of formation and transformation. Depending on the aims of a given project, the order in which the aspects are addressed in the actual process of analysis may differ.

NATURAL ENVIRONMENT

The **natural environment** is the combination of natural physical features making up a place and the patterns of their relationships. The natural environment is the inescapable context within and out of which urban form is necessarily created. Ultimately, urban form is a transformation of the natural environment and the product of a human response to specific conditions in a particular place. Therefore, to understand the form it is necessary to understand those conditions. The question to be asked is, to what extent is the shape and structure of urban form an adaptive response to the natural environment that takes advantage of the particular substances and patterns of the place for human purposes?

The principal elements of the natural environment that we use and to which we respond include:

- Geology, minerals and soils
- Landform (topography)
- Water features, including ground water (hydrology)
- Plant and animal communities

Climate is usefully separated into the general category of natural resource flows discussed in more detail below.

In many cases, what might be considered the natural environment has already been significantly

Figure 3.1
The context for and substance out of which the built environment is made is the natural environment, summarised in the elements of geology, topography, hydrology, flora, fauna and climate.

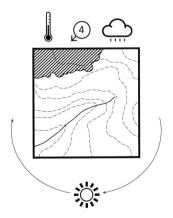

modified by humans, most obviously in the case of agricultural landscapes. Cultivated land is just as essential to urban settlement as routes and buildings — all are the product of humans applying energy to transform the natural environment. The natural and built environments are therefore not spatially separate but coextensive. The *difference* between them is a variable **gradient of transformation**. The difference between **urban** and **rural** areas is thus strictly one of degree in the density and intensity of hard built features.

In practice, the distinction is generally represented by defining different areas with a linear boundary. The distinction between rural and urban areas, for example, is often formally defined and mapped for the purposes of policy and public administration. While various definitions may be used, the maps produced can be a useful starting point for morphological analysis. Whatever specific definition is used, it should be clearly stated and used consistently.

USE

The aspect of **use** refers to the human activities that give rise to and are accommodated by particular elements of the built environment. Use is in effect the generator of the built environment but always in response to the specific conditions presented by the environment. Use and the built environment are interdependent and diversity in one gives rises to diversity in the other. Use is therefore fundamental to understanding the structure and character of places. We understand built form at a primary level in relation to its use. If we come across an unfamiliar form – some visible sign of order in the built environment – we usually ask, what is that for, what activity does/ did it accommodate? The basic units of use are the **agent**, the **form** and the **act** or **activity**.

Importantly, however, the relationship between form and use is flexible. A given form such as a building can be used in many different ways and a given activity such as 'working' or 'residing' can

Figure 3.2
This view of Castelvecchio Calvisio, Abruzzo, illustrates that the difference between the natural and built environments is not a binary opposition but best described as a gradient of transformation even if in practice it is necessary to draw distinct boundary lines between the built and the unbuilt.

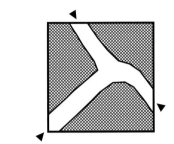

(a)

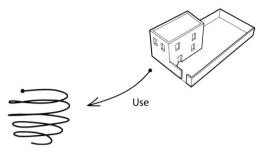

Use

Repeated use over time in the context of
(b) changing needs and environment

be accommodated by a number of different forms.
To a greater or lesser extent, active use involves
an exploration of the possibilities presented by the
form. Use, as a process, is divergent. The results
of the exploration can actively contribute to the
generation of new forms.

GENERIC FUNCTION
One of the most fundamental human activities
is movement. We are mobile creatures and the
characteristics of the way we move lead to the
generation of essentially linear forms within the
environment: tracks, paths, streets and corridors
among many others. As explored in Section
6, human movement and patterns of routes
historically precede settlement: nomadic ways
of life/habits preceded sedentary habits. The
formation of settlements therefore occurs within
the context of an established pattern of routes
and involves the creation of new routes to provide
access to new buildings.

From this observation it is possible and
fruitful to distinguish two broad categories of
generic function: movement and occupation.
As with the relation between form and use more
generally, the distinction between movement
and occupation is not hard and fast. Movement
necessarily occurs in occupation space and
movement space can be used for a range of

different activities that take place in a limited area
and constitute a kind of occupation.

MOVEMENT
Movement as an activity is generally divided by
mode, each with its own particular formal/physical
requirements and characteristics.

- Road
    - pedestrian
    - vehicular
    - cycle
- Water
- Rail
- Air

While the various forms of configurational and
network analysis are applied to the pattern of
routes and infrastructure as physical forms,
analysis of movement per se focuses on the act
of movement. The elements of analysis are thus
mode, speed, quantity or level of movement,
agent behaviour and the psychological/behavioural
parameters that contribute to measures such as
route or junction capacity.

OCCUPATION
The distribution and relative position of different
activities within a settlement constitute a

Figure 3.3
**Use refers to the
relationship of *purpose*
between human activities
and the objects of the
built environment that
facilitate the activities.
A basic distinction of
use arises with human
mobility and the resulting
differentiation of areas
that accommodate
the *generic functions*
of movement and
occupation (a). In terms
of an ongoing process,
use can be characterised
as a spiral of cyclical but
changing interactions
and mutual modifications
between activities and
the environment (b).**

fundamental dimension of the settlement's form and structure as well as driving the generation of different specific physical forms. Human activity is, however, notoriously diffuse, ambiguous and mutable as an object for classification and association with built form. What may be employment for one person can be leisure for another, paid office work is commonly carried out in the home and domestic chores can be seen as a productive economic activity. There is also significant variation within and across cultures. Given this fuzziness and diversity, the starting point in seeking to include the aspect of use in the composite view of urban form is to focus first on the **patterns of difference** between activities, the **clustering** of instances of the same or similar kinds of activity and typical **associations and interactions** between activities. The fundamental requirement is that whatever classification is used to distinguish different activities should be applied consistently.

The aim of the distinctions should be to capture the pattern of relationships and structure of activities within a settlement and their associations with different specific forms. A common underlying pattern is the diurnal cycle and the distinction of places for sleeping and waking activities – thus the distinction between residential and non-residential areas or buildings.

Other basic activities that might form the basis for distinguishing uses include:

- Production
- Exchange
- Social gathering

Such distinctions are the basis for the categories generally used within formal land-use planning systems. For example, the Use Classes Order in UK planning law includes four general classes,

- Retail
- Commercial/Industrial
- Residential
- Institutional

These are further subdivided into subclasses and there is also a catch-all, *sui generis* class. Other systems use a similar range of use categories.

Figure 3.4
George Street, Bath, illustrates both the clear distinction between movement and occupation spaces and the fundamental flexibility of the relationship between use and form. The footway allows for both movement and occupation without any physical differentiation, and the buildings accommodate a range of different specific uses.

SERVICING

The distinction made by architect Louis Kahn between served and servant spaces highlights a third generic function, which is servicing. This includes the circulation or movement of fluids, gases, electricity and heat/cold as well as storage and accommodation of various forms of equipment. The corresponding servant spaces include cisterns, *bâdgir/malqaf,* chimneys, flues, vents, ducts, plenums, cupboards, closets, plant rooms etc.

USE PATTERNS AND NEIGHBOURHOOD STRUCTURE

The distribution and relative positions of different uses within a settlement were the subject of some of the earliest morphological studies. These and subsequent analyses show there is a general tendency for some activities such as exchange and social gathering to create or locate in **clusters, centres** or **poles** to serve a **catchment** or **field**. Other uses tend to locate at the **periphery** or **fringe**, such as productive or institutional uses. Depending on specific circumstances, these uses can aggregate in a cyclical **fringe formation process** to form more or less well-defined patches, rings and corridors.

Larger settlements can form a number of centres or poles, in some cases with a main centre and subsidiary local sub-centres or a hierarchy of centres. Repeating patterns of associated uses, for example retail, education, worship, community and recreational facilities, can constitute sub-centres and may correlate with the more loosely defined and socially based unit of the **neighbourhood**. A starting point for identifying the neighbourhood structure of a settlement is therefore to locate the sub-centres and repeating patterns of associated uses.

SOCIAL AND ECONOMIC DRIVERS

If we are seeking to improve our understanding of settlements and apply that understanding in an intelligent way, then our descriptions, explanations and applications will have greater clarity and make more sense if they are situated within a definite context. Isolated concepts are more difficult to understand than concepts that are tied together in a network of ideas. The human activities that create and make use of the built environment necessarily take place within a wider context of social, political and economic activities. That is to say, creating and using the built environment are only part of a wider set of activities that make up a culture, so, in the same way that we seek to understand a given element of the built environment in terms of its position within a larger whole, we seek to understand the use and creation of the built environment in terms of its position within the culture of which they are a part.

At the general level, building up a picture of the social and economic context involves identifying the **values**, **ideas** and **intentions** typical of the wider population and the resulting **cultural habits, structures and technology** that they generate.

CONTROL

Control refers broadly to the ability to determine how and by whom a particular area of land is used. It involves a relationship between an 'agent' – an individual person or group that exercises the control – on the one hand, and the area of land that is controlled on the other. In general the relationship between the two is established either by physical occupation or social convention. There are thus different types and degrees of control, including:

- Occupation
- Leasehold/Rental
- Ownership
- Regulation (for example, planning controls, criminal law)
- Criminal coercion (for example, 'protection rackets')
- Sovereignty

Figure 3.5
Control is a socially established relationship between a person or group and a particular object or area of land, often in the form of ownership. The patterns of control, such as property boundaries established with the initial formation of a settlement, have a significant and long-lasting influence on the specific configuration and character of the built form.

There are also different types of agent:

- Individual
- Family
- Informal group
- Formal, private corporate entity
- Public body (agency, department etc)
- Government/sovereign

In systems that recognise private property, the right to build generally requires ownership or permission from an owner as well as permission from local government or a planning authority. In this context, the property holding or parcel thus tends to be the unit of building activity.

In such circumstances, the underlying pattern of control is a significant determinant of the physical built form that might arise in a given location and how it might be transformed over time. In effect, patterns of multiple ownership become much more resistant to change than a single or no owner.

Given the resistance of multiple ownership to change, the initial act of subdividing land has one of the most profound effects of any stage in the process of development. Once set out and made manifest in physical form, the patterns can remain in place for millennia.

BUILT FORM

As noted above, the built environment is essentially embedded within the natural environment. Built form is made up of those physical elements in the environment that have been transformed by humans and the relationships between them. The task of specifying what makes up the physical form of the built environment is therefore one of selecting out those features.

The basic elements of physical built form are streets, plots and buildings, broadly corresponding to the three essential elements of human settlements: routes, areas for cultivation and shelter. The pattern of streets, plots and buildings together is often referred to as urban grain. A more comprehensive set of elements that allows for a higher resolution of analysis includes the following:

- Urban tissue
- Streets
- Plot series and blocks
- Routes
- Plots
- Buildings
- Rooms
- Structures
- Materials

The elements form a compositional hierarchy based on the relationship of part to whole. Each element is composed of or contains the element below it in the list. Thus, urban tissue is ultimately composed of materials but to give a more comprehensive picture of the structure embodied between those two we can usefully identify elements and patterns at progressively higher **levels of resolution**. The hierarchy is not, however, accurately represented in a simple vertical list of elements.

A more accurate depiction is shown in figure 3.8. The diagram shows that there are different kinds of element that combine in

Figure 3.6
Flats, Madrid. In strict terms, control is an abstract relationship. The physical expression of control may therefore take many forms. It might be either an obvious barrier to access or a minor difference in surface material.

Urban tissue		
Streets (simple tissue)		
Plot series [blocks]		
Plots		
Buildings	Open areas	Street spaces
Rooms		
Structures		
Materials		

different ways. It also highlights the three types of void that constitute the 'usable spaces' of the built environment: rooms, open areas and street spaces.

The structure of the diagram helps to visualise the pattern of relationships presented by the built environment in a number of ways.

Within the structure of the hierarchy any element can be seen and defined in three ways: 1) in terms of its **position** within the hierarchy as a generic form and as a component within a form at the next level up; 2) in terms of its **outline** as an object; 3) in terms of its **internal structure** as an arrangement of parts. A building, for example, is identifiable as a component within a plot, an object with an outline, and an object with an internal arrangement of rooms.

The diagram can be seen as an abstract representation of the generic structure of built form, each level corresponding to a different generic type of form. It is extremely important to point out, however, that *the levels and corresponding generic types are neither normative nor absolute*. There are different **generic configurations** of built form that reflect the full diversity and variability of specific forms. As explored in more detail in Section 6, specific types of built form may have more or fewer levels, which can be accommodated within the generic structure by either **co-extensive levels** or **intermediate levels**. One of the fundamental ways in which different specific types of form can be distinguished is by identifying which generic types they contain.

The diagram also helps to illustrate the complementary relationships between the different approaches and methods that have been used for the study and analysis of different elements. As an example, the voids have been the subject of particular attention within the configurational approach using methods such as graph analysis, j-graphs, axial line analysis and isovists. The typo-morphological approach has tended to deal with the generic hierarchy as a whole as a context for design, focusing on the level of the building type and urban tissue but without examining the voids as a network in significant detail.

THE PLACE OF SETTLEMENTS IN THE GENERIC STRUCTURE OF BUILT FORM
The hierarchy does not extend to include villages, towns and cities because there is no unequivocal correspondence between those terms and a particular position with the hierarchy of generic elements. The distinction between village, town and city in the UK, for example, is not based on physical built form but the presence of a particular use (church, market, cathedral). 'Settlement' is a general term that as suggested above implies only the core elements of routes, cultivated land and shelter. More colloquially, there are different forms of settlement that correspond to different positions in the hierarchy, for example:

- A farmstead made up of a complex of plots and fields and an access route
- A village made up of a single street
- A town composed of a number of different tissues
- A polycentric urban area formed by the coalescence of several towns.

above left **Figure 3.7 The aspect of built form refers to the physical fabric of the built environment and its spatial configuration generated through the process of building. The result is a multi-level compositional hierarchy of elements that are combined to form progressively more complex entities.**

above right **Figure 3.8 The multi-level diagram represents the generic structure of built form and can be seen as a kind of 'cross section' through the different levels of order within the built environment.**

This suggests the need for a parallel distinction of settlements that cross-refers to and extends the hierarchy of built form as illustrated in figure 3.8.

It should be noted and emphasised here that the generic structure of built form should be taken as a reference point that aids in the systematic investigation of urban form. As the product of a particular point of view, it does not exclude other views of the same 'object', for example those from more experiential perspectives such as city image or townscape, or those relating to patterns of use and interaction. The hierarchy immanent in the generic structure as seen from this point of view overlaps with other hierarchies in other views. This issue is central to the basic principle of the composite view, which allows for both the simple hierarchies that give clarity from a particular view and the more complex 'semi-lattice' structures that arise with overlapping hierarchies.

INFRASTRUCTURE

Infrastructure as an aspect of urban form is the equipment used for movement and transport, natural and military defence and to supply services, energy and resources including water, sewerage, electricity, gas, street lighting and telecommunications, as well as systems for heat and waste.

With the exception of areal features such as fortifications and reservoirs, infrastructure functions as quasi-independent networks made up of links and nodes that over- or under-lays the patchwork of tissues. Such networks have distinct morphological characteristics, and to analyse and understand them and the performance of the systems, it is generally necessary to take into account the entire network or significant parts of it and to use distinct methods of analysis.

Infrastructure can be seen as quasi-independent because the infrastructure systems connect with the other generic elements at distinct points, for example a telephone cable connection to an individual building, and the links between the connection points, need not necessarily follow the structure of other elements. A fundamental exception to this is the network of spaces or voids embedded in the generic structure of built form. The network of spaces is a special case because the individual voids are generically both integral elements of urban tissue as spaces and constructed surfaces, but also integral parts of the movement network or **route structure**. Spaces such as streets have both a local and global function and, in terms of use, as set out above,

accommodate both movement and 'occupation', even if temporary. The dual nature of spaces is explicitly brought out with respect to streets in 'link and place' theory as set out by Boujenko, Marshall and Jones in *Link and Place*.[3]

When considering built form, there are thus two sets of elements, urban tissue on the one hand and infrastructure on the other, with the movement network being common to both.

- Urban tissue
- Route structure
- Infrastructure

To take account of the overlap and the dual nature of the movement network, it is necessary to render the sets in different ways, subject them to slightly different forms of analysis and then recombine the different views. Putting the patchwork of urban tissue together with the network of route structure and the various other kinds of infrastructure in a composite view illustrates the principle of the overlay. By rectifying the three with respect to a common reference – either abstract geolocational coordinates or specific physical reference features – and viewing them together it is possible to identify the contact points and associations that allow them to work together. The fact that they are represented by different kinds of component is not an issue. Rather, seeing the different types together – patches and lines – brings out the depth and functional richness of the built environment.

INTENTION

Most generally, intention refers to the **aim** of an agent in creating or changing some part of the built environment. The intention is a response to some need or desire to accommodate a more or less well-defined set of activities, use or purpose – it might be shelter or self-glorification. At the abstract level, intention can be seen as the relationship between humans and the *future* built environment. In that relationship the 'future built environment' necessarily takes the form of an **idea**. Intention therefore encompasses:

- The urge to respond to some situation
- The purpose to be accommodated
- The idea of the possible physical composition of the form

While intentions regarding the built environment can be reduced to an abstract but diffuse sense of

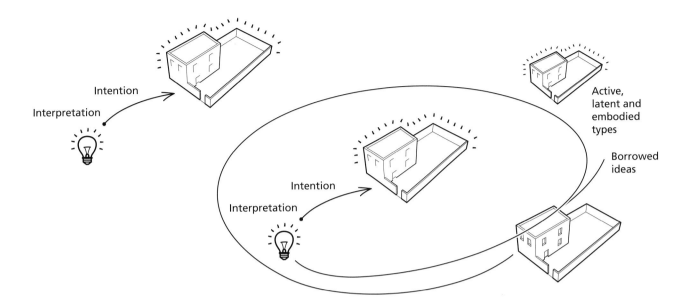

Intention

Interpretation

Intention

Interpretation

Active, latent and embodied types

Borrowed ideas

'wanting to make something for some purpose', they tend to take shape as **cultural habits**. That is to say, the need for shelter is universal but the specific intentions of an individual to provide shelter in a particular place and time will be conditioned by the culture in which the person grew up and lives. The expression of the intention is fundamentally cultural. As such, the intentions are **the product of learning**. One of the benefits of looking at intention in this way is that the combination of habit and learning account for the observation that in the built environment we find, at the same time, the continuity of traditions, the growth and diversification of forms through innovation, and the accumulation and transmission of knowledge.

Intention conceived as a cultural habit and product of learning corresponds with the notion of the **type** as used in typological approaches to architecture. The urge to build, the purpose and idea for a building are all necessary precursors to building it. This is to suggest that the type is usefully seen as a cultural habit that is the product of learning and, necessarily, the potential subject of modification in the ongoing process of learning. The persistence of a type within a culture is a function of the strength or **modularity** of the habit and its reinforcement by other associated habits. The more **integrated** the interactions between them, the more persistent the type.

As cultural habits, types are in effect common ideas held by a population. The common idea leads

to the reproduction of forms with common physical characteristics. It is those common characteristics that then form the basis for identifying types when analysing examples of urban areas.

The ideas of habit and learning also suggest there is a **momentum** to intention. It is one of the most active and living aspects of the built environment because it is a part of us as living beings. As there is a continual, cyclical drive to life, so there is a similar drive to build. The default state of the system is constant production and reproduction of buildings. It is easier to keep going than it is to stop.

In this context it is possible to identify three kinds of type:

- Active
- Latent
- Embodied

Active types are those that are in operation at a given moment. Latent types are those that are either one-off modifications to existing buildings or ideas held in the heads of a population but not yet acted upon – ideas of possible buildings. There are also possible buildings that have not yet been invented. Embodied types are those that have been realised and are either manifest in built form or as representations of built form. That is, we can work backwards from the relation between present intentions and future buildings. All existing buildings are a record of past intentions.

above left **Figure 3.9 Intention is the urge, purpose and generative idea that initiates the process of formation or transformation of built form.**

above right **Figure 3.10 The generative idea of an intention is necessarily derived from the experience and culture of the person or group who intends to build. Intentions are the product of learning (which is fundamentally social) and tend to operate as cultural habits.**

There is thus a **pool** of types and intentions much larger than the body of active ideas that allows for rapid adaptation when external circumstances change. An important point in this respect is that any given idea in the head of an individual is necessarily an **interpretation** of some embodied type or types. We can only get an idea of a possible building from our experience of existing buildings or components that might be combined to form one. That means, on the one hand, that active intentions are necessarily derived from one or a number of previous intentions and, on the other, that there will be variations in a given, shared intention – or cultural habit – because no two individuals' perceptions and experiences are the same.

It is also important to recognise that intentions for a particular project are not necessarily held in the head of a single agent. With increasing scale, complexity and specialisation, the intention for a project as a whole is more likely to be **distributed** over different agents and over time. In large and complex projects, no one person will have a picture of the whole project in all its detail in his or her head. The motivations and generating ideas for different aspects and elements are held by various agents and the overall idea for the project develops progressively over time with increasing specificity. The distributed idea of course opens up the possibility of **conflicting intentions** within a project and the problems associated with **design by committee**.

CONSTRUCTION

The aspect of construction encompasses the process of moving from the idea of a building – or, more broadly, the idea of development – to the fully realised physical form. Depending on the elaboration and complexity of the cultural context, the process can involve a number of steps, each of which presents potential limits and conditions for the creation of built form.

Assuming there is control of land and an idea for the project in mind, the next steps may include:

- Planning and technical approval
- Acquiring materials, a workforce and any other resources
- The act of building

The limits generally involve one or more of the following:

- Available materials and energy
- Available workforce, skills and supporting technology
- Physical/structural possibility
- Economic viability
- Social and political acceptability: planning regulations and policies
- Technical acceptability: building regulations

While the structure and complexity of any given system presents opportunities, there is an emphasis on limits in approval and construction because the move from idea to physical form is fundamentally 'convergent'. There are innumerable possible buildings we can entertain in our heads, but the economic realities, social and political acceptability and physical practicalities of actual construction reduce the number to a much smaller set of structures that can actually be 'delivered'. If the system involves a market with separate producers and consumers, a further limit is the perceptions of the participants in the market. A house-building company may have many designs but will only actually build houses it thinks the consumers will buy at a given time and place.

In effect, intention and the design process **generate** ideas and the regulatory and construction process **test** them for viability within a given context. There is also a significant amount of testing within the design process, which anticipates the testing of regulation and construction, based on learning and experience.

There are two general types of viability, internal and external. **Internal viability** refers to the structural integrity and coherence of the form. Do all the parts fit and hold together? In this respect, the capacities of materials and methods of construction available at a given time act as a limit on viability. Internal viability also refers to the suitability of the form in use. Does it serve its intended function – or some other unintended function – sufficiently well?

There are a number of dimensions to **external viability**, which refers generally to the extent to which a form works within a particular context. Dimensions include:

- Physical connections with the wider area
- Connections, integrity and coherence in use
- Economic viability
- Social and political acceptability

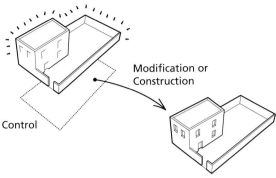

Figure 3.11
**Seen in the wider context
of the overall process, the
aspect of construction
involves the various
steps necessary to move
from the idea to the fully
realised physical form.
This can include the
regulatory regimes of
planning and building
regulations.**

The process of 'generate and test' is fundamental to both learning and evolution and we can get insights into its role in the formation and transformation of urban form by distinguishing the different ways it can be carried out. Paraphrasing Daniel Dennett's idea of the 'tower of generate and test', there are four broad steps in the tower.[4]

Building can be an **instinctive** behaviour such as nest building or burrow digging. In effect, the organism and building method are fully fused. The method of building is a way of life and succeeds or fails as one.

We can try out different methods of building directly so that the act of building is equivalent to a variable form of **behaviour**. We test the building by constructing and using it.

A further step is to internalise the testing through the **design** process. We generate ideas, think them through deductively to anticipate how they might work and select a building we think will be successful.

The next step is to use the experience embodied in the existing built environment as a **design resource** as well as borrowing ideas from other realms. These 'mind tools' provide us with and help us to select solutions intelligently and so again increase the likelihood of success.

PERCEPTION

Perception is the basic underlying relationship between humans and the built environment. It is through the feedback of perception that we are able to successfully interact with our environment and engage in adaptive behaviour. While it can be argued that we *only* have access to the built environment (or anything, for that matter) through perception, we can usefully distinguish for ourselves (and communicate) the *differences* between one perception and another.

Perception includes the gamut of human reactions and associations arising from the experience of being in a place. The range runs from

Figure 3.12
**Cité Internationale, Lyon.
The act of building is
a tangible test of the
physical viability of
the generating idea
within the environment.
Not infrequently,
construction involves
on-the-spot adjustments
and adaptations to
accommodate
unforeseen issues.**

the immediate sensory perceptions of sight, sound, smell (touch and taste) on to qualities, feelings, associations, images, memories, interpretations, inferences and judgements, to more considered and articulated commentaries.

At the more immediate end of the spectrum are the essentially cognitive interactions of mental image formation, memory and emotional responses. At the more inferential end are the attribution of different kinds of social and cultural meaning, significance or value. And while the spectrum is fundamentally continuous, it can be useful to identify what might loosely be called different *species* of perception:

- Cognition
- City image and memory
- Emotional effect
- Interpretation and meaning

The more directly cognitive species tend to arise in individuals, while the more inferential tend to emerge with social interaction and might be said to be 'socially coded' in the same way as language.

To a large extent, these species represent subjects of study in their own right either individually or as part of more general urban studies. The principal purpose of identifying them here is to show how they fit into the composite view of urban form.

THE VALUE OF DIFFERENT PERSPECTIVES

As a matter of convention, the aspects of form, use and control are viewed from the plan view, facilitated by the intermediary of plan drawings and maps. By contrast, city image and emotional effect are fundamentally rooted in our perceptions of a place from the direct **experiential perspective** of being in and moving through it.

While the difference is one of point of view, the example of binocular vision demonstrates that we can get additional information – and information of a different kind – by combining 'descriptions' of something seen from two different perspectives. In the case of binocular vision, the additional, different kind of information is depth perception – the spatial relations between things. One way to put it is that there is a yield or benefit from combining views from different perspectives or different kinds of description of the same thing. This yield is central to the morphological method of the composite image.

SENSORY AGENCY

Our perception of our environment is an essential part of the processes of responding to and learning from our experiences in creating and transforming the built environment. We are all **sensory agents** in the process. As we actively use our environment, we have the capacity to identify issues to which we must respond and adapt as well as to search out and identify potential solutions.

**Figure 3.13
Perception underpins our awareness of and access to the built environment but is also essential as the distinct perspective through which we experience places and attribute order and meaning to them (a). In terms of the process of formation and transformation, perception provides the essential element of feedback that makes it a complex adaptive process (b).**

(a)

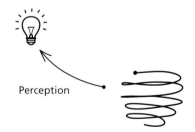

Perception

(b)   Repeated use over time in the context of changing needs and environment

CITY IMAGE

There are innumerable features we might pick out as we move through a place and compile a picture of it in our heads. In *The Image of the City*, Kevin Lynch used the pragmatic and robust method of asking people to draw maps of their neighbourhood in order to compare those maps and identify the features people most commonly select when finding their way in urban environments.[5]

The results are the five elements:

- Paths: channels of movement (axial reference)
- Edges: boundary lines (lateral reference)
- Districts: areas of distinct character or identity (area reference)
- Nodes: focal points and points of convergence, concentration or crossing (point reference)
- Landmarks: features that are singled out as prominent, distinct or significant relative to their surroundings (point reference)

The task of city image analysis is therefore to identify these elements within an area either through mental mapping exercises with people from the area or by inference from the definitions through map analysis and field surveys. One of the important conclusions made by Lynch is that all these elements are most effective when combined, typically taking the path as the core axial reference to which a sequence of lateral, area and point references are associated. Time and movement therefore become essential dimensions of the city image.

TOWNSCAPE AND TRADITIONAL TOPOGRAPHY

The townscape tradition is another perceptually based approach to the description, characterisation and, in the end, design of the built environment. Rooted in the concept of landscape – and therefore painting – townscape is explicitly visual in its emphasis. As set out in *Townscape* by Gordon Cullen,[6] the approach focuses on the experiential and emotional states induced by particular configurations or combinations of elements in the built environment. The core concepts of the approach are:

- Optics and serial vision (the static and dynamic sensory and experiential point of view and its characteristics)
- Place (the spatial/configurational structure that is experienced)
- Content (the experiential characteristics of the fabric defining the spaces), including:

- colour
- texture
- scale
- style
- character
- personality
- uniqueness

Townscape, in particular as practised by Cullen, is a structured approach to the more general, traditional discipline of topography, which is the 'detailed description of place'. The dynamic experience of serial vision provides a key organising principle which, like Lynch's approach, uses movement along a path as the primary axial reference to which a series of experiences is associated.

While the aim of both city image and townscape analysis is to specify and articulate the ground-level experience of places, in practice the methods make active use of maps and plans to record and annotate the features identified. The process of **transcription** or representation of ground-view perception onto a plan representation as common frame of reference is important in developing the composite view of form. Other kinds of perception such as social status and value can also be transcribed in the same way (which is only to use and confirm the value of methods used in GIS).

NATURAL RESOURCE FLOWS

The flow of energy and resources is a defining aspect of the built environment, which, to restate the basic definition, is 'the transformation of the environment through the application of human energy in the process of building'. We, in turn, get our energy and resources from our environment. A necessary starting point is therefore the flow of resources within the natural environment.

While the milieu of the natural environment necessarily extends to the solar system and the Earth's position and movement within it, from a local perspective the various potential sources of energy can be summarised in terms of an **energy budget** including the direct sources of **geothermal** and **solar** energy, which, along with gravitational attraction, induce the secondary forms of **the hydrological cycle, wind,** and **tidal** energy. The different patterns of insolation, hydrological cycles and wind speed and direction found in different parts of the planet are usefully characterised in terms of **climate.** Further sources come from the range of **metabolic processes** that have developed

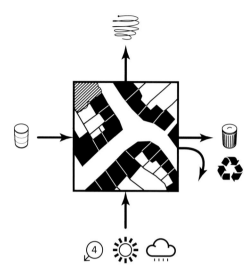

to form **energy** and **material cycles** involving **micro-organisms, plants** and **animals**.

It is important to note that the idea of a flow necessarily incorporates a time dimension. Resource flows are one of the temporal aspects of the built environment along with perception, development and evolution. This reinforces the principle that the built environment is the product of a process that takes place in time.

HUMAN DIRECTED AND INDUCED RESOURCE FLOWS

The matter of the planet and its energy budget, including the metabolic energy and material cycles, provide the energy and materials available to humans to create the built environment. While this perspective may appear overly wide and all-encompassing, it is essential to fully acknowledge that the built environment can only exist where there is a constant flow of resources. By definition the built environment requires the application of energy. This is the sense behind the formulation that the built environment is, in strict terms, only a temporary patterning of a constant flow of energy and materials.

Looking at the flows in more detail, there are three broad modes in the application of energy to create and sustain the built environment: the energy of **production, maintenance** and **use**.

That is, energy is required to put the built environment together in the first place, it is required when we use it and, because of the second law of thermodynamics and the general tendency toward disorder, it is required to keep it together. All biological order – and the built environment is a form of biological order – requires a constant flow of energy to be sustained. Thus, again, the idea that the built environment is only a patterning of the flow.

Looking at flows involves identifying the **source, channel, processes, rate** and **destination**. Looking at the wider system involves understanding the **balance** of different flows and the **interactions** between them.

In practice, the fundamental source of energy for the production, maintenance and use of the built environment is **human metabolic energy** (which we get from food). Humans have, however, developed a number of means of capturing and directing energy from other sources, including:

- Geothermal
- Solar
- Hydrological
- Wind
- Tidal
- Nuclear
- Plants (primarily by combustion)

Figure 3.14
Both the natural and built environments are dependent on a constant throughput of energy and resources. Examining the sources, rates and balance of flows is essential in seeking to understand how the process of creating, using and maintaining the built environment can be sustained.

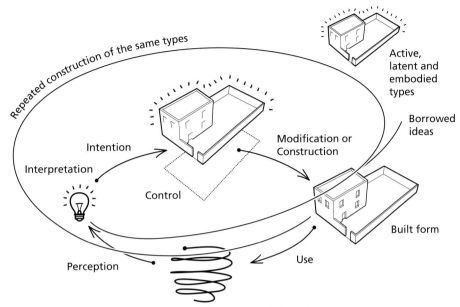

plant material (eg, wood, charcoal)
- fossil fuels
- Animals
  - draft animals
  - combustion of by-products
- Micro-organisms
  - combustion of by-products (eg, fermentation and anaerobic digestion)

Similarly for materials, the sources include:

- Mineral products
- Petroleum products
- Plant products
- Animal products

In taking account of the source, channels, rates, processes and destinations of the flows, it is useful to define a locality as a starting point for a simple input/output model. It is then possible to distinguish between **local resources**, available within the locality, and **external inputs**. For the production and maintenance modes, the outputs are the **physical forms** of the built environment and any by-products, which may be of some further use or not (waste). For the use mode, the outputs are the **beneficial use** of the physical form, often with reference to some standard or benchmark, and by-products including shared use, re-use, recycling and waste.

Within this framework it is then possible to compare different modes of production and physical forms (or 'morphologies') in terms of the efficiency of the channels and processes involved in production, maintenance or use.

DEVELOPMENT AND EVOLUTION

With the exception of energy and resource flows, all of the other aspects set out above have been defined primarily in terms of a relationship between physical forms or between forms and human agents.

If the different aspects of urban form can be seen as the different facets of an 'object' viewed from different perspectives, then **development** and **evolution** are the facets revealed by viewing urban form through time. The temporal dimension is fundamental to the morphological approach because the built environment is understood to be the result of a process of formation and transformation.

While the primary terms of reference are time and change, an essential distinction arises with the fact the built environment is the product of the habitual reproduction of forms according to human intentions and ideas.

Development deals with the life history of an **individual** form in the built environment such as a settlement or building (and any trace of its

Figure 3.15
The formation and transformation of the built environment involves both the development and growth of buildings, settlements and regions as well as the evolution of the ideas that generate them. The different aspects of urban form as set out above are essentially different parts and perspectives of that double overall process that in simple terms can be characterised as a process of learning.

existence), from conception and realisation, through active use, modification or transformation to decay and destruction or dissolution.

The basic terms of reference for development are the generic steps in the process:

- Foundation
- Extension
- Internal transformation
- Abandonment or destruction

Evolution involves the changes to the **generating ideas** or **types** that emerge from the reproduction and development of many examples over time. As set out in the discussion of the aspect of intention, the two processes of development and evolution are interrelated. Evolution of types generally occurs in response to changes in the context and environment, such as social or technological change, as realised through the reproduction, development and modification of many individual examples of the type over time. Changes from one example to the next might involve the incorporation of some or all of the developmental modifications to existing examples or the combination of elements from examples of different types and ideas from related areas. One way or the other, for the evolution to occur, new forms need to be produced and developed in accordance with new ideas.

The more detailed terms of reference for development and evolution are in effect the other aspects of urban form. The two interrelated processes of development and evolution bind the aspects together. The natural and built environments along with the social and economic context are the environments and context in which the development and evolution occur. Some form of control over land is a necessary precursor to the development of an individual form which then involves the intention, construction and use of the form, sustained by flows of energy and materials all led and monitored by the perceptual capacities of the agents involved.

At a given time the agents choose from the pool of ideas – the active, latent and embodied cultural habits – in response to the circumstances presented by the environment and context, and test them through the development process and active use. Examples that persist add to the pool of ideas and so potentially contribute to the evolution of the habits. Evolutionary changes can therefore involve the emergence and transformation of

types, a shift of a particular idea from latent to active to embodied types and potentially their complete disappearance.

The built environment as a whole does not evolve in this sense because there is no generating idea for the whole. Rather, types of element at various levels within the built environment evolve and, because of the persistence of both patterns and physical fabric, the result of the overall process in the long run is a complex composite of elements generated by a succession of ideas. The built environment is the product of **polymorphogenesis**.

THE REFERENCE ASPECT

While the processes of development and evolution afford a means of tying the different aspects together in a coherent *process*, it is still necessary to provide a consistent means both of reconstructing the process of development of particular places and of combining the aspects to develop a composite image of a settlement at a given point in time.

Of all the aspects identified, physical form and use are common to all the different approaches to urban morphology. As set out above, physical form strictly defined is the spatial relations of physical objects. Function, use and activity are interrelations between humans and some physical form, an interaction between someone and some thing. The aspect of use or function therefore *presupposes* and includes physical form within the definition. To talk about use, you need to talk about form. It is also the case that activities such as residing, worshipping, working and playing are, on their own, relatively fluid and flexible, both in their constituent elements and where they take place. Use is more evanescent and changes more quickly than form.

By contrast, physical form is the most tangible, ubiquitous and persistent of all the aspects. It is also the case that most representations of settlements primarily depict physical form, which is the easiest to represent by drawing and other graphic means. In cases where other aspects are represented, such as property boundaries on cadastral maps, in general the ultimate reference point is still physical features on the ground. If we are to compile a composite image of a settlement and reconstruct the process of development, the source material with which to do so is most likely to be representations of physical form. The tangibility, ubiquity and persistence of physical form make it the best candidate for the reference aspect.

In essence, physical form can function something like the registration marks in multi-plate printing. If the different aspects of urban form are seen as different colours, each with its own pattern applied to a separate plate, physical form can be used as the common feature to locate and bound the colours and align the different layers to generate a coherent image. This idea is by no means novel and is essentially the approach used in GIS and its precursors in overlay drawing. The equivalent for coordinating a time sequence of images is the peg bar of traditional animation. Built form performs the same registration function for illustrating the process of formation and transformation.

ASPECTS, DIVERSITY AND EXPERIENCE

In summary, it would be presumptuous in the extreme to even suggest that the aspects as set out above give a complete account of the full diversity of cities. Even if in theory settlements are finite, there is an infinite amount of general and detailed information and experiences that we might explore. The aim in identifying the distinct aspects is to come to a balance between consistency, comprehensiveness, coherence, generality and specificity in a way that is workable in practice. There can never be any truly 'full' account of a city that might be absorbed by an individual in a lifetime. Even direct experience is necessarily limited by time and point of view. The aspects as identified here and the composite views that can be generated with them are openly an approximation but one that provides significant insights and allows investigations into phenomena that might otherwise remain obscure. Most importantly, it allows for better communication and the growth of understanding within a community.

References

1 Kevin Lynch, *Good City Form*, MIT Press (Cambridge, MA), 1981, p 37.
2 Ibid, p 48.
3 Natalya Boujenko, Stephen Marshall, and Peter Jones, *Link and Place*, Local Transport Today (London), 2007. Print.
4 Daniel Dennett, *Darwin's Dangerous Idea*, Penguin (London), 1995. Print.
5 Kevin Lynch, *The Image of the City*, MIT Press (Cambridge, MA), 1960. Print.
6 Gordon Cullen, *Townscape*, Architectural Press (Oxford), 1961. Print.

Minimum Elements

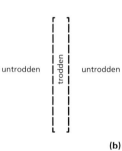

(a)   (b)

ELEMENTS

As in other fields of morphology, one of the starting points for achieving the aims of better communication and the growth of understanding is to identify the **minimum elements** that constitute the phenomena, expressed as generalised abstract entities. The task is then to identify the ways in which the elements are combined to account for the diversity and complexity of specific forms.

The method of identifying the minimum elements most consistent with the morphological focus on *process* is to take a developmental approach. From this perspective, the question becomes, from what has built form been derived and what is the minimum set of pertinent features we need to describe the primitive elements?

The starting point is **human activity** in an **environment**.

The features of the environment pertinent to the structure of built form are essentially those of three-dimensional geometry and the laws of gravity and mechanics. In terms of a geometric description of built form, the most fundamental morphological element is thus a **surface** on which activity can take place.

There are three fundamental modes of activity rooted in the human diurnal cycle and the need to move through the environment for resources:

*   Long-distance movement
*   Local activity
*   Sleep

These modes lead to three **primitive types of surface** in terms of shape, size and relative position:

*   Tracks
*   Core territory
*   Shelter

A surface implies a space. At its most primitive, the surface and the implied space are defined not by any constructed boundary but by the extent of an activity and any traces it might leave: footprints and the **difference** between trodden and untrodden ground.

The difference constitutes a **boundary**. However diffuse or well-delineated, any distinct space must have a boundary. Spaces are **codependent** with their boundaries.

Figure 4.1
Tracks can emerge from repeated acts of movement in the environment (a). The difference in surface between trodden and untrodden ground resulting from repeated foot traffic creates a boundary that implies a space (b). The tracks that emerge in this way are part of the proto-built environment.

Boundaries might thus be:

- Implied (corresponding to the limits of an activity taking place)
- Left (traces or marks left by an activity)
- Found (existing boundaries adapted for an activity)
- Constructed (including as implied by boundaries of control)

Whatever the nature of the boundary, all three types of primitive bounded surface – tracks, core territory and shelter – can be considered **structured spaces** or **voids**.

Deliberately creating a boundary to form a space involves the selection, manipulation and arrangement of **materials** from the environment to create **physical structures**.

The extent to which any given type of space is defined by physical structures is variable. There is a continuum from the simple **environment**, which would be land uninhabited and unstructured by humans on the one hand, and the fully **built environment** of a city on the other. In between is the **proto-built environment**, which is made up of the unconstructed, emergent forms that are implied, left and/or found and not deliberately built. Nor is it necessarily the case that all elements are defined by physical structures to the same extent at a given time.

When constituted by built structures, the three types of void can be referred to as:

- Street spaces
- Open areas
- Rooms

These terms should be interpreted as broadly as possible to allow for a wide range of specific forms. For example, street spaces include piazzas as well as urban thoroughfares; open areas include front and back gardens as well as campus environments; rooms include habitable spaces, corridors and stairs as well as service spaces such as ducts, flues and cupboards.

Once there is an upright structure enclosing a space, an essential component for these elements to function is an **opening** to allow for movement in and out and from one to another. **Access** and **movement** are therefore fundamental to the structure of built form.

An access point establishes an **internal orientation** for a structured space which in turn forms the basis for the ways in which structured spaces can be combined.

Colloquially, the faces established are:

- Front
- Sides
- Back

There are also different types of opening:

- Doors
- Vents
- Windows

The inclusion of vents and windows adds further considerations, limits and conditions to the ways structured spaces can be combined. For the purposes of establishing the minimum elements, the only necessary type is a door: an opening that allows physical human access.

The three minimum elements of the built environment are therefore:

- Surfaces
- Boundaries
- Openings

Figure 4.2
A boundary on its own only implies inside and outside. A boundary with an opening implies front, back and sides as well as inside and outside.

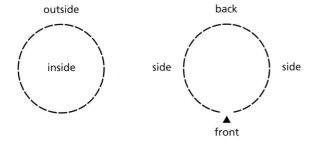

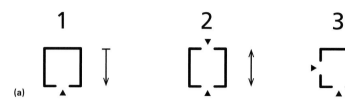

1   2   3

(a)

The **number of openings** establishes distinct types of structured space in terms of access. At a minimum there are three access types: single, double and multiple (three or more).

Each access type has a particular role within a configuration as a whole in terms of the potential range of generic functions it can accommodate:

- Occupation
- Through movement
- Distribution

These are, of course, not mutually exclusive. Above a minimum size, all spaces can be used for occupation and also accommodate local movement.

Distribution is a subset of through movement that allows for greater **choice**. The three access types apply to all three types of void: street spaces, open areas and rooms. The access types also form the basis for possible combinations of two or more structured spaces.

The structured space diagram assumes a number of graphic conventions. The boundary represents the **plan outline** of the form on the ground plane (the reference surface). The outline assumes and refers to all the physical structures and voids within the outline in all their three-dimensional detail both above and below the ground plane. Gaps in the outline and triangles represent access points.

Figure 4.3
Structured spaces can be distinguished as different access types on the topological basis of the number of openings: one, two and three or more (a). Further types are generated by exploring the possible combinations of any of the three basic types (b).

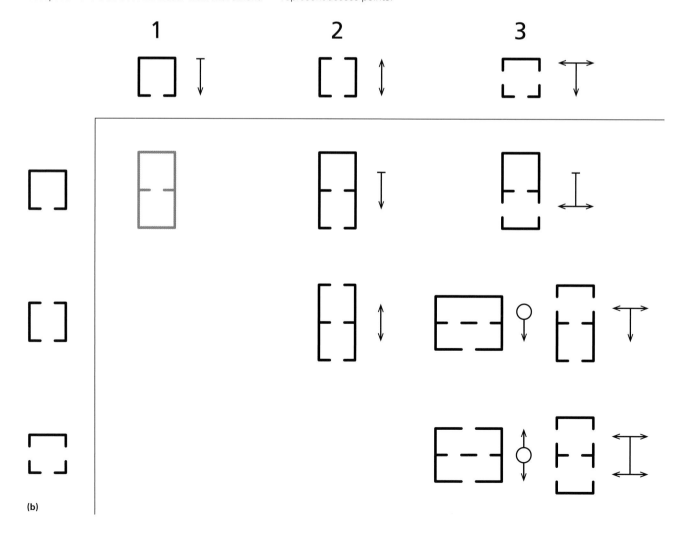

(b)

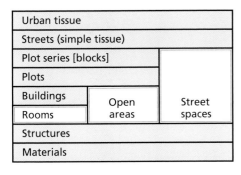

(a)

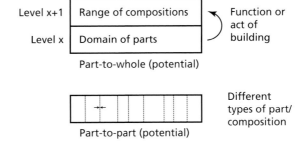

(b)

ANALYTICAL VIEWS

The basic **outline diagram** is in effect an abstract **analytical view** that isolates the minimum elements of surface, boundary and opening. Because the diagram abstracts and combines only the three minimum elements, it can be used to represent all different kinds of simple and complex structured space.

An important consequence of using the outline diagram to render all three types of void is that all parts of the built environment can be **positively** represented. That is to say, there is no 'negative' space within the built environment. A street space or open space within a plot is not leftover space between buildings but a positively structured surface. Any given surface is thus either inside or outside the built environment. Put another way, the only 'negative' spaces are those outside the built environment.

The fact that the outline diagram can be used to represent both simple and complex forms suggests that the abstract structured space is the **minimum unit of urban morphological analysis**. The three types of primitive bounded surface can be distinguished as **base** structured spaces and all more complex forms can then be described as aggregations of the base structured spaces. Because any aggregation is in turn itself a structured space, the underlying process that leads from the base structured spaces to more complex forms can be seen as a **recursive act**

of aggregation. The result of the process is a compositional hierarchy of built form, illustrated by a **multi-level diagram**.

The compositional hierarchy represents the **generic structure of built form**. The analytical view of the multi-level diagram is in effect a kind of cross section through the generic structure. The diagram extrudes out and exposes the different levels of order within urban tissue. The levels in the hierarchy and diagram correspond to **levels of complexity**.

A further, and likely the most familiar analytical view essential to morphological analysis, is the two-dimensional **plan view**, showing the spatial arrangement and extent of elements on the ground surface. The plan view can be presented as a composite of different elements or as a series of **element separations**. In the separations, only elements from a given level are shown, each element drawn in outline (see figure 4.5).

The element separations reinforce the idea that the compositional hierarchy represents a cross section through the generic structure of urban tissue. Each rectangle in the diagram represents all elements of a given type, represented in outline. Drawing a horizontal line through a level in the multi-level diagram 'cuts through' elements that appear in outline in the corresponding element separation. Thus, a line through the level of the plot cuts through plots and street spaces, both of which appear in outline in the plot level element separation.

Figure 4.4
The levels in the multi-level diagram of generic structure represent recursive acts of aggregation (a). Each move up a level therefore involves an increase in the level of complexity of the elements and each level constitutes the range of potential parts for elements one level up (b).

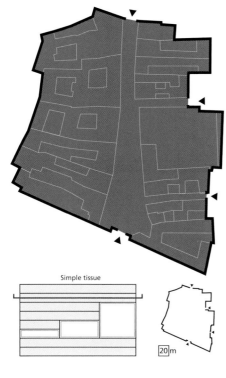

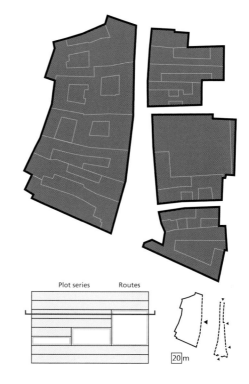

Simple tissue

20 m

(a)

Plot series   Routes

20 m

(b)

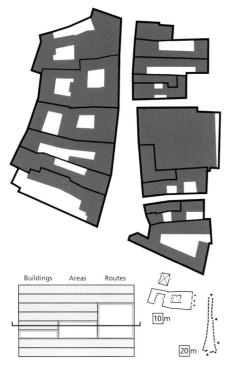

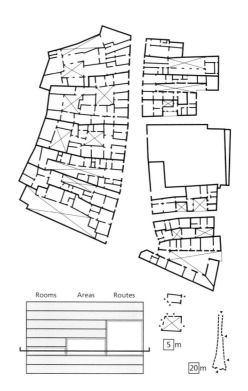

Buildings   Areas   Routes

10 m

20 m

(d)

Rooms   Areas   Routes

5 m

20 m

(e)

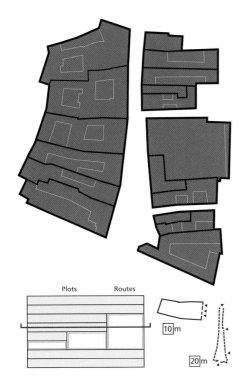

Figure 4.5
The series of diagrams
illustrates the relationship
between the three
main analytical views:
structured space,
plan view and generic
structure. Each plan
view is a different
element separation that
corresponds to a cross
section through the multi-
level diagram of generic
structure. Sliding down
the hierarchy increases
the level of resolution of
the view.

(c)

IDENTIFYING AND DESCRIBING BUILT FORM

Different purposes, aims and objectives in analysis call for different **levels of specificity** in the definition of form. The definitions might be more or less detailed and precise depending on the nature of the study.

The highest level of specificity is obtained by describing all the constituent parts of an element in sufficient detail to isolate a single unique object. For example, a single house can be distinguished from all others in terms of its location, shape, size, openings and internal arrangement down to materials and paint colours. The lowest level of specificity is given by the general definition of the built environment: all those parts of the environment materially modified by the application of human energy.

Intermediate levels of specificity can be set by varying the number and range of pertinent characteristics used in the definition. The three analytical viewpoints together – the multi-level diagram, outline and plan views – constitute a composite view that makes it possible to identify and describe elements of built form at varying levels of specificity in a consistent, structured way. Because there are clear, formal relationships between the three viewpoints, in combination they provide a means of specifying forms that is both precise and flexible.

The first step in setting an intermediate level of specificity is to identify the position of an element within the generic structure of built form (multi-level diagram). This is to define an element generally in terms of both its role as a part in a composition and its internal constituent parts. The position of an element within the generic structure established the **generic type** of the element. Each level in the hierarchy therefore represents a generic type of built form.

Within each level or generic type of form, the **specific type** of an element is defined in terms of three key attributes:

• Specific position within a composition
• Outline, including points of access
• Internal structure

Position is determined using the plan view, identifying the relationship of adjacency with other elements of the same type within a distinct composition one level up the hierarchy. An example is a corner plot within a plot series.

Outline is defined using the outline diagram, set in terms of:

- Shape (using a geometric descriptor)
- Size (dimensions)
- Proportions (ratios of dimensions)
- Points of access

The plan view is used to identify types in terms of the **internal structure** of an element's constituent parts:

- Specific type of parts
- Number of each type
- Arrangement or configuration

Specificity can be increased still further by identifying the shape, size, proportions and internal structure of the parts at one or more levels down.

The effect of the move from position to outline view and from outline to a view that includes the internal structure of an element is to adjust the **structural perspective** and to increase the **level of resolution**. The level of resolution of analysis is therefore the total number of levels of structure taken into account. A low level of resolution would include only one level in outline. A high level of resolution would, for example, include the internal structure of elements three levels down the hierarchy. There is thus a general correspondence between level of resolution and specificity. Higher levels of resolution allow for higher levels of specificity.

Using a combination of the three structural perspectives means the definition of built form can be both inclusive and precise. Many different specific elements might occupy a particular position, but each can be distinguished by its outline and internal structure. By the same token, it is possible to distinguish elements with the same internal structure that occupy different positions.

In summary, elements can be distinguished by their:

- Position in the hierarchy of generic structure (generic type) (multi-level diagram)
- Position within the specific structure of a form at the next level up the hierarchy (specific type) (plan/plan separation)
- Outline (shape, size and proportions and points of access) (outline diagram)
- Internal structure (number, type and arrangement of parts) (plan/plan separation)

Figure 4.6
The three different attributes for defining specific types of form: position, outline and access, and internal structure. These can be seen as different ways of viewing the element or structural perspectives: looking up the hierarchy, straight on and looking down the hierarchy.

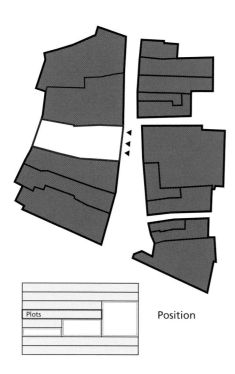

Position

Outline and access

Internal structure

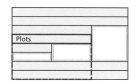

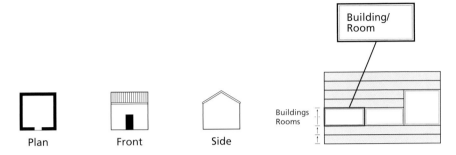

Plan   Front   Side

AMBIGUITY: CO-EXTENSIVE AND INTERMEDIATE ELEMENTS

It is of the utmost importance to understand that the generic structure of urban tissue as depicted in the multi-level diagrams used up to this point is only one of many **generic configurations**. Actual examples of built form, even within a relatively homogeneous area, show an enormous range of variation. The multi-level diagram as shown so far should therefore be seen only as a **reference diagram**.

Two concepts that are essential to account for actual variations in a consistent and coherent way are **co-extensive elements** and **intermediate elements**.

Examples of co-extensive elements or **co-extension** are 1) a single-room building and 2) a single building occupying an entire plot. In terms of the compositional hierarchy, the phenomenon occurs when a single entity functions at two levels at the same time. It is thus a case of ambiguity. A single-room building is both a 'room' and a 'building'. In terms of the recursive process of aggregation, a co-extensive form corresponds to 'an aggregate of one entity'.

Co-extensive elements are represented in the multi-level diagram by removing a division between levels so the lower level extends further up the hierarchy. This highlights the fact that co-extension involves the 'removal' or 'loss' of a level of order in the generic structure, resulting in a generic configuration with a lower level of complexity relative to the reference diagram.

Examples of intermediate elements or **compression** are apartments in an apartment building or sub-series of plots within a series. An example at the level of structures is a masonry arch. In each case, a composition of elements functions as an element at the same level rather than the next level up. The arch, which is a composition of stones, does not constitute a full structure in itself but functions as a part with other individual stones in a composition making up a wall. An apartment, which is a configuration of rooms, is not a building in its own right but a part in a larger building.

Figure 4.7
Within the context of the compositional hierarchy of built form, a single-room building is equivalent to a set or class of one member – a singleton or unit set. It is both a building, because it stands as part of a plot, and a room because it is composed of structures – floor, walls and roof, without any more complex parts.

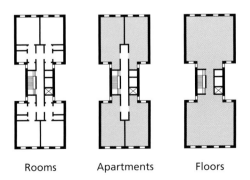

Rooms   Apartments   Floors

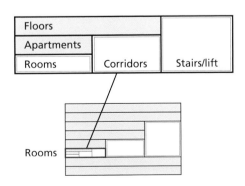

Figure 4.8
An apartment is a composition of rooms that is only one of a number of similar compositions making up a building, along with shared corridors. Within the context of the hierarchy of built form, the apartment occupies a level between rooms and buildings.

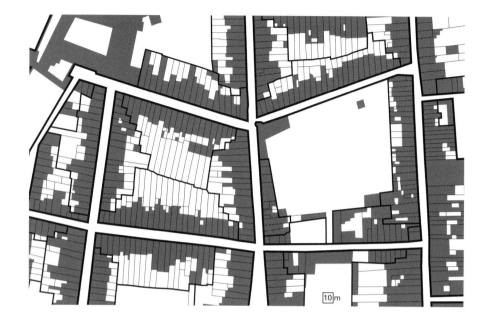

left and opposite top
Figure 4.9
Urban tissue with blocks
made up of single-
frontage plot series with
single-access plots is
common throughout the
world. Many different
specific types share this
generic configuration
that corresponds to the
reference diagram.

left and opposite bottom
Figure 4.10
Tissue with a number
of isolated apartment
buildings within a single
plot with multiple access
points is also extremely
common. The generic
configuration of these
tissues compresses the
levels of order into the
building with fewer levels
associated directly with
street spaces. From an
objective, descriptive
standpoint, the difference
with respect to the
reference diagram is only
that: a difference.

Within the multi-level diagram, an intermediate form is represented by an additional, intermediate level inserted within one of the reference levels. The presence of intermediate levels in a generic configuration involves an increase in the level of complexity relative to the reference diagram. In terms of the recursive process, an intermediate element is an aggregate within an aggregate of the same type.

There are forms that involve both co-extension and compression, so it is possible to find cases where two forms may have different generic configurations but the same level of complexity. The difference is then the 'location' of the complexity within the hierarchy.

The idea of generic configuration is perhaps best illustrated by comparing two distinct types of urban tissue: an **articulated grid** with individual buildings on plots (figure 4.9) and an **interlocking grid** with several multi-occupancy buildings on large plots (figure 4.10).

The difference between the two is highlighted by the multi-level diagrams. The example of the articulated grid includes elements at all the reference levels, while the example of the interlocking grid includes intermediate levels within the building and a co-extensive level between the simple street/tissue. The examples have different numbers of levels, and they are found at different positions within the hierarchy relative to the three voids. On this basis, generic configuration can be defined as the number of levels and their relative position in the hierarchy with reference to the three principal types of structured space – the room, open area and street space.

GENERIC STRUCTURE AND THE STATUS OF THE BLOCK

The above highlights that while the block can unequivocally be defined as an aggregate of plots surrounded on all sides by street spaces, it is ambiguously related to those street spaces when taken as an isolated entity. A block can be either (1) the result of combining several plot series, each connected with a different single street, or (2) an aggregate of plots that may be connected to two or more streets. One way or the other, the block occupies the same level as the plot series in the generic structure, but as a **resultant form** (for this reason 'blocks' is set in square brackets in the diagrams).

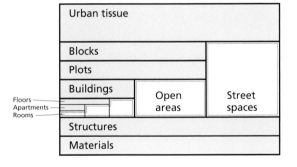

PART 2

Methods

The General Process of Analysis

Urban morphological analysis encompasses a wide range of specific methods, from rapid appraisal and identification of character areas to in-depth investigations of historical development, environmental performance and theoretical investigations of possible forms. The various methods necessarily involve different levels of resource, time and effort. It is therefore essential to identify the aims and objectives of the analysis at the outset in order to select the most appropriate methods and focus the effort on the most relevant aspects. It is equally essential to establish the scope of the study based on the principal aims and objectives and the resources available.

Most of the common purposes have been outlined above in the Introduction. The starting point is to pose a number of questions:

- What is the project seeking to achieve?
- Who is the audience?
- How will the results be used?

While the full range of methods rightly includes theoretical investigations, the focus of this handbook is on the analysis of settlements on the ground. With this limitation in mind there are some general indications that apply to most cases and so it is possible to identify a common framework and general process of analysis.

In very broad terms, the process involves the following sequence of stages:

- Identify place or type, purpose and scope
- Information gathering
- Desktop analysis
- Field survey
- Interpretation, synthesis and communication
- Final outputs

These are best seen as elements in an iterative process in which later stages can feed back into earlier stages. For example, it is often the case that the results of the field survey and different forms of synthesis contribute to desktop analysis. More generally, it is useful to set the steps in the broader context of the idea that a morphological study involves **analysis**, **comparison** and **synthesis**.

In all cases there is great benefit in the long term in having a clear, succinct written statement of the purpose of the study and the aspects it should cover.

PLACE, PURPOSE AND SCOPE OF THE STUDY

The general starting point for any morphological analysis will be a more or less well-defined idea of the place or type of form to be analysed and the purpose of the analysis.

More specifically, the steps at this stage are to:

- Identify the place or type of form
- Identify the aims and objectives
- Assess the available information
- Identify the scope of the study
  - study area(s)
  - aspects
  - level of resolution
  - specific methods
- Identify the principal outputs

This may involve an iterative process that starts with a broad location or generic type and a very generalised purpose that need to be limited and refined with the formulation and distillation of more specific aims and objectives. This iterative process should also extend to include an assessment of the information available to determine whether it will serve the purposes of the study, whether new information is required, or whether the objectives need to be changed to better suit the available information.

Careful formulation of the aims, objectives and scope of the project at the outset is particularly important because some methods of analysis can be very resource intensive. This underlines the benefit of making an initial assessment of the available time, skills and information in order to make best use of the resources available.

The list of specific applications in the Introduction provides an indication of the potential aims and objectives of different kinds of projects. Each has different needs focusing on different aspects and at different levels of resolution. One of the ways to help focus the aims and objectives is to identify at a very early stage the outputs of the project. The overarching question to answer is: what specific material is needed at the end of the project to achieve the aims and objectives? Considering the outputs at an early point in the process helps to avoid open-ended objectives that can result in undertaking significant amounts of work without any defined purpose or means of assessing its value.

What is the project seeking to achieve?
Who is the audience?
How will the results be used?

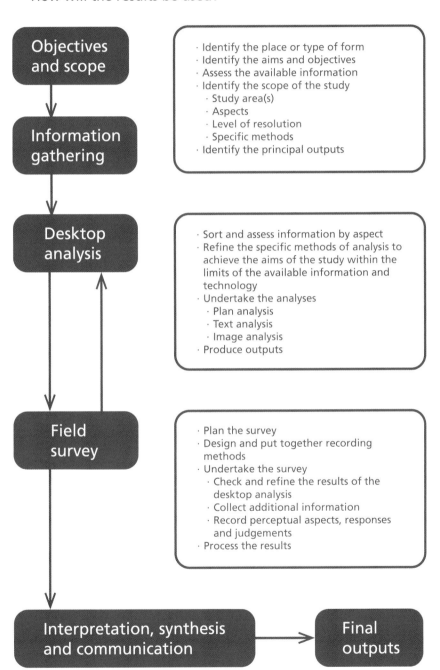

Objectives and scope

- Identify the place or type of form
- Identify the aims and objectives
- Assess the available information
- Identify the scope of the study
  - Study area(s)
  - Aspects
  - Level of resolution
  - Specific methods
- Identify the principal outputs

Information gathering

Desktop analysis

- Sort and assess information by aspect
- Refine the specific methods of analysis to achieve the aims of the study within the limits of the available information and technology
- Undertake the analyses
  - Plan analysis
  - Text analysis
  - Image analysis
- Produce outputs

Field survey

- Plan the survey
- Design and put together recording methods
- Undertake the survey
  - Check and refine the results of the desktop analysis
  - Collect additional information
  - Record perceptual aspects, responses and judgements
- Process the results

Interpretation, synthesis and communication

Final outputs

Figure 5.1
Diagram showing a general sequence of steps that make up a morphological study.

GENERAL TYPES OF STUDY

There are two general types of study that determine how the scope of the study is defined. **Place-based** studies focus on a single area or settlement, while **element-based** studies investigate different examples of the same element such as building types or urban tissues from different places (within either a single settlement or cultural area or different settlements and areas). A further type, which tends to be element-focused, is **regularity-based** studies that investigate repeating patterns of interaction, formation and transformation as well as correlations between various measures of form, use and performance.

SCOPE

The scope of a project can be defined in terms of the specific boundaries of the **study area** or **type of form**, the specific **aspects of urban form** to be investigated (as set out above), the **level of resolution** of the study and the **time frame** to be employed. All of these will be limited by the time, funding, expertise and information available. The scope for a project should therefore be drawn up with those limitations clearly in mind. In general, the parameters can be adjusted to allow a fine-tuning of the scope of the study to suit different specific circumstances, aims and objectives.

At a conceptual level, as indicated in figure 5.2, we start with our immediate experience – the current state in all its detail. This narrow, near focus

is expanded outward by applying the more abstract concepts of levels of resolution, time sequence and different aspects of urban form, each of which is a distinct view. One way or the other the scope should be fixed at the outset of the project to ensure that it remains focused and deliverable.

THE STUDY AREA

To fit with different purposes and circumstances, it is useful to distinguish different kinds of boundary in terms of the way the boundary relates to the area in question.

ARBITRARY BOUNDARIES

Often the simplest and most convenient way to define the study area is to fit the settlement or area of interest into a rectangular or square boundary. The boundary is arbitrary in the sense that it does not directly follow any features of the settlement being studied. An arbitrary boundary such as a square kilometre might be used in element-based studies or those involving sampling of larger areas or controlled comparison of different areas.

GIVEN BOUNDARIES

In some cases the study area will be defined by existing boundaries such as the **administrative** or **jurisdictional** limits of local authorities, municipalities or regional bodies. The boundary is 'given' most often because the study is undertaken by or for the authority or other body

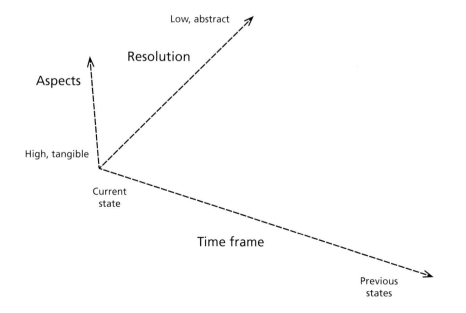

Figure 5.2
Diagram showing the relationship between the different dimensions or views that make up the scope of a study.

whose interest is only the area over which they
have control. A given boundary might also be
used when revising an existing designation such
as a conservation area or policy area. If the given
boundaries cut through areas in an arbitrary way,
it may be worth extending the study area some
distance beyond the given boundary to show the
continuity of important elements.

ELEMENT OR FEATURE BOUNDARIES
There are also cases in which it makes most sense
to define the study area by following the outline of a
particular element such as a settlement, tissue or plot.

ASPECTS

The scope of a study can be adjusted to suit
different purposes and objectives by selecting
which of the different aspects of urban form to
include. A minimal study might involve only built
form and a general indication of use, while a
comprehensive monograph of a settlement might
include all the aspects with a detailed account of
the process of development and evolution of local
types of building and tissue.

LEVEL OF RESOLUTION

The **level of resolution** of a study refers to the
smallest element taken into account in the study.
A study of building types, for example, may only
involve the overall form and internal floor plans
of buildings, treating the structures as 'indivisible

Figure 5.3
The study area
establishes the spatial
extent of the project.

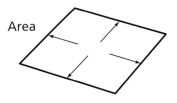

Area

Figure 5.4
The different aspects
included form one of the
dimensions of the scope.

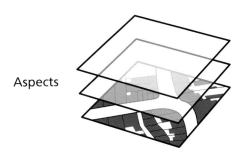

Aspects

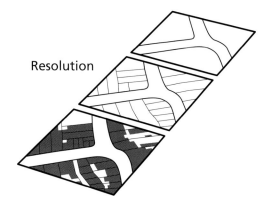

Resolution

Figure 5.5
The level of resolution
chosen for the study
forms a further dimension
of the scope.

solids' and not identifying different types of structure or materials. An assessment of a town or village might include the position of the settlement within the landscape down through tissues and individual streets, plots, leaving the building as the 'solid' and so not distinguishing different types of building in terms of internal arrangement, structures and materials.

A comprehensive morphological analysis or character assessment would include the nine principal elements of form. In practice, the limited availability of information on all aspects (for example, internal layout of buildings or structures), necessitates covering some elements in less detail, by inference, sampling, reference to types or omitting some levels.

As with the aspects, the scope of a study can be fine-tuned to suit the objectives by selecting the most relevant level of resolution.

TIME FRAME

Similarly, the time frame of the study can be focused or extended to suit different aims. In some cases, such as studies using urban tissue as a reference for environmental performance, it is only necessary to identify the different tissues making up the fabric as it currently stands. While it may be helpful to use historical information to clearly identify different tissues and knowing the historical period of the examples may help to explain differences, it is not the 'period of origin' that is being tested but the current physical structure. By contrast, in studies seeking

to establish the historical development of a settlement, the time frame obviously needs to extend from the foundation of the settlement to its current state – or some part of the process relevant to the aim of the study.

In this respect, it can be said that all morphological studies have a **time dimension** on the principle that form is always the product of a process. The **time frame** of a study is the period of time over which the study explicitly seeks to establish the state of the settlement or relevant elements.

MIXED BOUNDARIES, ASPECTS, RESOLUTION AND TIME FRAME

In some cases it can make sense to mix different boundaries, aspects, resolutions and time frame. For example, if the aim of the study is to understand the role of specific parts of a settlement within its current state and identify principles for planning and design, the study could cover a wider area (with an arbitrary boundary) at a low level of resolution for the current state of the settlement, looking only at built form and use to establish a wider context in which particular tissues function. The study could then go on to focus in on the specific, relevant tissues at a higher level of resolution as well as patterns of control and the construction process, setting the time frame to start with the origin of the tissues up to their current state.

Similarly, an element-based study might take a settlement as a whole or a 'transect' as

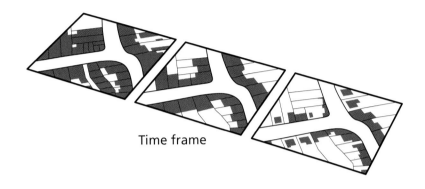

Time frame

a wider source area within which sample areas are identified with arbitrary (kilometre square) boundaries looking only at the period of origin for each sample.

The possible variations are effectively boundless. What is of significant importance for the rigour of a given study and the wider use of studies collectively is to ensure that the variables of study area boundaries, aspects of form, level of resolution and time frame are clearly and explicitly stated.

ASSESSING THE AVAILABLE INFORMATION

As stated above, there is often a direct connection between the aims and objectives of the project and the information necessary to realise the objectives. It is therefore important to identify and assess the resources available at the outset of the project when formulating the aims and objectives. The quality and resolution of the information is also of significant importance in this respect. There are increasing numbers of compiled datasets available that are useful in morphological analysis. These datasets need to be assessed, however, to determine if they will serve their intended purpose. The assessment should examine the quality of the data from both traditional archival and digital sources in terms of:

• Completeness
• Currency
• Accuracy
• Consistency

In many cases it will be necessary to either process the information in some way, such as cleaning or conversion from one format to another, or to use the data indirectly by inference or manipulation. This can be time-consuming and a judgement needs to be made whether the processing costs are lower than compiling the data directly.

INFORMATION GATHERING

The information-gathering stage is crucial to the success of a project in a number of ways. The principal steps in this stage are to:

• Plan the information-gathering process
• Identify the reference platform and output resolution
• Put together a working set-up
• Compile the information

While it is obviously necessary to have basic information before undertaking any analysis, experience shows that discoveries can be made during the process of analysis that prompt the need for additional information. Without knowing the study area in detail, it is difficult to anticipate what will be judged to be the most important or significant aspects and features. Thus, in the same way that identifying aims and objectives benefits from an iterative process cycling between identifying the outputs and assessing the available information, gathering information can often benefit from an iterative process with the actual analysis of the information.

Figure 5.6
The fourth dimension of the scope is the time frame. The diagram shows the current state on the left to highlight the fact that the study begins with our current experience of the study area. We can only extend the time frame by compiling information about its previous states if such is available.

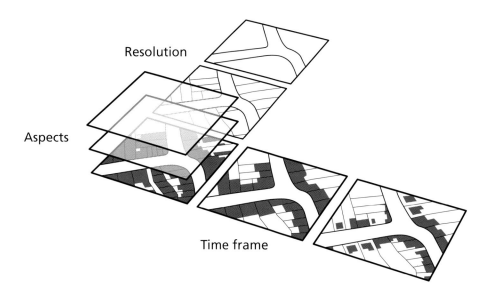

Resolution

Aspects

Time frame

This is particularly the case with the two distinct stages of the desktop analysis and field survey. It may seem an obvious point, but it is worth emphasising that the desktop analysis is best done before undertaking the field survey. The results of the desktop analysis are likely to reveal things that will help to focus the field survey and ensure the information gathered is the most relevant to the project as it progresses.

The information-gathering process should therefore be planned in a way that parallels the analytical process from lower resolution, wider area information to higher resolution, more tightly focused information. A staged process of gathering information is particularly important if the later stages involve sampling of areas in order to manage project resources. The early stages of analysis will be helpful in identifying the most appropriate areas for sampling the information.

THE REFERENCE PLATFORM, DATA FORMATS AND RESOLUTION

A fundamental principle in the practice of morphological analysis is the need to establish a fixed frame of reference for the analysis. In simple terms, for plan analysis this means specifying a map projection and scale or scales suited to the area being covered. All the information then needs to be compiled or produced using the

same projection and scale. The choice of scale still matters with digital mapping because when viewing large areas, high-resolution data becomes illegible and more compute-intensive – and so working becomes very slow.

It is also worth assessing at an early stage the range of different data formats that will be used and identifying the required software to view, convert and manipulate the data. In short, it is necessary to know if it will be possible to get all the data into the same frame of reference.

A related issue is the output resolution. Before beginning to compile information it is necessary to know the resolution of the final outputs, for two main reasons. One is that the outputs need to be legible – neither too low nor too high a resolution for the medium of communication. The other is that it would be a waste of effort if very-high-resolution data is compiled when the outputs are of such a low resolution that the detail is not visible.

THE WORKING SET-UP AND WORKFLOWS

Whether using paper or digital maps or both, it is very advisable to think through the working set-up to ensure the process is as efficient and enjoyable as possible. This involves considering the physical space and surfaces available, organisation of equipment, digital workflow threads and storage of raw data, interim and completed analysis,

Figure 5.7
Together the three
dimensions of aspects,
resolution and time frame
constitute the scope of
the study along with
study area.

and outputs for easy retrieval. A consistent and systematic approach is extremely beneficial but should not be so rigid that it cannot be adjusted to adapt to emerging issues or contingencies.

PROJECT PLAN

A final task to conclude the project inception is to write up and record the **project plan**, setting out:

- The aims and objectives of the study
- The principal sources of information
- The scope of the study
  - study area
  - aspects to be included
  - level of resolution
  - time frame
- Specific methods to be used
- The initial and final outputs
- The project programme

TYPES OF ANALYSIS AND THEIR ORDER

The types of analysis correspond broadly to the aspects of form as set out in Section 1.

There are no hard and fast rules for the order in which the various tasks of analysis should be carried out. There are, however, some general sequences that can make the whole process easier and more efficient.

The basic principle that underpins the logic of the sequences is that patterns of elements higher up the hierarchy of generic form tend to change more slowly and constitute a **frame** within which smaller-scale patterns emerge and change. It therefore makes sense to analyse the wider patterns first and progressively increase the level of resolution and detail of analysis. Pragmatically, the process involves cycling up and down the hierarchy, looking first at wider patterns, increasing the level of resolution and investigating the internal detail of the elements identified and then reassessing the wider patterns in light of the detail.

The principal types of analysis and the order that takes advantage of this logic are as follows:

- Natural environment and site
- Growth and transformation
- Social and economic drivers
- Control
- Route structure
- Built form
- Use and neighbourhood structure
- City image, townscape and open space network

Further details of each type are set out in this order in the following subsections.

Not all of these methods will be appropriate for every project, as is true of the range of methods at the field survey stage. Clearly the methods used will depend on the purpose of the study. For conservation designation and management or reconstruction, for example, studies are likely to be much more detailed than those used as an evidence base for strategic planning. Appraisals for use in masterplanning and design might be more selective in picking out particular aspects and elements for more detailed investigation.

FINAL OUTPUTS

Because urban morphology has a role as both an independent and as an auxiliary discipline, there are different levels of output. When urban morphology is used as an auxiliary support for another field or discipline, the analysis required may only be the minimum necessary to identify the basic structural units: urban tissue, plan units or character areas or types at other levels such as streets, blocks or plots, depending on the application.

The basic, minimum outputs might include:

- Plan drawings of tissues or types
- Tables of dimensions and measures
- Elevation, section and/or 3D drawings and/or photographs

The final output of more self-contained studies will likely include additional material such as:

- A map set with single aspect and composite views
- Text descriptions of the elements and process of development
- Quantitative measures
- Diagrams and drawings of detailed elements
- Explanatory text

Desktop Analysis

The overall aim of the desktop stage is to identify the specific elements that constitute the study area or areas. This involves separating out the different aspects of urban form and identifying the range of particular elements of each aspect that make up the study area. In most cases this also involves examining the steps in their formation and transformation. As an example, one of the principal tasks in a place-based study is to distinguish the different urban tissues within the study area based on their location and extent and the patterns of streets, plots and buildings.

The general steps in the process are:

- Sort and assess information by aspect
- Refine the specific methods of analysis to achieve the aims of the study within the limits of the available information and technology
- Undertake the analyses
- Produce outputs

A range of methods and different kinds of information are used, including:

- Plans
- Text documents
- Geospatial and other data sets
- Photographs and other images

There are thus four broad kinds of desktop analysis:

- Plan analysis
- Text analysis
- Quantitative analysis
- Image analysis

PLAN ANALYSIS
Probably the most central and familiar method of morphological analysis involves the analysis of maps and plans. This can include both two-dimensional plans and three-dimensional representations such as axonometric or perspective bird's-eye views.

Plan analysis takes advantage of both the systematic representation of information based on accurate methods of surveying and the conventions of orthographic projection and the wealth of information about different aspects of urban form represented on plans and in the increasingly available geospatial data sets. In short, plan

analysis is the systematic extraction and sorting of geospatial information.

TEXT, QUANTITATIVE AND IMAGE ANALYSIS
Plan analysis is generally supported and augmented by investigations using text documents, statistical/quantitative data sets and images. The types of documents used include:

- Legal documents, accounts and administrative records
- Planning documents
- Local histories and topographic descriptions
- Demographic and census data
- Government, institutional and commercial data sets
- Urban, economic and political histories
- Photographs, film and video

The principal aims of text, quantitative and image analysis are to:

- Fill in gaps in plan information
- Understand the quantitative characteristics of development
- Identify the agents and original intentions motivating the creation of built form
- Establish the institutional and social structures that facilitate or constrain development and transformation
- Set out the wider social and economic drivers for development

The focus in this section is on **plan analysis**. Archival, text and image analysis are necessarily dealt with in much less detail or referred to as indicative tasks, principally in seeking to identify the social and economic drivers for the formation and transformation of built form.

Types of plan analysis covered below include:

- Natural environment and site
- Overall growth and transformation
- Control
- Route structure
- Built form
- Use and neighbourhood structure
- City image, townscape and open-space network

SOURCES OF PLAN INFORMATION
Readily available cartographic sources vary in nature and content from country to country. In the UK, in addition to digital and paper Ordnance Survey (OS) maps at various scales, high-resolution aerial photography is also now ubiquitous through the Internet. Paper and web-based road atlases are also a significant resource. In European and other countries, cadastral and other administrative and/or insurance and property maps provide a key source for cartographic information on property boundaries and, by inference, physical features. Digital cartographic/geospatial data sets are also increasingly available for use in GIS programs, often under open licences. These can include information on aspects such as:

- Land-form elevation
- Geology
- Habitat
- Land use
- Infrastructure
- Heritage assets

Sources for historical cartographic information also vary in kind from country to country. Historical cadastral records are often available in European countries, Sanborn fire insurance maps in the US and early editions of OS maps in the UK. Other sources in the UK include:

- Estate maps
- Enclosure maps
- Tithe maps
- Parliamentary projects (turnpikes etc)
- Bird's-eye views
- Conveyancing plans/deeds
- Planning applications
- Archaeological records

Sources of text and image documents on specific places are still more variable, but useful sources include:

- Local histories
- Topographic descriptions
- Tourist guides
- Architectural guides
- Postcards
- Panoramas
- Estate inventories
- Estate agents' brochures

Many record offices and archives have local history sections and keep place-based catalogues of material.

SET-UP
Good working practice in starting the plan analysis is to prepare the **working set-up** and workspace, allowing for laying out a number of maps and plans and other sources. The next step is to compile the **basic working materials**:

- The most current paper or digital plans of the study area, as detailed as possible. Ideally the plans should depict **street lines** (frontage and/or kerb), **plot boundaries** and **building outlines**. These features are usually shown in maps at the scale (or scale equivalent) of 1:500, 1:1000, 1:1250, 1:2500.
- Maps showing the topography, geology and vegetation/habitat within the study area
- Plans, elevations and sections of building types at 1:100 or 1:200 (as available)
- Sequence of available historic maps
- Atlas or maps showing the wider context OR
- GIS, earth viewer
- Tracing paper for overlays; pencils, coloured pencils, markers or pens OR
- GIS, CAD or other vector drawing program allowing for overlays
- Photographs, postcards and other depictions
- Online street viewer (recognising potential issues of currency of information)
- Text descriptions.

THREE CORE TECHNIQUES: THE OVERLAY, PLAN SEQUENCING AND ELEMENT SEPARATION
The **overlay** is a technique common to GIS, CAD, illustration and image manipulation. It is fundamental to urban morphology because it enables clear and accurate comparison of different states and aspects of a single form: a settlement at different times in its development; different aspects of a settlement such as site, land use, social and legal boundaries or movement patterns, among any number of other aspects.

For the sake of clarity, in very simple terms the overlay involves first undertaking an **aspect separation** by identifying all elements of a given aspect and putting them on a separate plan or overlay. It is then possible to view two or more different images, each with different information about the same object or area on semi-transparent media and looking at them simultaneously by laying

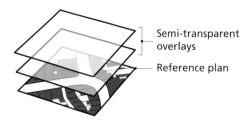

Semi-transparent
overlays

Reference plan

one on top of another and aligning the images. *Fundamental to the method is using the same view, projection and scale, most sensibly using an accurate plan of the most current state of the study area as the reference plan*.

Overlays are commonly used in producing images for plan sequencing and investigating the correlation between different aspects of urban form. As shown in figure 6.11, it is often helpful to use different colours for each layer. The overlay gets to the heart of one of the key aims of morphology, which is coordinating the findings of a wide range of disciplines around the unifying aspect of form.

A similar method is to **toggle** rectified images on a computer screen (or flip back and forth between aligned paper plans). Toggling involves opening the drawings as image files (so they are in random-access memory) and quickly switching between them using a keyboard shortcut (often alt-tab). Because toggling is dynamic (and as long as the images are exactly the same size in the same position), differences between the images appear as movement, which is much easier for the eye/brain to detect. Toggling also generates a short-term composite image in the brain through persistence of vision.

Perhaps the most essential *urban morphological* method is to visualise the process of formation and transformation of a settlement over time by a chronological sequence of images, usually historical plans, to create a **cartographic time series** or **plan sequence.** The technique is also referred to as **map regression**. Sequencing using overlays helps in illustrating the outward growth and internal transformations that occur with the development of the settlement.

A third fundamental tool of morphological analysis is **element separation** based on the compositional hierarchy of built form. The method involves producing a number of plans of an urban area, each showing only a single generic type of form. The result illustrates the area at

progressively higher **levels of resolution**. One of the principal benefits of the method is that it allows clear visualisation of the distinct patterns of forms at each level in the hierarchy. As shown in Section 4, the element separations correspond to sections through the multi-level diagram of generic structure. The multi-level diagram is therefore an important tool for investigating and keeping track of levels of resolution.

These three general techniques are used in various ways in the more specific methods set out below.

NATURAL ENVIRONMENT AND SITE

The natural environment is the **substance** or **substrate (base matrix)** out of which the built environment is created. There are a number of ways in which the characteristics of the natural environment therefore have a role in the location, shape and internal structure of the built environment.

Natural features, including stocks and flows of energy, materials, plants and animals, constitute assets or resources that attract human attention, activity and use. At the same time, some of those same features – and others – present constraints to human activity and settlement.

ENVIRONMENT, ADAPTATION AND LEARNING

One way or the other, in creating the built environment, humans necessarily **respond** to the natural environment in order to take advantage of the assets and avoid, mitigate or remove the constraints. In broad terms, the responses are forms of culturally rooted **adaptive behaviour**. More generally it can be seen as a process of **learning**. We either change our habits and behaviour – including the things we build – to adapt to the environment, or change the environment to adapt it to suit our habits and behaviour.

The logic or rationale for any adaptation involves three elements:

Figure 6.1
The aspect separation and overlay are the analytical techniques used to investigate the different aspects included in the scope.

- The initial intentions for an activity or act of building
- The assets and constraints presented by the environment or context for the activity or building
- The resulting form, which is a cultural response to the assets and constraints

The aim of the analysis is to follow this logic when looking at the built environment in relation to natural features. The underlying question is, to what extent is the location, shape and size and internal structure of any particular part of the built environment an adaptive response to the natural environment?

The key natural features for analysis usually include:

- Underlying geology
- Soil
- Topography or landform
- Ground water, water courses, floodplains and water bodies
- Vegetation, habitat and ecosystems

Another fundamental element of the natural environment to consider is the climatic regime of a place, including:

- Insolation
- Wind speed and direction
- Temperature regime
- Precipitation pattern

The basic method of analysis involves the following steps:

- Compile map information on built features, natural features and climate
- Create base maps and overlays at the same scale
- Examine and compare the information, if necessary isolating one or a limited number of types of features at a time (eg, topography)
- Seek to identify consistent patterns or regularities in relationships or associations, between built forms (at various levels) and the natural features or resources in terms of:
    - proximity
    - orientation
    - alignment
    - overall form (outline and extent)
    - internal structure

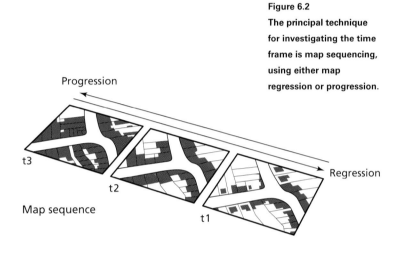

Figure 6.2
The principal technique for investigating the time frame is map sequencing, using either map regression or progression.

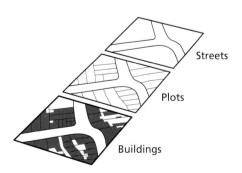

Figure 6.3
The graphic analytical technique of the element separation along with diagrams of generic structure are used in exploring the levels of resolution included in the scope.

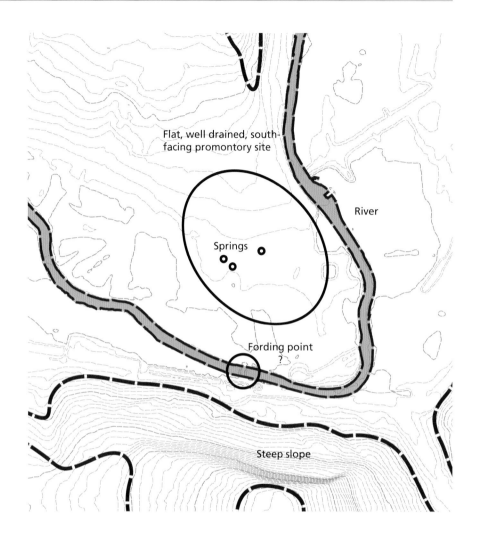

Flat, well drained, south-
facing promontory site

River

Springs

Fording point
?

Steep slope

SOURCES OF INFORMATION

High-resolution mapping and aerial photography are the principal starting points for compiling information. Data sets for a wide range of subjects such as topography, habitat and land cover are increasingly available for use with GIS, which allows easy comparison with map layers. For elevation data, Lidar technology has proved particularly useful as it allows processing to reveal surface features beneath buildings and tree cover. Similarly, processing techniques allow the use of satellite imagery to distinguish different habitat types. While these sources are useful for larger areas, the level of resolution of the data is generally too low for smaller study areas.

NATURAL FEATURES, STOCKS AND FLOWS AS ASSETS AND CONSTRAINTS

In setting out the elements of the natural environment, it is helpful to think in terms of both **features** and **stocks and flows**. As a feature, a river can be a constraint to movement and, if it tends to flood, also to building. It can also be an asset as a feature, for example as a means of transport or fortification. As a flow, the river is an asset because it can provide a water supply, outfall for land drainage and, historically, often contributed to waste disposal.

The focus here is openly on the features, stocks and flows to which some cultural response is made, either as an asset or a constraint. What is considered an asset or constraint, however, is fundamentally dependent on cultural context and so varies with time and place. Wildlife habitat, for example, has not historically been taken as a constraint, but is increasingly seen as such in some parts of the world. Similarly, topography that aids defence against attack is no longer generally considered an important asset.

Figure 6.4
The principal natural features of the site of the city of Bath highlighting the limits of the steep slopes and river, and attractors of the hot springs, fording point and flat south-facing slope protected by the bend in the river.

ATTRACTORS AND LIMITS

When looking at features, stocks and flows as assets, the result is generally to identify the natural **attractors** to the creation and extension of settlements or transformation of elements within them. Examples include sources of fresh water, level ground with good drainage, nearby cultivable land and building materials, defensible sites and river fording/crossing points. These can be inferred from basic principles but ideally, particularly with variations in cultural context, should be supported by textual or other archival evidence.

There is variability in the extent to which natural features act as constraints to the creation of the built environment. The variation is dependent on the intentions, resources and technology available to the people and culture who undertake the building. The shoreline of a river, lake, bay or sea, for example, in many cases presents a **hard** or **fixed limit** to urban development. Other features that typically present hard limits include very steep slopes and sheer cliff faces, floodplains, poorly drained land and weak or shifting ground. Features that present softer limits include high-grade soils, mineral reserves, wildlife habitat and valued landscape (protecting assets creates constraints).

As the examples of Boston and San Francisco – among many other cities – show, however, what were once hard limits can be overcome with the appropriate level of resources, technology and the need or desire to extend the urban area. The shorelines of the Charles River and San Francisco Bay were altered by filling to accommodate urban extensions (see figure 6.10).

INFLECTIONS

Notwithstanding the ability to overcome limits, in cases where a limit is taken as fixed, there is a general tendency for development to be adapted to its position on or near the limit. Built features such as streets or boundaries tend to follow the lines of the limits, so that types and forms that would be used in unconstrained locations are **varied** or **inflected** in response to the constrained location. Inflection can also occur in response to an attractor. Inflected types are sometimes referred to as **variants** or **synchronic variants**.

THE NATURAL MORPHOLOGICAL FRAME

The combination of natural features that are taken as hard limits at a given point or period in time and to which development is adapted can be referred to as the **natural morphological frame**. It can be the case that the inflected forms built in response to the frame at a given time persist even after a given limit has been removed or overcome. The outlines of historical morphological frames can thus sometimes still be identified within the fabric of the settlement as **traces** or **persistent features**.

Some natural constraints such as slopes are extensive rather than specifically limiting. Similarly, some features that are both assets and constraints, such as solar exposure, are ubiquitous. An example of the principle of inflection in response to a constraint is the orientation and alignment of routes in relation to topography. Specific responses may vary depending on the culture and available technology.

Because of the basic physics of moving bodies, steeper slopes present a constraint when

Figure 6.5
Routes in the city of Bath that have been inflected in response to the presence of the river, which acts as a limit and forms part of the natural morphological frame.

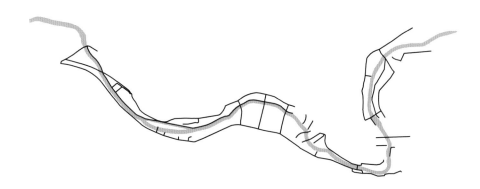

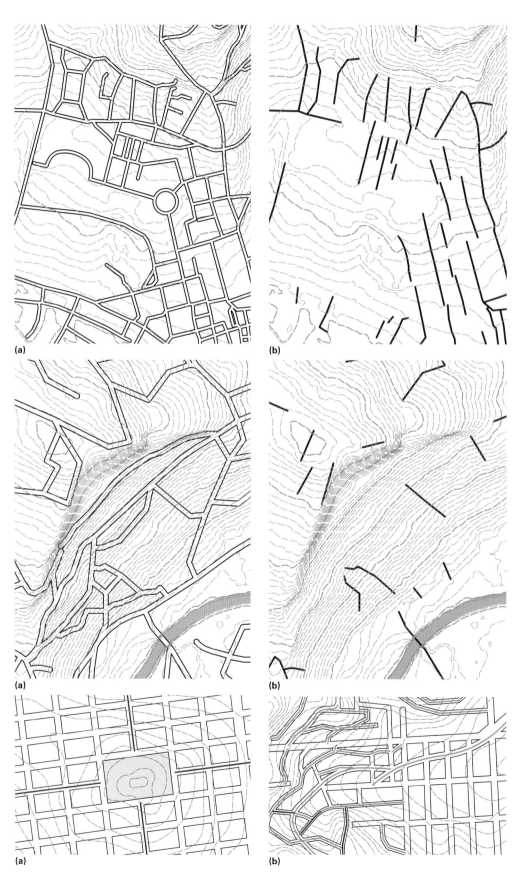

(a)

(b)

(a)

(b)

(a)

(b)

top **Figure 6.6**
Routes in the city of Bath inflected in response to moderate slope: a) all routes in relation to contours, b) routes at right angles to contours, c) routes diagonal and parallel to contours. Note the relatively high proportion of routes perpendicular to contours.

middle **Figure 6.7**
Routes in the city of Bath inflected in response to steep slopes: a) all routes in relation to contours, b) routes at right angles to contours, c) routes diagonal and parallel to contours. Note the relatively high proportion of the latter.

bottom **Figure 6.8**
Routes in San Francisco showing different responses to slope. While the grid appears to 'ignore' the topography, there are a number of subtle responses that take slope into account: a) a block centred on a local peak, treated as open space, b) breakdown of the grid and inflection of routes to run mainly parallel or diagonally to contours, c) significant inflection following the shape of the contours.

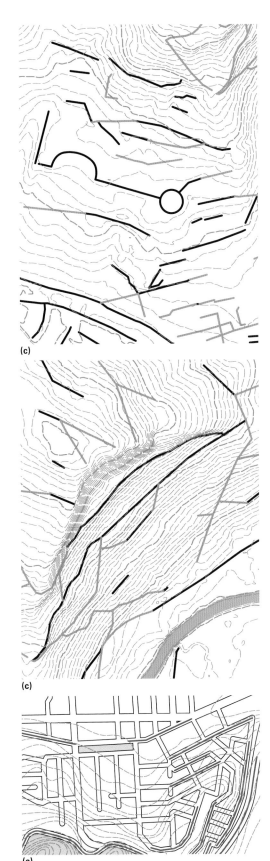

(c)

(c)

(c)

seeking to allow for efficient, comfortable and safe movement as well as to ensure the stability of the structure of the route. The response to steep slopes is therefore to adjust or **inflect** the alignment and orientation of the route to remain within certain limits. The characteristic response in many locations is for routes to run either parallel or perpendicular to the contours, with routes running diagonally generally for longer-distance movement up steeper slopes and to fit within an established pattern of routes relating to plot sizes. The resulting inflection of the routes in response to the slope creates patterns that vary with the characteristics of the topography. It can therefore be said that the adapted pattern has a **bias** in response to the natural features.

LOCAL MATERIALS

A further part of the analysis of the natural environment is to identify the **natural building materials** that are and have been used in the locality. The analysis should identify the type, source and use of natural materials and the extent to which there is a **local building culture** in terms of techniques of working the materials and using them in construction.

OUTPUTS

In summary, an analysis of the natural environment and site should identify the principal natural features, stocks and flows to which creation of the built environment has been adapted, in terms of:

- Hard and soft limits and constraints
- Assets and attractors
- Ubiquitous features, stocks and flows
- Inflections and variants created in response to natural features

These can be summarised in a plan of the current natural morphological frame, adaptive inflections and any historical frames and their traces.

OVERALL GROWTH AND TRANSFORMATION

An analysis and account of the historical development of a settlement or selected area or element of the built environment may be either the central focus or a supporting technique for a morphological study. Irrespective of the purpose of the study and the value placed on historical features, it is a simple fact that all human settlements have a time dimension. They are all created at a particular point in time and are the product of an ongoing process. Once built they continue to be extended and modified and may stagnate or decline.

The specifics of the process have a profound and fundamental effect on the physical structure of a settlement. The order of the steps establishes its composite structure at any given time and limits future possibilities. One of the most effective ways of understanding the resulting patchwork structure is to retrace the process of development.

There are three basic components in an analysis of historical development:

- Growth and/or contraction in extent
- Transformation and/or persistence of internal structure
- Social and economic drivers

PLAN SEQUENCING

The primary technique used for the analysis of growth and transformation is **plan sequencing** as introduced at the beginning of this section. The aim of the analysis is to get a picture of the development process of a settlement or element such as a tissue at a level of resolution appropriate to the objectives of the project by tracing the progressive changes in its physical extent and any internal transformations.

The sequencing can be done in either direction, by **progression** from earliest to most recent, or by **regression**, in reverse order. The minimum form of the technique is to simply reproduce the historic maps *at the same scale* in chronological order. This allows people to do their own visual comparison. The initial steps are as follows:

- Compile historic maps of the study area
- Establish the chronology of the maps
- Reduce or enlarge them to the same scale
- Rectify the map images as necessary to compensate for differences in projection, orientation, surveying techniques and accuracy. This is now relatively easily done by using the various tools in image manipulation software

GROWTH IN EXTENT

The analysis of changes in extent can be undertaken at a relatively low level or resolution, distinguishing only between the built-up and unbuilt areas. It can, however, be useful to include

(a)

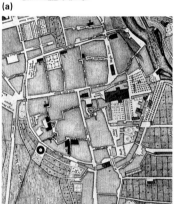

(b)

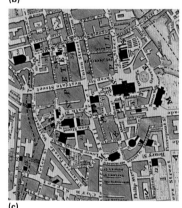

(c)

(d)

Figure 6.9
A sequence of historic plans of the city of Bath: a) Speed's map of 1610, b) Wood's map of 1735, c) Cotterell's map of 1852, d) first edition Ordnance Survey map of 1885.

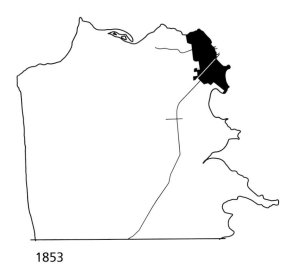

1853

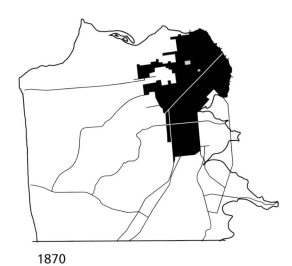

1870

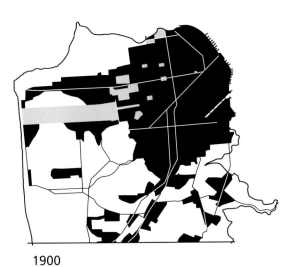

1900

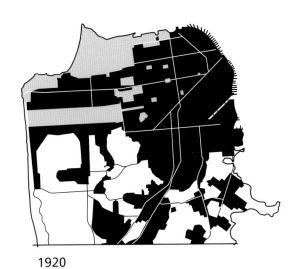

1920

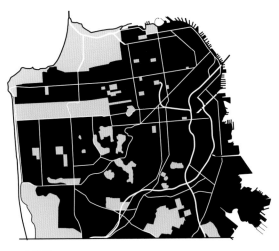

1970

Figure 6.10
A sequence of
diagrammatic plans
showing the changes
in outline extent and
selected internal features
depicting the growth of
San Francisco from 1853
to 1970. In this case the
built-up area is shown
in outline with only
principal internal routes.
As depicted in Moudon's
study, the full street
patterns were included.

some internal structure as points of reference, in particular the main routes. More specific steps involve the following.

- Trace the physical extent of the settlement or other element for each period
- Compare the steps in order to identify:
  - the increase or decrease in physical extent from one state to the next
  - the seams between stages of development
- Set out each step in chronological order to form the time series or sequence

In the absence of comprehensive mapping, it is necessary to work backwards by inference based on the dating of any retained features and characteristic patterns.

The function of establishing changes in extent of a settlement or element may be principally to provide background information to more detailed analysis of particular components (see for example Moudon's classic *Built for Change*[1]). In other cases, the process of growth and historical development may be the principal focus of the overall study. In either instance it can be beneficial to complete the analysis of changes in extent before analysis of the natural environment and site, in order to set out the basic framework for more detailed analysis such as identification of natural morphological frames at different stages.

INTERNAL TRANSFORMATION

What is evident from the investigation of plan sequences is that the development of settlements involves not only increases and/or decreases in extent but also **internal transformation**. What is also evident is that the transformation is generally not uniform but variable. Some elements and patterns of elements are changed while others **persist**. The aim of this stage of the analysis is to identify which parts and features have changed and which have persisted.

PERSISTENCE

The phenomenon of persistence of element patterns was identified in the early 20th century at about the same time by the Italian Gustavo Giovannoni and the Frenchman Pierre Lavedan.[2] Both noted in the sequence of historical maps of cities that street patterns tend to remain relatively unchanged over time. Early studies also demonstrated that the initial transformation from rural to urban often incorporated pre-existing routes and boundaries. More detailed studies show that the patterns of plot boundaries also tend to persist but change more frequently than streets, while buildings tend to change more frequently than plot boundaries (see Robert for further new research[3]). The growth and transformation of settlements thus show **differential rates of change at different levels of generic structure**. This follows from the fact that changing or creating a street (public highway) involves changing a large number of abutting individual plots and buildings. Changing a plot boundary involves making changes to one or more adjacent parcels, while change within a single plot does not affect any other properties or structures at all.

Transformational analysis seeks to identify the variable change and persistence of features and involves the same basic technique as growth analysis but adds a number of steps.

- Trace the internal structure of the settlement or other element for each step in the sequence
- Compare the steps in order to identify:
  - the changes/persistence of specific features, elements or patterns in existing built-up areas
  - the incorporation of pre-existing features from land on which an extension is built
  - inflections in response to pre-existing features
- Highlight either persistent or changed features within each subsequent or preceding plan

Figure 6.11
Overlay plans showing the current state of central Bath (in red) and: a) the state in 1610 and b) 1885. Despite being drawn in axonometric, Speed's map is surprisingly accurate.

(a)

(b)

A specific technique is to use a semi-transparent version of the current state of the study area as an overlay on top of each historic map in the series (with a new overlay for each stage). As with growth analysis it is possible to work in either direction by progression or regression. One way or the other it is essential to use the most accurate map (likely the most recent) as the reference plan to which others are aligned. An advantage of working from the earliest to latest is that retained and persistent features are easier to identify. An advantage of working back from the latest is that more recent plans tend to be more accurate and boundaries can be easier to place. In complex cases it can be easier to spot changes by comparing adjacent plans in the series rather than comparing just the most recent with any particular stage. It is best, however, to record the steps on the most recent version as a reference. The choice of how to highlight persistence and change will depend on the extent of the latter. If there is little change, it is easier to highlight. If the change is extensive, it is easier to outline the change and highlight the persistence. Obviously it is essential to use a consistent method for designating the two, for example using one colour for change and another for persistence.

When putting together plans to communicate the results, it is important to indicate the reference date for persistent features. This can be done by either creating separate drawings for each stage or distinguishing dates of changes by colour. Because settlements are fundamentally a palimpsest, this technique can become quite complex.

A technique to help clarify the results and a general aid to transformational analysis is to use element separations. These make it possible to work systematically through the streets, plots and buildings, helping to simplify the individual steps and clarify the changes at the different levels.

THE BUILT MORPHOLOGICAL FRAME
As set out in Section 3, most development does not occur on untouched natural sites but is a transformation of an environment that has already been modified in some way. Most development therefore involves a cultural response to both natural and built features: the tracks and field boundaries of open countryside or dense urban tissue of a settlement centre. As in the case of natural features, pre-existing built elements can present both assets and constraints to subsequent development. The combination of existing built features therefore constitutes a **built morphological frame**. As with the natural frame, there is a logic to the response involving the intentions behind the development, the assets and constraints presented and the adaptive response. The principal choices in deciding what to do with built features are:

- Removal
- Substitution
- Partial modification
- Full retention

The range of costs involved with removal and the benefits of retention mean that removal tends to be the least likely choice. It is easier and so more common for features to be modified or retained. This manifestation of the principles of **least effort** and **greatest convenience** (Zipf[4]) leads in turn to the tendency for persistence. The pre-existing built features may function as limits or as assets that are incorporated into the development. In either case there is a tendency for the new forms to be inflected variants of unconstrained forms in response to the retained features. With hard limits such as fortifications or railways, for example, inflected or variant types of street, plot and building are often found along the line of the feature and some distance from it.

Again, as with natural features, the fixity of persistent features is not absolute. Changing circumstances, resources and technology, as well as the need for new forms and activities or the inconvenience of outdated forms, may warrant removal of previously hard limits. As with natural features, the surrounding inflected forms built in response to the earlier frame may persist.

TRACES
There are different ways in which features persist, all of which are **traces** of previous states.

- **Material trace**: retention of the feature and its physical fabric
- **Substitution trace**: retention of the outline or alignment of a feature, substituted by another physical element
- **Inflection trace**: retention of surrounding forms that were initially inflected in response to a feature that has been removed or transformed
- **Association trace**: retention of a combination of elements in a consistent relative position or association

Features that tend to persist include:

- Pre-urban
  - Infrastructure
  - Roads and tracks
  - Drainage features
  - Field boundaries
  - Isolated buildings and monuments

- Urban
  - Infrastructure (eg, fortifications and railways)
  - Streets and squares
  - Public open spaces
  - Plot boundaries
  - Monuments and special buildings

Depending on the extent to which the subsequent forms retain and/or adapt to the features of the frame, the development shows degrees of **frame continuity** or **discontinuity**. Comprehensive or *tabula rasa* redevelopment generally results in an area of **discontinuity**.

OUTPUTS

In summary, an analysis of the growth and transformation of built form within the study area should give an account of the development process in terms of:

- Areas of extension or contraction
- Areas of transformation
- Persistent features and types of persistence
- Inflections and variants created in response
- A narrative of the main stages of development and rationale for adaptive changes and inflections

These points can be summarised in a series of plans showing the areal extent of growth, the historical morphological frames and their traces supported by narrative text. It is worth recalling that the morphological frame is the combination of features taken as limits or incorporated into changes made at a given time.

As noted above, some cases may present a challenge as far as clearly communicating the analysis of growth, persistent features and morphological frames. One method is to produce a sequence of drawings representing the changes from one period to the next. Another is to show only the outer extent of the settlement and

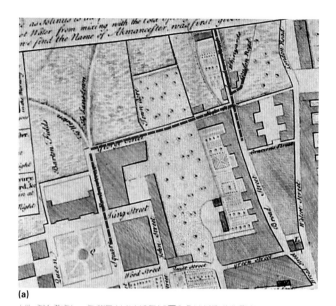

(a)

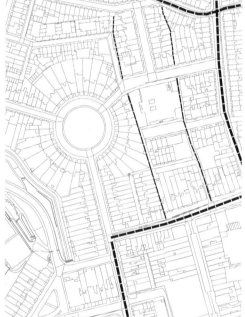

(b)

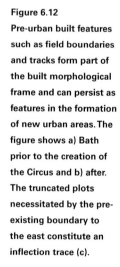

Figure 6.12
Pre-urban built features such as field boundaries and tracks form part of the built morphological frame and can persist as features in the formation of new urban areas. The figure shows a) Bath prior to the creation of the Circus and b) after. The truncated plots necessitated by the pre-existing boundary to the east constitute an inflection trace (c).

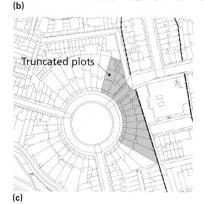

Truncated plots

(c)

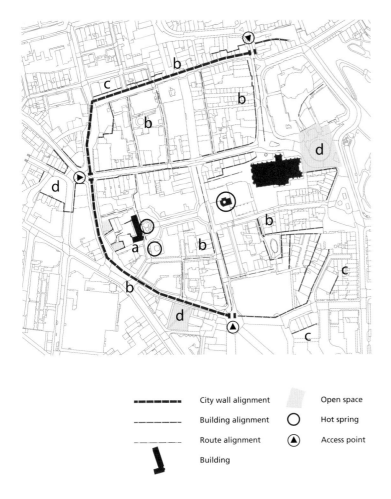

Figure 6.13
Plan of central Bath
showing the traces of
the principal features
that have persisted from
1735, some of which have
persisted from earlier
states such as the line
of the city wall, which
dates back to the original
Roman foundation. The
plan identifies different
types of trace: a) material
traces, b) substitution
traces, c) inflection traces
and d) association traces.

━ ━ ━ ━ ━ City wall alignment	▨ Open space
─ ─ ─ ─ ─ Building alignment	○ Hot spring
─ · ─ · ─ · Route alignment	▲ Access point
▮ Building	

(a)   (b)

Figure 6.14
Another example of
persistence, showing
the trace of the line of a
railway within the block
and plot structure in
San Francisco. The land
occupied by the railway
(a) has become a series
of distinct plots within a
number of blocks (b).

retained or incorporated features at each stage in a single drawing. The different dates and types of persistence can be shown with a different colour, tone or line type.

A simple and effective tool for the narrative account is a timeline. This can be combined graphically with a sequence of plan diagrams to tell the story in an easily accessible way. One way or the other it is best to present historical development together with social and economic context.

In some cases, the analysis may extend to identifying the logic or principles that have been applied in responding to existing built features, modifying them and adapting new forms to them. As with the analysis of the natural environment and site, the basis for the analysis is the logic of adaptive behaviour:

• Intentions
• Conditions, assets and constraints
• Response

SOCIAL AND ECONOMIC DRIVERS

While it is fairly easy to visualise the growth and transformation of a town through a sequence of maps, it is much easier to *understand* the changes when the sequence is set beside an account of the social, cultural and economic changes and specific events that stimulated or triggered them.

The story is much richer and sheds more light on the evidence if the physical and social are tied together. It is only by examining the agents and mechanisms of change that it is possible to properly explain the changes. Similarly, understanding the mechanisms involved makes it easier to identify repeating processes that may be common to a number of settlements and so represent more general developmental regularities. The most obvious example of this on the larger scale is the connection between economic cycles, building cycles and the physical growth of towns. Identifying such regularities at various scales is a key goal for research.

It should be said that detailed investigation and primary research into social, cultural and economic history are likely to go beyond the scope of most studies unless they are principal objectives of the project. Often it is sufficient to provide a brief narrative that focuses on general trends and changes as well as specific events with a direct bearing on growth and change in the fabric of a settlement:

• Demographics
• Economics
• Politics
• Cultural trends
• Technological development

When the study focuses on the historical development of a particular settlement or area, the investigation of social and economic context should set out:

• Main stages of development and events
• The agents involved
• The principal intentions
• Key considerations

OUTPUTS

In principle, the investigation into the social, cultural and economic context for either a particular state of a study area or its longer-term growth and transformation can be as concise or extensive as necessary to suit the aims and objectives of the study.

In most cases it will be a narrative account used in association with the analytical plans and the text narrative of the development process. In cases where the wider cultural context is less central to the study, the information on the social and economic context can be added to the timeline setting out the stages of development.

CONTROL

Control is one of the core aspects of urban form along with environment, form and use. The most basic type of control is the occupation of a space (surface), either moving through it or remaining within it. At this primitive level, use – movement and occupation – is itself an exercise of control.

It is only at this generic level, however, that the two are effectively the same. With the diversification of culture, and its associated built forms, distinguishing between use and control and different kinds of each becomes increasingly important. The distinction between use and control is perhaps most evident when looking at the processes of formation and transformation. Patterns of control, exemplified by land ownership, tend to change less frequently than either patterns of use (types of activity) or generic types of built form lower down the hierarchy. A property, as a unit of ownership and control, acts as a kind of container for uses and forms. The different occupants, activities and buildings come and go

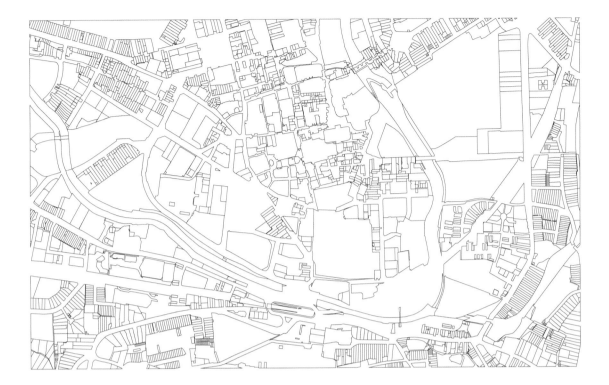

but the container remains in place to accommodate each subsequent use or form.

Because of the inertia of control, the pattern put in place with the initial formation of a settlement acts as a significant constraint on possible built forms that might be placed within the pattern and possible transformations or modifications of the resulting urban tissue. In terms of process, there are a number of different ways in which this becomes manifest. In some cases, the land is subdivided first and plots built up individually over time. In other cases, a large number of buildings might be constructed by a single agent on a large parcel and, in strict legal terms, separate properties are only created once they are first sold. The strength of property as a resistive element is perhaps most famously illustrated in the case of the rebuilding of London after the Great Fire in 1666. Despite the opportunity presented by the destruction of much of the built form and the existence of plans for a reconfiguration, the previous patterns were reinstated primarily because individuals did not want to lose the value of the property they owned.

One of the reasons patterns of control change more slowly than patterns of activity is that changes in control necessarily involve more than one agent and more than one property. Inertia increases with the number of agents and entities involved. It also increases with the size of the agents. As part of the general tendency toward least effort and greatest convenience, the resistance of the social binding of control contributes to the fundamental morphological regularities of **persistence** and **differential rates of change**.

While it is most commonly the case that a unit of control corresponds to a physical plot (and unit of land use), this is not always the case. Because of this general correspondence, as with use, there is the potential for a conflation between physical form and units of control. Control is strictly an abstract relationship between an agent (individual or group) and an area of land or physical form. It is not the physical form itself. In some places there are complex levels of ownership and there is a difference between the unit of occupation and unit of ownership. In other cases there is no distinct physical boundary corresponding to the boundary of control one way or the other. Physical structures may change with no change in control and vice versa.

In order to undertake an analysis of control, it is therefore necessary to distinguish the three parts of the relationship:

- Controlling agent
- Type of control
- Entity controlled

Figure 6.15
Plan of Bath showing only the property parcels as recorded by the Land Registry.

TYPES OF AGENT

The types of controlling agents are likely to include:

- Individual
- Corporate/group
    - Commercial
    - Public
    - Institutional

Depending on the nature of the study, it can also be relevant to identify the size and structure of the corporate/group agents. Again, these distinctions are particularly important when looking at change over time. Larger organisations and institutions tend to be more conservative and act more slowly. Forms under their control therefore tend to persist and change more slowly.

TYPES OF CONTROL

There are two broad types of control based on whether the agent is physically present or not. On the one hand, there is **occupation** and **physical control**. On the other hand, there are different forms of **socially established control**, which involve socially sanctioned relationships between an area of land and a person or group that continue to hold whether the agent is present or not.

Analysis of patterns of control is not treated in detail here. Morphological investigations of control have tended to focus on the effect of different configurations of control that might be exercised or sensed by a person occupying or moving through the configuration. Methods used include those set out by Hillier and Hanson in *The Social Logic of Space*[5] and John Habraken's investigation of control in *The Structure of the Ordinary*.[6] Associated and alternative ideas from environmental psychology include defensible space, personal space and prospect/refuge.

SOCIALLY ESTABLISHED CONTROL

There are many types of socially established control that bear on built form depending on the culture and legal system, but they generally include:

- Rights of property and tenure
- Building regulation
- Environmental health and safety
- Land-use regulation
- Environmental protection

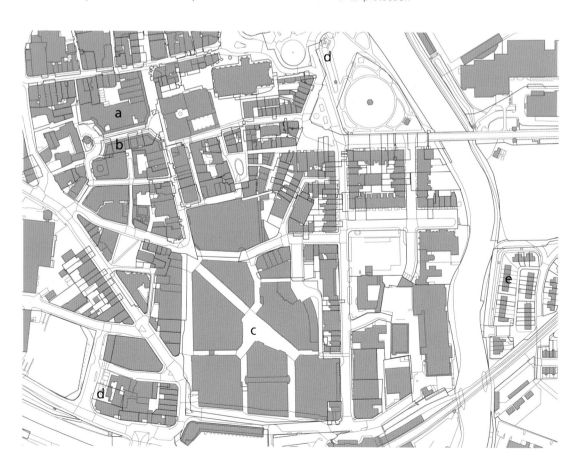

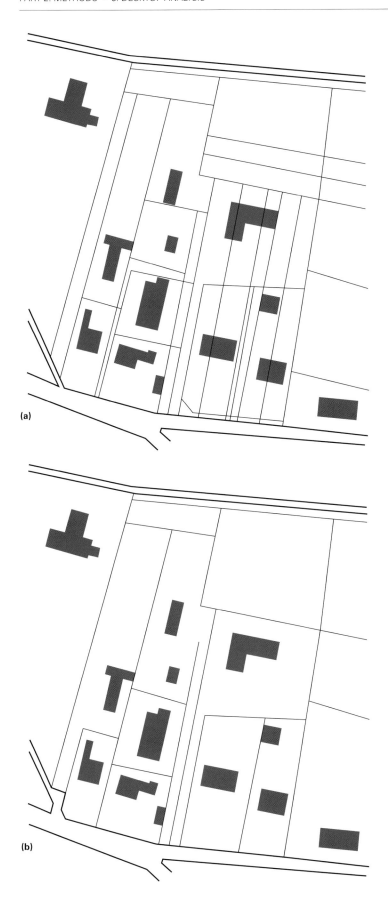

(a)

(b)

opposite **Figure 6.16**
A detail of Bath showing
an overlay of property
parcels and built form,
demonstrating the
variability between the
boundaries of the two: a)
multiple plots/buildings
within one ownership,
b) different parts of a
single building in separate
ownerships, c) a tissue,
including buildings, plots
and street spaces in a
single, private ownership
d) property boundaries
that do not follow any
physical feature, e)
mixed public and private
ownership reflecting
'right-to-buy' legislation.
Also, in some areas the
property boundaries are
not recorded.

left **Figure 6.17**
Representation of a
French cadastral plan
(a) and physical built
form (b). Comparison
highlights that there are
more property boundaries
than physical boundaries,
reflecting the role of
the cadastral plan as a
record of different types
of property holding and
subdivision for purposes
of taxation.

THE PUBLIC HIGHWAY

An important primary distinction in types of socially established control is rooted in the distinction between the generic functions of occupation and movement. Control of occupation space tends to be **restrictive** – access is restricted by default – while control of movement space tends to be **permissive** – access is allowed by default. In more formalised contexts this corresponds with the distinction between private land, controlled by a single agent, and public highway, controlled by a public authority for the benefit of all individuals. Even when movement space is technically private, it tends to be permissive within the group allowed onto the land. The distinction between restrictive occupation space and permissive movement space corresponds in turn with the general difference in configuration between the discrete parcels of occupation space and continuous networks of movement space.

PROPERTY AND TENURE

Types of property and tenure include:

- Occupation (as a socially recognised relationship – sanctioned or not)
- Freehold ownership
- Leasehold/rental

One of the most basic effects of having defined areas of occupation and formal systems of property and tenure is a degree of **modularity** focused on the plot or lot as a unit of control. As noted above, in the context of changes over time, and the difference between occupation and movement space, plots tend to persist and act as a container for different uses and buildings. In this respect, the plot can be considered to be a **module** of urban tissue (though there are other types and degrees of modularity).

The different types of property and tenure vary in terms of the degree and extent of control exercised and the specific aspects controlled (as codified by the legal system). Most importantly, this can involve a number of different layers of control. For example, a residential plot can be owned by the freeholder, rented and occupied by the leaseholder who allows friends to occupy rooms in the house by informal agreement.

REGULATION

Historically, concerns for public health and equity have prompted many cultures to acknowledge that there is social benefit in regulating the use of land and the location, form, shape and size of built form. Depending on the culture, there are many different kinds of regulation, including:

- General planning policy
- Development control, zoning and coding regulations
- Environmental health and safety regulations
- Conservation areas and heritage protection zones
- Building regulations (types and quality of construction)
- Covenants and restrictions associated with property and tenure

All these types of control tend to act as **limits** on the use and/or type of form that can occur within a defined area. The result tends to be a correlation between characteristic types of built form and areas of control. Boundaries of distinct types of form often correspond to boundaries of control. Types of form also tend to persist so long as the controls remain in place. Examples include high building zones in cities such as Boston and Paris, conservation areas, extensive areas of leasehold such as Mayfair and Marylebone in London and planned unit developments.

GOVERNMENTAL AND ADMINISTRATIVE CONTROL

The more general forms of control associated with different legal systems and types of government and administration tend to be more relevant for comparative studies looking at differences between urban form in different countries or regions. Examples include the difference between countries with and without private property, between countries with Common Law and Civil Law legal systems (the United States and United Kingdom on the one hand and most Continental European countries on the other) or between countries with discretionary and legally binding planning systems (UK and some Commonwealth countries on the one hand and the US and Continental European countries on the other).

THE ENTITIES CONTROLLED

Given the range of different types of control, the entities involved may be equally varied. As noted, occupation tends to use the individual structured space as a unit (rooms, convex spaces or street spaces); the plot, as a unit of property, tends

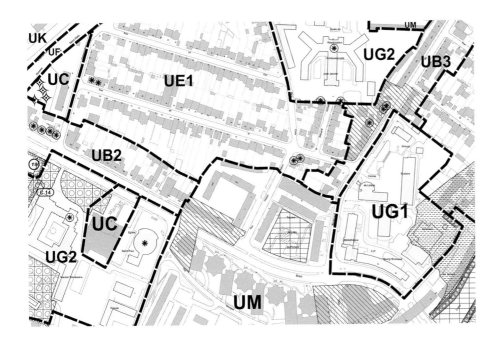

to be the entity most commonly used in the analysis of ownership and other forms of socially established control; regulatory control tends to operate over wider areas from the individual tissue to settlements and whole areas of administrative control such as a municipality, district, county, state or country.

SOURCES OF INFORMATION

Because of the fundamentally abstract nature of socially established control, the primary sources for establishing patterns of relational control are necessarily documentary.

For property and tenure, sources include:

- Cadastral records
- Insurance plans
- Parcel maps
- Subdivision plans
- Property deeds and title documents
- Estate maps

Cadastral records are used in many countries for the purposes of taxation and recording property title. When interpreting cadastral maps and other title documents, it is important to note that the entities on the map do not necessarily correspond to physical forms. A standard physical form may be broken down into several cadastral entities, either by type of form (building, garden, courtyard) or into arbitrary units for legal reasons. Several forms may also fall within the same cadastral entity, such as in the case of a freehold divided into separate leaseholds corresponding to standard plots.

Sources for boundaries of regulatory control will include policy, administrative and legal documents including:

- Development plans
- Zoning plans
- Administrative boundary plans

When plotting and transcribing information for analytical purposes, the boundaries and/or areas can be distinguished graphically by either type of control or type of agent or both. For example, a plan might show leasehold and freehold ownership by public and private agents.

Depending on the nature of the study and level of resolution, it may also be worth compiling a gazetteer to list specific agents associated with specific properties and the type of control involved.

Figure 6.18

Extract of the zoning plan for the city of Rennes in France. In this case the zoning boundaries deliberately follow tissue boundaries (see the case study in Section 9, Zoning plans and regulations: Rennes and Porto) and the attendant regulations control principally the aspects of form and use. As with property, however, boundaries of regulatory control do not necessarily follow physical features.

OUTPUTS

The task of analysis generally involves the following steps:

- Identify the types of control relevant to the study
- Identify and map the boundaries of control for each type (the entities controlled)
- Identify the controlling agents

The aim should be to compare boundaries and regimes of control with other aspects in order to find correlations and associations. To what extent do boundaries of control correspond with physical boundaries or areas of use? To what extent does control contribute to making areas different or similar? What is the role of control in the formation and transformation of areas and settlements?

Again, depending on the nature of the study, the investigation is likely to involve:

- Establishing the correlations and correspondence between control and the other aspects of form
- Investigating the effect of control on other aspects of form and interactions between aspects

- Comparing the effects of different kinds of control within a given system or hierarchy of controls
- Comparing different systems of control

ROUTE STRUCTURE

Highways, roads, streets, tracks, lanes and footpaths are all fundamental to the way human settlements work. Simplistically, you need to be able to get *to* a building to use it and you need to be able to get *from* the building to a range of locations to acquire the other things you need. Movement is essential to our daily lives and ultimately our survival. For towns, it is equally essential to get people and goods in and out to sustain the life of the town. Towns generate roads and are generated by them[7].

Routes can be seen in at least three ways:

- As a movement network (infrastructure)
- As an element of urban tissue
- As a defined area of 'land use' and control

The distinction between routes as part of a network or part of urban tissue is a matter of how we choose to aggregate street spaces as one of the three types of minimum elements of urban form.

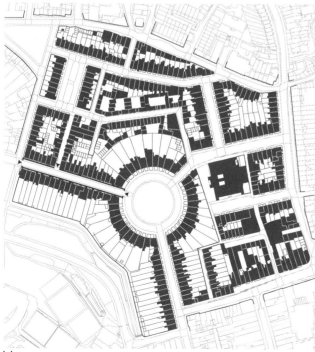

(a)

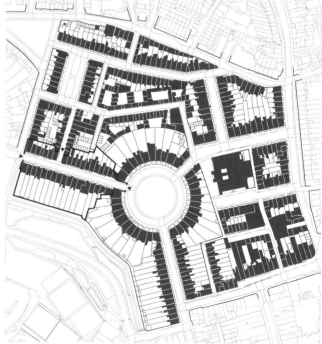

(b)

There is, on the one hand, the 'vertical' aggregation of elements as represented by a vertical section through the multi-level diagram of generic structure. This 'embeds' the street space into urban tissue. On the other hand, there is the 'horizontal' aggregation of spaces implied by the 'Nolli Section' through all the three types of void. This is essentially to isolate the spaces, which necessarily interconnect to allow movement through the built (or proto-built) environment. As figure 6.19c shows, a network of routes can be rendered using the three access types of structured space (single, double and multiple openings – see Section 4), where a link is a single or double opening space and a node is a space of three or more openings. By convention in route structure analysis, the single and double opening spaces are rendered as a line and multiple opening spaces as a node or simply a junction of three or more lines. Note that even though single and double opening spaces are rendered as lines they can still be treated as vertices for the purposes of graph analysis.

In terms of use, as explored below, street spaces accommodate not only the generic function of movement but also a range of other occupation functions or activities that constitute the aspect of use.

Examining routes first as a network provides many insights into the role of individual streets as part of the urban fabric and in relation to other land uses. Also, looking at the network as a whole provides a context and frame of reference for the other two perspectives and for the different aspects of urban form.

There is extensive literature setting out the theory and practice of traffic modelling and network analysis and there are many software applications to undertake the analysis. The method presented here is a simple starting point taking a configurational approach that builds on the work of Marshall's *Streets and Patterns*[8] and provides a basic differentiation of routes, as types, based on their position relative to other routes within the network. It is topological and discrete and works on the basic morphological principle of relative position of parts. Because it focuses on configurational *types* where other approaches such as Space Syntax[9] and Place Syntax[10] focus on *measures*, the methods are complementary. Route structure analysis provides a basic profile of route types within a system that serves as a frame of reference for correlating the many other measures and attributes from size and capacity to mode of use, control and priority or centrality and proximity.

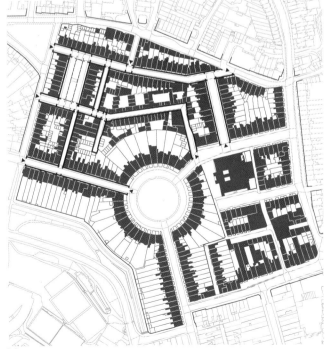

(c)

Figure 6.19
Street spaces (a) can be included in a 'vertical' aggregation to form a tissue (b) or 'horizontally' to form a street network (c).

ROUTES AND THE ORIGINS OF THE BUILT ENVIRONMENT

As suggested in Section 4, routes are one of the most primitive elements of the built environment. The habit of forming **paths**, along with the habit of establishing **territories, shelters**, dens or burrows are the quintessential elements of the proto-built environment created by a range of animals and out of which the built environment has developed. Some of the most striking and persistent features of the human proto-built and built environment are prehistoric routeways. As shown in figure 6.20, early, emergent routes can become formalised – and remain as traces even with less frequent use.

Routes are a direct result of a distinct underlying logic:

- We have a constant need for resources of different kinds
- The resources are dispersed and unevenly distributed
- We need to move to get to resources or take them where we need them
- It is easier to follow an existing route than constantly create new ones

The last term is the equivalent to the general principle of **least effort**. Any individual will seek to use the least effort necessary to achieve a particular aim. For example, it takes less effort and energy to walk along a smooth path than over rough ground. It is easier to walk along harder ground where you can see where you're going rather than on soft or wet ground with obstructed views. It is less effort to walk on flat rather than sloping ground. Familiar routes are easier to follow than unfamiliar ones.

It should be noted that least effort is *not* necessarily equivalent to **least total energy**. It is less effort for an individual to use a car than to walk, even though the total energy used in driving is greater. The rule might also therefore be termed the **greatest convenience**.

Routes emerge out of our **habitual behaviour** in the environment. And because of the general principle of least effort, the pattern of routes established at the initial stages of occupation of a territory has a strong tendency to persist. Once established, a given route will be preferred and reinforced because it is familiar and less effort to use. When new routes are added, they must necessarily connect to the existing routes, which further reinforces their status and tendency to persist. The accumulated effort and energy that goes into creating a route and the dependence established by its habitual use means there is a high cost in effort, energy and resources to change it. The rule of least effort is reinforced by a rule of inertia.

If an easier alternative is built, old routes tend not to be removed but left and only slowly 'fade' from disuse over time. Routes are only actively removed when the land has greater value for some other purpose. Route patterns are emergent, persistent and cumulative. All these contribute to the general persistence and differential rates of change in the built environment as discussed in the previous section.

THE GENERAL PATTERN OF ROUTES AND SETTLEMENTS

The results of the process by which routes emerge and persist is a general differentiation of areas on the ground that accommodate the two generic functions of **movement** and **occupation**: linear surfaces for movement and intervening areas of various shapes and sizes for occupation. In addition to this differentiation, a fundamental concept for understanding the structure of route patterns is the **centre**. There are many reasons for the general pattern of nucleated and polycentric settlements, but one way or the other there is a strong tendency for the emergence of centres, that is, concentrations of activity that serve or draw on a wider **catchment**. The formation of centres presupposes routes to get to them and, in turn, centres can generate new routes to widen or extend access to them and increase the size of the catchment. The cumulative result is the familiar pattern in the landscape of settlements linked by roads.

To begin to articulate the pattern, it is possible to distinguish different types of route purely with reference to the position of a route in relation to centres and to other routes in the network. The first step in the analysis is therefore to identify the centres.

For the purposes of this stage of analysis, the minimum definition of a centre is any concentration of occupied buildings (departure or destination points) irrespective of use. Typically this corresponds to built-up areas as identified on most maps. On this basis, a 'centre' might be a hamlet, village, market town, city or metropolitan region. The principal variable to consider is the size threshold for what constitutes a 'concentration'. Depending on the scope of the study, the method

Figure 6.20
Site of the Roman city
of Peltuinum in Abruzzo,
Italy, straddling an ancient
transhumance route.
The line of the route can
be seen as a track in the
middle of the image (a
newer, surfaced route
lies to the left). It is likely
that a route along the
valley pre-dated the
Roman settlement, which
'captured' the movement,
later formalised in the
late Middle Ages as the
***Tratturo Magno*.**

for establishing the threshold might be a rank-size rule or density profiling. More simply and directly the built-up areas as identified on maps can be used, with smaller-scale, lower-resolution maps generally using a higher threshold of size for identifying settlements than larger scale, more detailed maps. In the UK, the open-source Meridian 2 map set is very useful for the purpose.

PRIMARY ROUTE TYPES BY POSITION

However the centres are defined, the first step is to treat them as a simple structured space, that is, in terms of the surface, boundary and access points. As shown in the following diagrams, the access points can be indicated by the point where a route connects to the centre. The next step in the process of analysis is to identify and colour code different route types based on their relation to centres. The process of analysis necessarily disregards any existing ranking of centres or routes on the basis of designation, size, capacity etc. The aim is to identify route types **solely on their relationships to centres or to other routes**. The analysis is therefore strictly **topological**.

In essence, the first stage of the analysis is carried out at a low level of resolution, distinguishing only built-up areas and the routes that are connected to but lie outside them. From this perspective there are four types of **strategic route:**

- **Tangential**
  Routes connecting several centres tangentially. The connection to the built-up area is only indirect and the priority is for through traffic along the tangential route. Examples are limited-access dual carriageways, motorways and freeways/expressways.
- **Primary arterial**
  Routes connected to a centre on each end (bicentric).
- **Secondary arterial**
  Routes connected to a centre on one end and a through route on the other (monocentric).
- **Pericentric**
  Routes connected on each end to one or another of the higher-level strategic routes (tangential, primary or secondary).

Once the external strategic routes have been identified, the next step is to trace the arterials into the built-up areas, extending them along continuous routes until they either end in a T-junction or emerge

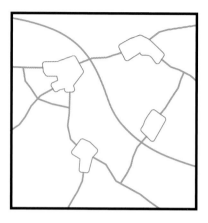

Figure 6.21-a
A pattern of routes and settlements treating each settlement as a structured space with the route lines indicating points of access.

Figure 6.21-b
Tangential route running between settlements.

Figure 6.21-c
Primary strategic routes connecting one settlement to another.

out of another side of the built-up area. Internal pericentric routes can be added after the internal arterials are identified.

EXTENSIVE URBAN AREAS

Areas of extensive urbanisation such as metropolitan regions and conurbations can present a complex pattern of routes that is not easy to decipher. In most cases, extensive areas have developed over time, often by the fusing or 'coalescence' of previously separate settlements that would have been connected by strategic routes. The centres and strategic routes then become embedded in a continuous built-up area. Greater clarity can be brought to the analysis of such cases by undertaking a route analysis of strategic routes for each stage of the town's development as represented in a map sequence.

With the growth of a settlement by outward extension, there is also a general tendency for the creation of more pericentric routes to avoid congestion in the original centre. Similarly, the type and role of a given historical route may change with growth and reconfiguration of streets. A common change is for arterials to be truncated toward the historical centre and diverted onto pericentric routes (either new or existing). Strictly, the routes remain strategic types if they provide a continuous route out of the built-up area.

A technique that can be used to overcome the issues raised by a study area that lies entirely within a singe built-up area is to undertake a **relative route structure analysis**. In this case, an area or **peripheral zone** is defined around the study area and primary strategic routes are defined as those with one end in the study area and the other beyond the peripheral zone. Secondary strategic routes are those with one end within the peripheral zone and the other in the study area. The 'radius' of the analysis can be increased by increasing the size of the peripheral zone and adding a secondary peripheral zone within it. Secondary routes would be those that extend into the outer secondary zone.

LOCAL ROUTE TYPES BY POSITION

The next step in the process is to distinguish different types of local route, again identifying types in terms of a given route's relation to other routes and the possible combinations of different access types of structured space set out in Section 4.

There are four basic types of local route in terms of topological connections:

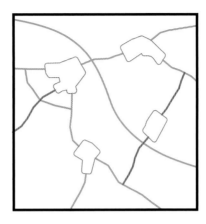

Figure 6.21-d
Secondary strategic routes connecting a settlement with a route.

Figure 6.21-e
Pericentric or tertiary routes connecting any of the higher strategic routes.

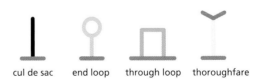

cul de sac   end loop   through loop   thoroughfare

Figure 6.22
Local route types based on the possible combinations of single, double and triple opening structured spaces (see figure 4.3).

(a)

(b)

Figure 6.23-a
The three types of
strategic routes of a small
market town.

Figure 6.23-b
The sub-systems of
thoroughfares.

Figure 6.23-c
The sub-systems of
through loops.

- **Thoroughfare**
  Route connected to a different route
  on each end
- **Through loop**
  Route connected on both ends to the
  same route
- **End loop**
  Route connected to a route on one end and
  itself on the other
- **Cul-de-sac**
  Route connected to another on one end only

SUB-SYSTEMS

Examining even a small number of places shows
that these types are combined in many different
ways. It is possible and not uncommon, for
example, to find a loop on top of a loop and many
cul-de-sacs along a cul-de-sac. It is also possible
to have a grid of thoroughfares at the end of a cul-
de-sac. These are **sub-systems** that form a distinct
level of structure between the local and the global.
There are four types of sub-system, corresponding
to the four types of local route.

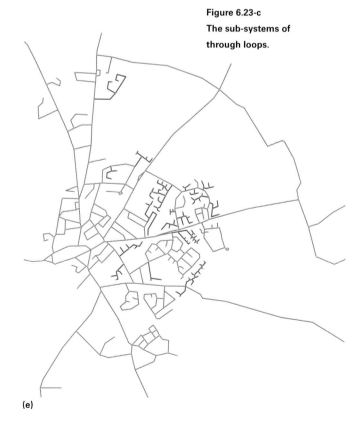

(e)

(c)

(d)

Figure 6.23-d
The sub-systems of end loops.

Figure 6.23-e
The sub-systems of trees.

Figure 6.23-f
Cul-de-sacs.

Figure 6.23-g
All types combined.

(f)

(g)

(a)

left and opposite top
Figure 6.24
A route structure analysis of Bath, showing vehicular access (a) and pedestrian access of street spaces (b). The principal difference is in the historic centre, where traffic management and pedestrianisation has created loops that limit vehicular access to the centre.

- **Thoroughfare**
  A set of interconnected local routes with three or more external connections to at least two different strategic routes
- **Through loop**
  A set of interconnected local routes with only two external connections, each to different routes, or multiple connections to a single strategic route or thoroughfare
- **End loop**
  A set of interconnected local routes with a single external connection
- **Cul-de-sac tree**
  A composition of only cul-de-sacs with one external connection

The most effective and familiar method of representing the types is to colour code them using the heat map convention. In most cases it is best to code the strategic routes and whole sub-systems. Colour coding whole sub-systems necessarily ignores the type of some of the component links. The result, however, gives a clearer general picture which can be augmented if appropriate with a separate more detailed coding of individual local links.

ACCOUNTING FOR DIFFERENT MODES
It is important to establish from the outset which modes of movement are to be included in the analysis:

- Vehicular
- Cycle
- Pedestrian

An analysis including only vehicular movement may be very different from one that includes routes only accessible to pedestrians. It can be extremely revealing to undertake analyses of both vehicle-only and pedestrian-only routes and compare the results.

The working assumption is that the routes included in the analysis are part of the public highway and cycleway/footpath networks. In some cases it may also be worth including private routes.

WORKING TIPS

- Use an overlay on a map of the study area; alternatively make several copies of the map and map the different types separately
- Identify the built-up areas using an atlas, online map or earth viewer
- Using coloured lines (pens, pencils and/or a drawing package), colour code the different types, tracing the extent of the route from built-up area to built-up area, built-up area to junction or junction to junction
- Use different line types for the different modes, for example:

(b)

bottom **Figure 6.25
The shapes created by the
alignment of routes are
not taken into account
in defining types. The
connection at the top of
the loop-shaped route
shown makes it a part of a
thoroughfare sub-system.
The third connection
means it is not a
loop type.**

- vehicular – solid, wider
- cycleways – long dash, narrower
- footpaths – short dash, narrower

• Extend the designation into the built-up area
following the line of the route until it comes to
an end (T-junction) or carries on out of the
built-up area

• When extending the line of strategic routes into
the built-up area, assume 'inertia' at junctions
(with the priority, straight or along the arc)

• Work from both ends of the hierarchy of
types: down from the primary and secondary
strategic routes and up from cul-de-sacs. Areas
of ambiguity can be resolved by testing from
both directions.

• Because the method is *topological* it is
important to disregard the shape of routes
in identifying types. For example a route that
forms a distinct loop shape and is connected at
its ends to the same route but has a connection
to a third through route is not strictly a loop
type but part of a thoroughfare sub-system.
In this regard it can be useful to re-render the
invariant relations of the network in an abstract,
dimensionless representation.

INTERPRETATION AND USE OF THE RESULTS
Route structure analysis establishes a simple, discrete hierarchy with the broad distinction between strategic routes, sub-systems and local routes as well as the types within each general category. These distinctions can be refined and elaborated with the use of other topological and Space/Place Syntax measures such as closeness and betweenness centrality. The interesting question then becomes, what are the correspondences and associations between type and measure? At a basic level, however, the picture painted by identifying the different types and sub-systems can be used as a general indicator for a number of different aspects of urban form including:

- Relative levels of movement
- Permeability and choice
- Growth and the relation between strategic routes and sub-systems
- The structure and type of urban tissue, character and legibility

The relation to the structure of urban tissue is of particular importance. Route structure analysis is in effect the first step in the identification of types of urban tissue.

OUTPUTS
The output of the route structure analysis should be a map or series of maps of the colour-coded route structure and an interpretative narrative. Most commonly, separate maps are coded to show the strategic routes and sub-systems for vehicular movement and pedestrian movement.

BUILT FORM
As set out in Section 3, the aspect of built form encompasses the full range of physical features making up the built environment, from materials and structures through to metropolitan regions. The purpose of this section is not to look at all the intervening levels in detail, but to focus on **urban tissue** as a means of setting out general methods that can be abstracted to apply at different levels. Urban tissue offers a useful focus for analysis because it occupies a mid-point in the range of generic forms. One the one hand, it is composed of and characterised by all the elements below it in the hierarchy of generic form. On the other hand, urban tissue is the principal **unit of urban growth** and is therefore the key to understanding the larger-scale structure of settlements.

Examining the historical development of a number of different settlements shows that the process of growth does not run at a continuous rate but tends to run in cycles or stages of more or less building activity. Periods of more rapid growth are followed by periods of relative stasis. A further feature of growth is that development within a particular period of growth tends to be similar in character in terms of layout and design. Urban growth is also most often cumulative.

The result in the long term of the **variable** and **periodic accumulation** of different types of urban fabric is a patchwork of distinct areas of urban tissue. That is, most settlements are complex composites of different tissues. The overall pattern can be complicated further by the partial redevelopment of areas either by small-scale piecemeal development or larger redevelopments with the differential persistence of various features. The process involves, in a figurative sense, adding patches, scraping away at them and partly or wholly replacing them. In this respect urban fabric can be characterised as a **palimpsest**. The additions and changes of previous periods persist and subsequent changes add to or modify what exists at a given time. As noted, the specific design of development tends to change over time in response to many factors. That is, while an individual settlement **develops**, the generative ideas and concepts that inform development **evolve** over time. But the expression of that evolution is unlike smaller cultural artefacts such as hand tools or motor cars, which are produced as a single whole object based on a single idea with each version representing a discrete evolutionary step. Because a city, town or village is a cumulative 'object' or 'artefact', it is necessarily the product of a series of different ideas, each of which gives rise to a different part of the overall whole. Human settlements are thus **polymorphogenetic** accretionary artefacts.

Analysis of urban tissue is thus the key to isolating the series of generative ideas that constitute the evolution of urban form and to unpicking and understanding the development and larger-scale structure of individual settlements.

URBAN TISSUE, PLAN UNITS, CHARACTER AREAS AND GEOGRAPHICAL REGIONS
It is worth clarifying the terms that are often used to refer to similar or overlapping concepts. 'Urban tissue' as used in this book is derived from the Italian concept of *tessuto urbano* (Muratori,

Caniggia and Maffei, Cataldi, Petruccioli, among others[11]) and the French *tissu urbain* (Castex et al, Panerai et al among others[12]). The concept is defined as a distinct area of a settlement in all three dimensions, characterised by a unique combination of streets, blocks/plot series, plots, buildings, structures and materials and usually the result of a distinct process of formation at a particular time or period (see also Scheer for the application of the idea in North America[13]). The term 'plan unit', as developed by Conzen,[14] refers to a distinct area of a settlement as viewed in plan only and characterised by a distinct combination of the plan element complexes of street pattern, plot pattern and building pattern.

Strictly, the terms 'character area' and 'geographical region' refer to a distinct area within a settlement characterised by its physical form in combination with, variously, site characteristics, land use, patterns of control, vegetation and city image features. The term character area tends to be used more loosely, referring also to urban tissue, plan unit and other distinct areas defined by a range of other specific characteristics.

GENERIC TYPES, SPECIFIC TYPES AND EXAMPLES

The aim of urban tissue analysis is to identify the range of different specific types of tissue found in the study area. A **specific type** of tissue is an area showing a distinct combination of streets, plot series, plots and buildings. There may be one or more **examples** of the type that share the same characteristics. For example, the analysis may result in identifying a type such as 'suburban villa tissue' with separate areas built with the same type in a number of different particular locations.

Specific types of built form can be identified within each of the **generic types** that constitute the distinct levels of generic structure, for example, urban tissue, plot series, blocks, plots and buildings. Because of the nature of the

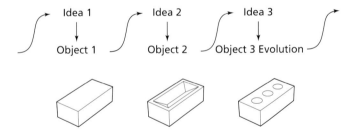

(a)   Evolution of simple artefact

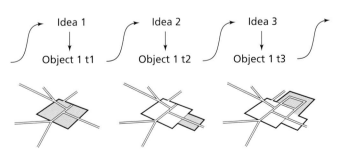

(b)   Polymorphogenetic development of cumulative artefact

Figure 6.26
The evolution of an isolated artefact, such as a brick (a) results in the production of a series of discrete objects (strictly, populations of objects). The development of settlements (b) involves the growth of a single object over time by the addition of parts, each of which is built according to an evolving idea of urban tissue. The corresponding populations of tissues are only ever part of one or more settlements (or, rarely, a settlement in its own right).

compositional hierarchy of built form, identifying a specific type at a given level essentially involves identifying the combination of constituent types that make up the type.

A place-based study will generally focus on urban tissue and therefore also cover the constituent generic types for a single place. An element-based or typological study, in contrast, would focus only on a particular element, for example blocks or plots, either within a single settlement or a number of different settlements.

BASIC TECHNIQUES

The most basic technique for identifying distinct urban tissues is simple comparative geometric analysis using a plan of the current state of the study area. The process involves visually comparing different parts of the plan to identify distinct geometric patterns as formed by the lines depicting the principal plan elements:

- Streets (highway boundary and kerb lines – and any other features within the public highway such as central reservation/median strips)
- Plot series and blocks (regular combinations of plots)
- Plots (plot boundaries)
- Buildings (ground-floor plan outline)

Further detail is added through the field survey to include:

- Building type (storey height and internal configuration)
- Structures and details
- Materials

The aim of the examination is to identify and outline areas that are internally consistent and distinct from other areas. The technique is fundamentally comparative and iterative, seeking to find both similarities and differences between different areas within a settlement and/or between different settlements. The boundaries between tissues separate one consistent pattern from another.

The analysis can be done in a comprehensive and systematic way by looking at the tissue as a whole and, progressively, each of its constituent elements, from three distinct **structural perspectives**:

- The **position** of the element as a whole within the wider context as a part or component of a larger element (a generic type one level up) and its relationship to other features and aspects
- The overall shape and size of the form expressed in terms of its **outline** (geometrical shape, dimensions, proportions of the outer boundary) and the **points of access** that establish the orientation of the element
- The **internal structure** of the element – the number, type and **arrangement of parts**

So, as shown in figure 6.28, a plot can be identified in terms of its position within a plot series or block – mid-series, end or corner; its overall size and shape (width and length); the specific arrangement of the parts that compose it.

Similarly, types of urban tissue can be distinguished in terms of the position of the tissue within the settlement and in relation to others (centre, middle or fringe), the shape and size of the tissue and its characteristic configuration of streets, plot series, plots and buildings.

Note that identifying the specific type of parts for the internal structure of an element is in effect to repeat the same analysis one level down the compositional hierarchy.

In summary, the basic steps in the process are:

- Visually compare patterns and distinguish distinct areas
- Draw outlines around distinct areas
- Specify differences at different levels of scale
- Make a systematic description of the defining characteristics

Figure 6.27
The relationship between generic types, specific types and examples is that of class-to-member. A generic type is a class of object, a specific type is a member or subset of the class, and examples are the members of the subset.

Generic type   Specific type   Examples

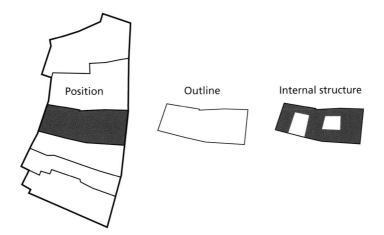

Position   Outline   Internal structure

Figure 6.29 shows examples of different tissues from different positions within the same settlement.

SUPPORTING TECHNIQUES
A number of other specific techniques can be applied in helping to identify individual tissues:

- Route structure analysis
- Plan sequencing
- Element separations
- Metrological and morphometric analysis
- Land-cover mapping

As noted above, route structure analysis often provides a significant start in identifying distinct areas because one of the features used to define tissues is the topological types of street. Sub-systems of route types such as thoroughfares, loops, and cul-de-sacs are in effect tissues defined at a low level of specificity.

Because the generating idea for urban tissue tends to evolve over time and the patterns of tissues persist once built, an effective technique for identifying different tissues is to use a map sequence to pick out each distinct area at the stage at which it was added (as far as map evidence allows). The map sequence can also help in highlighting transformations of areas that constitute distinct tissues.

In cases of very fine-grained and complex tissues it can be helpful to view the main elements in isolation by using element separations. Distinct areas of each element can be identified and then overlaid to identify common composite areas.

BACK BOUNDARIES, SHARED STREETS
AND DIFFERENT TYPES OF GRID
In theory, a tissue analysis would progress

uniformly across the study area from one side to another. In practice it is often the case that there are parts of the study area that do not present obviously distinct tissues. In such cases it is helpful to start by drawing partial boundaries where the differences are most evident. Plot patterns are generally the most distinct (as aggregates of closed polygons) and the boundary between two adjacent patterns tends to stand out more clearly. Because plots are necessarily associated with street spaces, the boundary between adjacent plot patterns tends to occur on the 'back boundary' between two tissues.

A specific technique that can be used to progressively close a boundary around a tissue is to draw a solid line (heavier than the map lines) along the back boundaries between distinct patterns. The next step is to draw the tissue boundary from the back plot boundary to the street, which often occurs near the junction of two streets. The underlying principle is that plots are bound to a specific street space by the 'glue' of access and orientation. The tissue boundary is then drawn so that all plots remain connected to their appropriate street space, leaving a dashed gap at the point where the line comes to the street space. The gaps can also be highlighted as access points by arrows. For complex tissues, the boundary should extend around a consistent combination of similar simple tissues.

In some cases a street may have two different plot series, one on either side of the street space. To capture that distinction and at the same time acknowledge the connection of each series to the same street space *established by access*, dashed lines can be added along the frontage of the plot series. This clearly indicates the public highway is shared between two different plot series. In this case, the street is a **shared element**.

Figure 6.28
Diagram of the three structural perspectives in the definition of built form: position, outline and access, and internal structure. The perspectives are clearly related to the generic structure of built form and levels of resolution. The resolution of the definition increases in the move from position to internal structure.

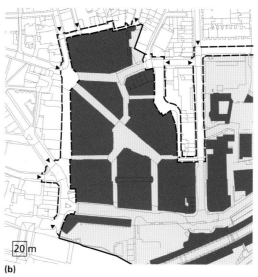

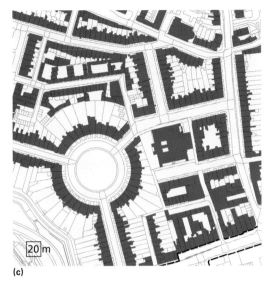

(c)

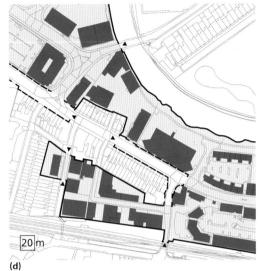

(d)

opposite top and above

Figure 6.29

Examples of different specific types of tissue from Bath: a) central, relatively dense, mixed-grain, the initial foundation of Roman origin with many subsequent transformations; b) outside edge of the initial foundation, **coarse-grained, uniform, the result of recent redevelopment of partially bombed and redeveloped site; c) mid-settlement, fine grain, uniform, with strong geometric shapes, an 18th-century urban extension; d) middle fringe/riverside, mixed, coarse-grained resulting from extension, bombing and redevelopment.**

opposite bottom

Figure 6.30

A detail of the route structure of Bath (a) and an overlay of the route structure and tissues (b). The pattern of routes, in terms of both type and geometry, is a key defining characteristic of urban tissue, which shows in the distinct pattern of routes in each tissue.

Figure 6.31
The process of identifying tissues is facilitated by starting with the more obvious boundaries – a line with a clearly different pattern on either side. These tend to be the back and side boundaries between distinct tissues. The dashed red lines indicate that the boundaries are provisional.

Figure 6.32
Once key back boundaries are identified they can be extended to the street. Where there is a distinct pattern either side of the street space and the two tissues both have access from the street, the boundary for each should extend to include the whole abutting street width. The boundaries of the two, in effect, overlap rather than run down the centre of the street. This is shown by using a dashed line where there is a shared street space.

UNIFORM AND MIXED PATTERNS

In visually scanning and comparing parts of a plan, the easiest areas to identify are those that are uniform, in which the component elements, particularly the plots, are essentially the same shape and size.

Typically, uniform areas are the result of a single effort of design and construction by the same agent. Many areas, however, are the product of a number of agents acting over a period of time with different intentions often involving transformations of existing structures. The result of longer-term, piecemeal and ad hoc development is most often a more mixed or heterogeneous tissue.

At the same time, as suggested at the outset of this section, urban fabric can be characterised as a palimpsest. A significant part of the development process involves **transformation** of previous development by either small-scale **modification** or **selective redevelopment**. Settlements and buildings are subject to a range of different modifications from repair and replacement of elements to internal alteration to extension and major reconstruction at all levels of scale. For obvious reasons, transformations are most highly concentrated in the oldest parts of settlements: the historical cores and the historical routes leading to them. One way or the other, areas subject to transformation also tend to be more heterogeneous.

VARIATION, RANGE AND LIMITS

Even in cases where individual streets, plots and buildings are built according to the same design, there tends to be some **variation** from one instance to the next, either through deliberate design or in response to some particular site circumstance. To accommodate the variation and avoid ending up with an unworkable number of distinct types based on small differences, the defining characteristics should be stated as a **range** within definite **limits**. Increasing the range of variation will decrease the total number of types and each type will cover a larger area. Conversely, narrowing the ranges of any or all characteristics will increase the number of types, each of which will cover only a small area.

below left **Figure 6.33 Example of a mixed or heterogeneous tissue.**

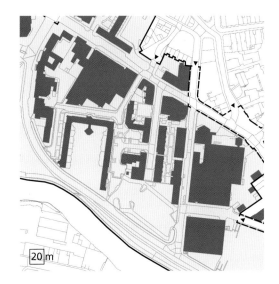

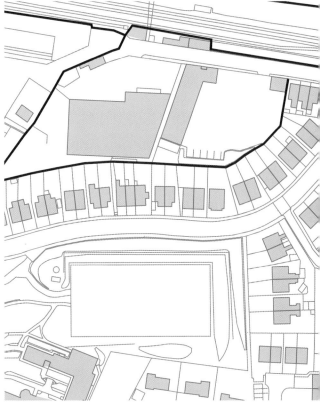

CHARACTERISTIC MIX, PREDOMINANT TYPES AND EXCEPTIONS

Areas can also be consistent without being uniform where they show a **characteristic mix** of elements such as areas of piecemeal development or transformations. A typical example of a mixed type is a strategic route leading into a town that has undergone piecemeal development over a long period of time. Again, to avoid multiplying the number of tissues, where there is a consistent mix of elements, the definition can be made more inclusive by identifying a range of included types. The mix may be consistent in terms of the numbers of each different type or be characterised by one or more **predominant** types and/or **exceptional** types. Similarly, another example would be a development that includes a number of slightly different house types, a shop and a school building. Rather than separating out all the types, they can all be included in one tissue as a characteristic mix with a few predominant and exceptional types.

LUMPING AND SPLITTING AND SUB-AREAS

The process of analysis can often produce a large number of distinct tissues even at a relatively low level of resolution. The differentiation of distinct tissues is a kind of **splitting**, which, if carried too far, becomes unworkable and defeats one of the objects of the analysis, which is to clarify the larger-scale structure of a settlement or study area. As just noted, however, decreasing the level of specificity of the analysis decreases the number of types. This has the effect of **lumping** tissues together into larger areas. Lumping and splitting can be balanced by adjusting the level of specificity of analysis in a systematic way in terms of:

- Total number of pertinent characteristics in common
- Range of variation in constituent types of internal parts
- Range of variation in shape and size of internal parts

Figure 6.34
In cases where there is significant variation and heterogeneity, the results of analysis can be clarified by grouping or lumping tissues that are distinct but still share some characteristics in common. In this case the common feature is the house/plot type. The lumped areas include either semi-detached or terraced houses, with some exceptional plots.

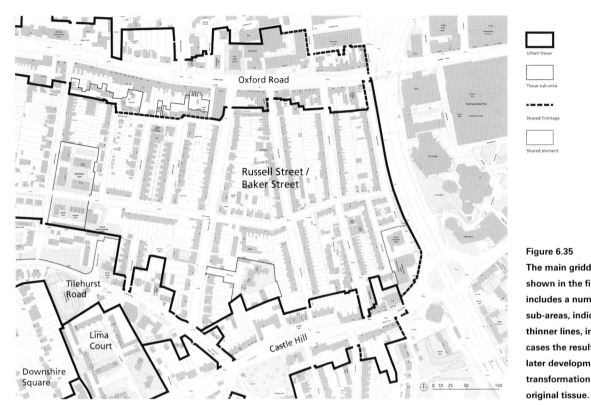

Oxford Road

Russell Street /
Baker Street

Tilehurst
Road

Lima
Court

Downshire
Square

Castle Hill

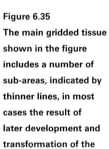

Urban tissue

Tissue sub-area

Shared frontage

Shared element

Figure 6.35
The main gridded tissue
shown in the figure
includes a number of
sub-areas, indicated by
thinner lines, in most
cases the result of
later development and
transformation of the
original tissue.

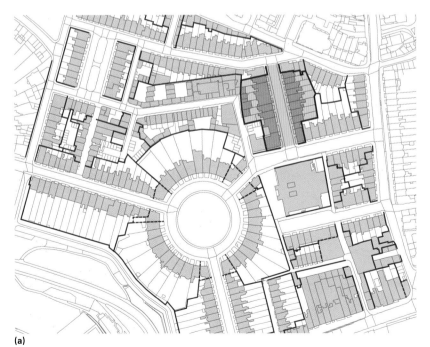

(a)

left and opposite **Figure 6.36**
Simple tissues can be
combined into various
arrangements of
interconnecting streets
forming a complex tissue.
The illustration (a) shows
an articulated grid,
where each plot series is
attached to a single street
and the resultant blocks
are split, a configuration
highlighted by the access
diagram (b).

The specific balance struck will depend on the nature of the place and the purpose of the study. A key point is to ensure that the areas lumped together share some specific features. Two further ways of dealing with mixed areas and variations are to identify exceptional areas within a consistent tissue as **sub-areas** and to identify 'families' of similar tissues. The sub-areas might be single plots, small groups of plots or relatively extensive areas. Graphically they can be distinguished by using a thinner boundary line. Families of tissues can be coloured using variations of the same hue (see figure 8.5) so they read together as a group. Both these methods increase the clarity of the analysis while still recognising distinct differences.

SIMPLE AND COMPLEX TISSUE
The simplest unit of urban tissue is a single **street**: a route with a plot or plot series on one or both sides. The street defined in this way is a **simple tissue** and has a high degree of modularity, often forming the unit of development in many different cultures. Depending on the circumstances, a simple tissue can form a distinct tissue on its own or be combined to form a **complex tissue**. Various arrangements

of simple tissues are possible, from cul-de-sac trees to loops and grids. In all these cases, the tissue is **articulated** if the individual plots have only one point of access and the resultant blocks can be split, with each plot series unambiguously attached to a single route.

A different kind of complex tissue arises when plots have more than one point of access and are therefore ambiguously related to two or more street spaces. This kind of tissue tends to occur when the generating idea for the tissue was a grid, in particular when the plot and block are co-extensive. In this case it is not possible to outline simple tissues. The blocks and streets work together as **interlocking elements** to form a complex tissue. The resulting **interlocking grid** is the unit of development and the boundary of the tissue lies along the edge where the consistent pattern of street spaces, blocks and plots ends, which may be either the back boundary of plots or a shared street. Again, as noted in Section 4, the distinction between articulated and interlocking grids highlights that the block is an aggregate of plots or plot series. As an isolated entity, however, the block is a resultant form ambiguously related to one or more of the bounding street spaces.

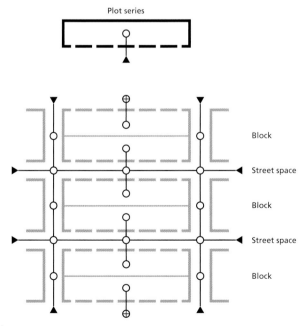

(b)

20 m

(a)

INFRASTRUCTURE

A further element to consider, particularly in relation to the larger structures of a settlement, is surface level infrastructure. Sub-surface and overhead infrastructure is also a consideration in looking at urban form but not dealt with here in relation to urban tissue. Common types of surface infrastructure include:

• Motorways
• Railways
• Bridges, viaducts and tunnel openings
• Fortifications
• Aqueducts
• Canals
• Reservoirs
• Waterway control and flood alleviation works
• Surface features of sub-surface and overhead service networks (water, electricity, gas, telecommunications)

Routes more generally are also a type of infrastructure but have a dual role as both a movement network and a principal constituent of urban tissue – two aspects explored, for

example, in Boujenko, Marshall and Jones's *Link and Place*.[15]

Many types of surface infrastructure are **linear** and either enclose or cross through the settlement as a whole and/or individual tissues. In a detailed plan analysis it is important to account for all land associated with an element of infrastructure. In most cases, infrastructure should be treated as equivalent to urban tissue or a plan unit that forms an integral part of the settlement as a whole. This is particularly important for features that have a role as part of the morphological frame and present a limit to other features.

METROLOGICAL AND MORPHOMETRIC ANALYSIS

A number of methods have been developed for identifying specific types of built form that focus on quantitative, dimensional characteristics. **Metrological** and **morphometric analyses** are used to aid in distinguishing types of form for a range of specific purposes, including establishing the chronology of growth where cartographic and other documentary evidence is lacking, understanding the general evolution of urban

Plot/block

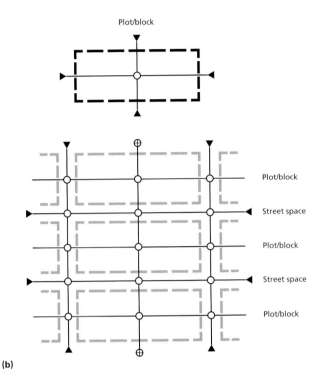

Plot/block

Street space

Plot/block

Street space

Plot/block

(b)

Figure 6.37
In tissues with
interconnecting streets
and large, multi-access
plots (a), the blocks
cannot be split into plot
series attached to a single
street space and so form
an interlocking complex
tissue (b).

form, differentiating areas for the assessment of environmental performance and for the purposes of urban-planning policy and management, to name a few.

Metrological analysis of plot series was developed by historical geographers such as Sheppard, Lafrenz and Slater[16] in seeking to reconstruct the initial layout and early growth of medieval new towns. The principles underpinning metrological analysis are:

- Planned development tends to show some metric or dimensional regularity of street and plot patterns
- Different patterns tend to be used in different periods through the evolution of types – polymorphogenesis
- The initial regularities tend to remain in place through persistence

Based on these principles, it is possible to draw inferences about the early states of towns from the existing fabric of towns and more recent cartographic evidence. The process of analysis involves the following steps:

- Establish the units of measure and specific dimensions of the plot patterns used in particular periods, ideally through archival documentary or archaeological evidence. Most frequently this will be the plot frontage, depth or area
- Measure existing plot boundaries using the original units to identify multiples or fractions of the units and dimensions used
- Infer initial patterns from the correspondence of persisting boundaries to the known regular measures and dimensions
- Distinguish different areas of uniform patterns corresponding to the known regular measures used at different times

The principal inference is that the areas of different regular patterns represent phases in the growth or transformation of the settlement. As noted by various authors, care needs to be taken in the inferences: different plot dimensions might be used at the same time, regularity is not a guarantee of planning and planned patterns may look 'irregular' from our point of view. What we consider to be 'organic' may have been planned.

An example of morphometric analysis that draws directly on biological morphometrics and systematics is the work of Dibble et al.[17] As the authors rightly point out, establishing the characteristic dimensions and ratios for urban tissues from different periods is the necessary background work for investigating the evolution of urban tissue as a socio-cultural type. The aim of the work undertaken so far is twofold. On the one hand they have sought to identify the dimensional attributes that are the most diagnostic for dating the period of origin of urban tissue. So far this has been done using broad historical distinctions between 'historical', 'industrial', 'new towns' and 'sprawl'.

The attributes identified as most diagnostic through a cost-benefit analysis include:

- Block built front ratio
- Block covered area ratio
- Regular plot covered area ratio

On the other hand, the aim has been to identify the signature values of the attributes for each of the historical periods.

Similarly, for very large areas or those with less distinct differences, a range of attributes can be selected and areas analysed using computational methods to identify clusters of common sets of attributes. An example is the work of Pierre Gauthier on Montreal Island.[18]

LAND-COVER MAPPING AND REMOTE SENSING
A set of related techniques focusing on the analysis of attribute sets derived from satellite imagery and aerial photography have been developed primarily within the field of urban ecology as well as land-use or land-cover mapping (see, for example, Voltersen et al and Walde et al[19]). Digital image-processing algorithms such as histograms of oriented gradients and edge orientation histograms are used to distinguish different **urban structural types** (UST) or **urban structural units** (USU). These methods have been developed primarily for the purposes of assessing environmental performance and applications in environmental management. The unit of analysis tends to be the block and the range of attributes used to define types generally includes:

- The geometry, density and spatial configuration of buildings
- Land-use classes (social, cultural and economic)
- Environmental properties (type of vegetation and water bodies)

The land-use classes are determined either by inference from the form or separate mapping exercises (see section on Use below). While the UST is similar in definition to urban tissue, the inclusion of land use makes it more similar to a character area. As emphasised by Osmond,[20] one of the key contributions of these methods is the systematic inclusion of vegetation and other natural features. A limitation of this approach is the relatively low resolution of the resulting types.

TEXT DESCRIPTIONS
A fundamental part of the analytical process and an essential component in communicating the results is a text description for each tissue identified in the analysis. The descriptions specify and articulate the structure of the tissues that makes them distinct. That is, the descriptions set out the **defining characteristics** of each tissue. Ideally the descriptions are themselves structured and consistent across all the tissues covered. Using a tabular format and a controlled vocabulary helps in this respect and keeps the descriptions concise and focused. A sample description of the tissue shown in figure 6.44 is set out in table 6.1. A very effective supplement to a table is a brief narrative description that situates the tissue in the physical and cultural context in which it was created and transformed.

Adding key dimensions to the description helps communicate the full sense of the tissues and allows for easier comparisons and application. Dimensions might include linear measures, area measures and ratios or indices. There are innumerable specific measures that might be made, depending on the aims and purpose of the study. The following set out the broad parameters of urban tissue and correspond to measures commonly used in applications such as planning and urban design.

opposite and overleaf
Table 6.1
Text descriptions of tissues set out in detail the defining characteristics of the tissue. A tabular format helps by using positional information to keep the descriptions succinct, clear and systematic.

LOCATION	READING
PERIOD OF ORIGIN	EARLY TO LATE 19TH CENTURY
GENERAL TYPE	SEMI-FORMAL URBAN GRID OF EIGHT STREETS
SIZE	12 HECTARES
ACCESS POINTS	ACCESS FROM OXFORD ROAD, CASTLE HILL, TILEHURST ROAD

POSITION	EDGE OF THE HISTORIC CENTRE BETWEEN TWO PRIMARY ROUTES

TOPOGRAPHY	
PATTERN	GENTLE EAST–WEST RIDGE
ORIENTATION	NORTH AND EAST-FACING
SLOPE	3.6 PER CENT SLOPE

VEGETATION	MAINLY MEDIUM STATURE TREES WITHIN PRIVATE SPACE/BLOCK INTERIOR, PRINCIPALLY BACK GARDENS; SOME FRONT GARDENS

STREET	
ROUTE TYPE	THOROUGHFARES, INCLUDING DIRECT CONNECTIONS BETWEEN PRIMARY ROUTES; SOME CUL-DE-SACS
PATTERN	SLIGHTLY VARIABLE, SKEWED GRID WITH MOSTLY REGULAR, RECTANGULAR PATTERN, THE PRODUCT OF SEVERAL STAGES OF DEVELOPMENT
ALIGNMENTS	STRAIGHT, LONG STREETS RUNNING UP SLOPE, SHORT STREETS ALONG CONTOURS
JUNCTION SPACING	LONG SIDE: 137–210M (180 COMMON); SHORT SIDE: 50–125M (70, 80 COMMON)
SECTION: FRONTAGE-TO-FRONTAGE	VARIES FROM 6.8 TO 15.5M (9, 12 COMMON)
SECTION: FACADE-TO-FACADE	VARIES FROM 16 TO 22M (18 COMMON)
WIDTH TO HEIGHT RATIO	3:1 TO 2:1

Highway (route/street space)	
Components	Carriageway and footway both sides
Parking	On-street parking on both, sometimes one side
Planting	No significant planting in the public highway (see plots)
Materials	Tarmac carriageway and footways

Blocks	
Types	Predominantly perimeter, enclosing private back gardens, some mixed/emergent blocks, some regular designed
Shape	Rectangular with some variation/skewing
Internal separation	Varies from 10 to 50m (30, 40 common)

Plot series	
Types	Predominantly regular series of terraces, some semi-detached pairs and single plots, some parking court combinations
Shape	Predominantly regular rectangular
Size	Regular series vary from 6 to 24 units (12, 16 common)
Orientation	Active front on street frontage, reinforces street hierarchy – Russell Street, Baker Street, north–south routes, east–west streets, some flag plots, rear buildings and parking courts
Building line	Predominantly continuous with small variations, set-backs vary from 0 to 5m (1, 3 common)
Frontage	Continuous, with varied boundary feature
Vertical alignment	Varied, stepping of buildings predominantly every two units
Skyline	Generally continuous but varied, formed by eaves, chimneys, some dormers, ridge lines, some gables

PLOTS	
TYPE	PREDOMINANTLY REGULAR RECTANGULAR SINGLE BUILDING, SOME FLAG PLOTS, SOME MULTI-BUILDING CAMPUS TYPES
SIZE	WIDTHS PREDOMINANTLY 4–5M, 6–8M, 10–12M, 14–22M, SOME LARGER, DEPTHS PREDOMINANTLY 18–22M, 30–33M, 45–50M
SHAPE	PREDOMINANTLY RECTANGULAR, NARROW FRONTAGE, LONGER DEPTH
BUILT AREA	PREDOMINANT DEPTH 8–14 METRES, AREA BETWEEN 40 AND 80 SQUARE METRES AND SOME LARGER
ACCESS	FRONT PEDESTRIAN ACCESS, LIMITED FRONT VEHICULAR ACCESS (SEMI-DETACHED AND DETACHED TYPES), SOME REAR PARKING COURT
COMPONENTS	SMALL FRONT GARDEN OR AREA-WAY, PRINCIPAL BUILDING, BACK GARDEN, PARKING, SOME SIDE GARDEN OR PARKING, SOME SMALL SHEDS IN BACK GARDENS
FRONTAGE	PREDOMINANTLY IRON RAILINGS, SOME WITH LOW BRICK OR STONE WALL
VEGETATION	MIXED ORNAMENTAL SPECIES OF MEDIUM TO SMALL STATURE TREES, SHRUBS, ANNUALS AND GRASSES, PRINCIPALLY IN BACK AND SIDE GARDENS, SOME SHRUBS AND GRASS IN SMALL FRONT GARDEN SPACES

BUILDING	
TYPES	TERRACED AND SEMI-DETACHED TOWN HOUSES, SOME DETACHED VILLAS AND FLATS
SHAPE	PREDOMINANTLY RECTANGULAR IN PLAN, FLAT FRONT, REAR PROJECTION
HEIGHT	2, 2.5 AND 3 STOREY (5–9M TO EAVES)
DETAILS (STYLE)	LATE GEORGIAN, VICTORIAN, PRINCIPALLY CLASSICAL
MATERIALS	WALLS PREDOMINANTLY RED BRICK WITH SOME POLYCHROME BRICK, TILE HANGING, SOME PAINTED RENDER AND SOME STONE; ROOFS PREDOMINANTLY SLATE, SOME TILE AND INFREQUENT FLAT ROOFS

LINEAR MEASURES

- Junction spacing (J)
- Street width
  - frontage to frontage – reference line (Sw)
  - facade to facade (Sw + set-backs)
  - carriageway (Sw - footways) (Cw)
- Block dimensions (J - Sw)
- Plot width
- Plot depth
- Building depth/width
- Building spacing or separation (Sp)
- Building height

AREA MEASURES

The principal area measures are shown in figure 6.39 set within the context of the generic structure of urban tissue.

Total land area (A), total plot area (P), total building coverage (B), green roof (Gr), total external plot area (O), green area (G), building storey height (H), total area of public highway (S), average width of public highway (Sw), average carriageway width (Cw)

- A = Total land area
- P = Total plot area
- B = Total building coverage
- Gr = green (vegetated) roof
- O = Total external plot area
- G = green (vegetated) area
- H = Building storey height
- S = Total area of public highway
- Sw = Average width of public highway
- Cw = Average carriageway width

Calculated measures and key relationships include the following:

- S = A - P
- O = P - B
- A = P + S
- P = B + O

Depending on the aims of the study, green areas can be distinguished between those within the public highway or on individual plots as well as between cases where there is surface level vegetation, a tree canopy or both.

- Gross floor area (GFA) = B*H
- Linear distance of streets (Sl) = S/Sw
- Area of carriageway (Ca) = Sl*Cw

Dimensions are fundamentally variable continuous quantities. Depending on the objectives of the study it may be necessary or appropriate to use sampling and to state the quantities as either an average or a range (or both). There may also be clustering and sub-ranges of dimensions with the clusters identified as predominant types.

INDICES AND RATIOS

Common indices and ratios include:

- Street Area Index = S/A
- Floor Space Index (FSI, FAR, FSR, plot ratio) = (B*H)/A or GFA/A
- Coverage, Ground Space Index (GSI) or coefficient = B/A
- Open Space Ratio (OSR) = 1-GSI/FSI
- Green Area Index = (G + Gr)/A

The floor space index, ground space index and open space ratio have been combined in the Spacemate tool developed by Berghauser Pont and Haupt[21] (see Section 9.1). The aim of the tool is to give a more broadly based and useful measure than simple dwelling density.

ELEMENT DENSITY MEASURES

Number of elements per unit area:

- Street segments
- Intersections – ratio of node to link/vertices to edge
- Plots
- Buildings
- Access points
- Households
- Inhabitants

ORIENTATIONS AND INFLECTIONS

The description should also note where key elements of the tissue have been oriented or inflected in response to other features. Those features might include:

- Lines of access and movement
- Topography
- Prevailing winds
- Views
- Solar/celestial positions or paths
- Cosmological/religious features
- Land use
- Densities

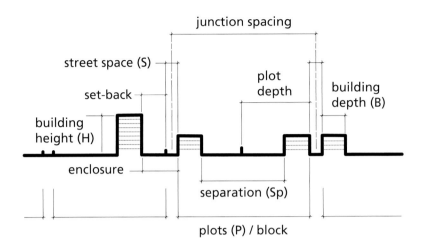

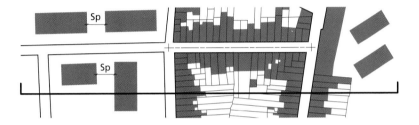

Figure 6.38
Diagram setting out the
key linear measures of
urban tissue.

Urban tissue		
Streets (simple tissue)		
Plot series [blocks]		Street spaces
Plots		
Buildings	Areas	
Rooms		
Structures		
Materials		

(a)

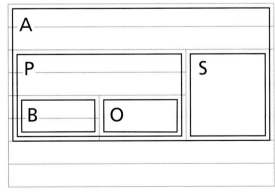

(b)

Figure 6.39
The multi-level diagram
of generic structure (a),
and the diagram inscribed
with the principal area
measures (b).

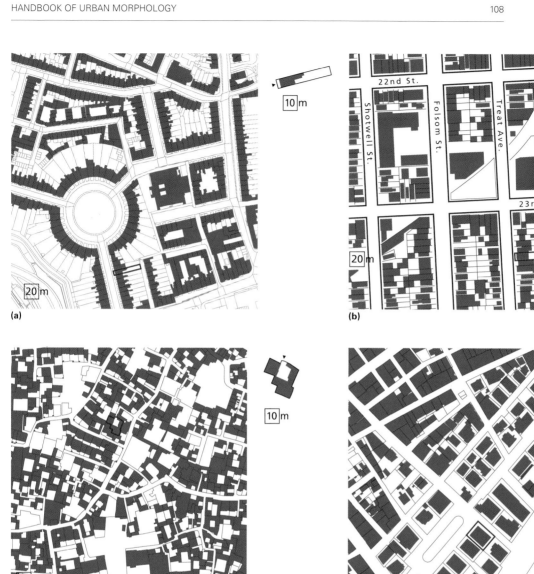

(a)

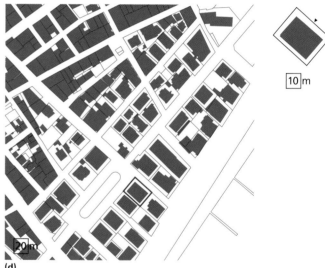

(b)

(c)

(d)

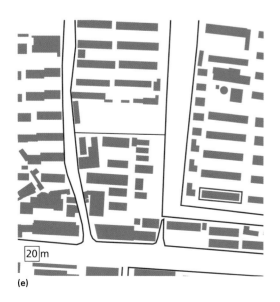

(e)

(f)

COMPONENT ELEMENTS AND THE PLOT AS THE MODULE OF URBAN TISSUE

As the sample text description table makes clear, describing or defining a tissue is in effect to specify its component parts. In principle, each component could itself be defined in the same way, in terms of position, outline (including points of access) and internal parts. In cases where the focus of the study is on urban tissue, the component descriptions are likely to be less detailed and rely on shorthand terms or a controlled vocabulary.

A common exception to this is the plot type. The overall form and internal structure of urban tissue is fundamentally determined by the ways in which individual plots can be combined based on maintaining points of access for movement, access to light and air as well as more culturally mediated standards such as privacy. These combinatorial constraints apply principally to the plot and reinforce its role as the **module of urban tissue**. It can therefore be very helpful to include more information on the plot type in order to shed light on the structure of the tissue. This is particularly true of what Scheer refers to as *static tissue*, which is deliberately designed to accommodate a particular 'building type'. It is worth noting that in this context, building type and plot type are often conflated because the concern is for both the building and its associated open space. In terms of generic types of form, the two taken together constitute the plot but the term 'building type' is the more common usage.

GROUPINGS OF TYPES

At this stage, the principal aim is to identify the full range of different tissues within the study area. As noted above in the discussion of lumping and splitting, the process also necessarily involves identifying families of similar tissues that might form a single group (at a lower level of resolution) in an effort to arrive at a clear overall structure. Thus, in addition to identifying the full range of different types, the desktop analysis of tissue also involves identifying tissues that potentially go together to form the larger-scale structures of the wider urban area. This subject is dealt with in more detail in Section 8 but at this stage it is worth noting one of the more important general distinctions, which is between uniform tissues on the one hand, and mixed or heterogeneous tissues on the other. This difference can signal the role of the tissue in the process of development and therefore also in the overall structure of the settlement.

OUTPUTS

The outputs of this stage in the analysis are a draft plan drawing outlining the *types* of tissues, the specific *examples* or areas of each type, draft descriptions and measures. Depending on the aims of the project and nature of the study area, outputs might also include a more detailed specification of the predominant plot types that form the module of the identified tissues.

The draft types from the desktop analysis along with the descriptions are checked and completed with information gathered in the field survey, in particular information on the third dimension, plot types, building types, structures and materials as well as townscape and other perceptual features.

USE AND NEIGHBOURHOOD STRUCTURE

The activities that animate places and bring them to life are fundamental to the way places work as well as to their character. A core component of urban morphological analysis is to investigate the distribution of land uses within a settlement. As set out in Section 1, the aspect of use covers the two main generic functions of movement and occupation as well as servicing. The principal concern here is with the different activities that fall under the category of occupation.

Depending on the scope and aims of the study, analysis of occupation can be undertaken at four broad levels of resolution:

- Individual spaces
- Individual plots
- Aggregations of plots
- Sectors or zones

At each level, the identified element is taken as the unit of activity type or use category. That is to say, any differentiation or variation within the unit is ignored for the purposes of analysis. Thus, a sector or zone identified as residential might contain other uses such as schools and small-scale retail.

The initial task of analysis is to identify the **current activities** accommodated by a particular form or area, irrespective of its original or intended use and irrespective of the form or conventional 'building type' such as 'house', 'theatre' or 'church'. This follows from the fundamental flexibility of the relationship between form and human activities. One of the points of

Figure 6.40
Examples of tissues from different parts of the world, highlighting a typical plot or lot, which, as a physical entity, constitutes the principal module of urban tissue: a) the Roman/medieval core of Bath, UK; b) the Mission District in San Francisco, California; c) the historic centre of Isfahan, Iran; d) a coastal edge of centre location in Mersin, Turkey; e) the edge of the historic centre of Nanjing, China; f) Borgo San Frediano, south of the Arno, Florence, Italy.

interest in the subsequent analysis is to examine the variable relationship between form and use.

As with the general process of analysis, investigation of use typically involves a desktop analysis followed by field survey. In cases where there is little or no documentary or digital evidence, it may be necessary to rely entirely on a field survey.

For a standard analysis of use at the level of the plot, the appropriate categories are likely to be the general use classes as employed in planning:

- Retail/commercial
  - shops, bars/pubs, cafés and restaurants, retail offices
- Office
- Industrial/manufacturing, distribution and storage
- Hotels
- Residential institutions
- Residential
- Institutional
  - churches, schools, hospitals, museums, libraries
- Leisure/entertainment

Movement and servicing can also be included in the analysis, either as a generic designation or different types. As a general rule it is good practice to assign a use to all built-up land within the study area. At the level of the plot upward, servicing generally includes those areas of land that are built up but not intended for – or actively exclude – regular access such as electricity substations, pumping stations, surface-level pipelines and reservoirs.

DATA SOURCES
There are increasing numbers of land-use data sets available, in various formats, produced by both commercial and government organisations. Many local authorities now maintain GIS data of local services and facilities which can be very useful. Similarly, there are online sources for many different categories of use, making it possible to compile land-use data relatively quickly. Information can also be collected 'manually' from online, street-level photography. All these sources vary in currency, coverage and level of resolution so it is critical to match the data to the scope and resolution of the study.

A significant amount of information can also be gathered from ground-level mapping of plots and buildings either directly from labels or by inference

from plot and building type. Working by inference from types must be qualified by the caveat underlined above: the relationship between physical form and use is not fixed. One way or the other, desktop collection of land-use data should ideally be checked in the field survey.

Studies that include examining changes of use through time will necessarily need to make use of archival and documentary sources or inference from building types to identify past land uses.

CENTRES AND NEIGHBOURHOOD STRUCTURE
Interpretation of the raw data once it is mapped is based on a number of basic principles and regularities revealed through observation and theoretical modelling. These can be summarised under the general concept of **centrality** and the secondary notions of **poles** and **nodes**. Centrality is the subject of significant investigation in its own right and is in turn part of the still wider subject within geography and planning of the interactions between movement, use and the physical form of cities. The very modest aim here is to establish the basic logic that underlies the differentiation of use patterns to identify characteristic structures. The objective is then to include the structured pattern of use in the composite view of urban form in order to gain insights into the process of formation and transformation as well as the resulting structure and character of the settlement at a given point in time.

Centrality operates as a general tendency in a number of different ways and at different levels of scale.

- A single activity, use or shared resource in a particular location that is the destination for a number of different people in the surrounding area. Examples include a well in a village, a place of worship or sports facility
- Clustering of similar and/or associated usually non-residential uses in a location or area. Examples are local and neighbourhood centres usually made up of retail and community facilities that serve a more or less well-defined catchment
- Network centrality as expressed through measures such as closeness and betweenness, usually applied to route networks but also social networks
- An isolated settlement within a rural/non-urban context or component centre in a polycentric metropolitan area

Figure 6.41
Local pattern of land use in Reading, UK. The non-residential uses are concentrated along the Oxford Road and Tilehurst Road, both strategic routes.

Figure 6.42
Land-use pattern in the historic centre of Hereford, UK. The pattern shows a definite clustering of commercial and institutional uses that contributes to the distinction of two parts of the centre: the commercial city and the Cathedral city.

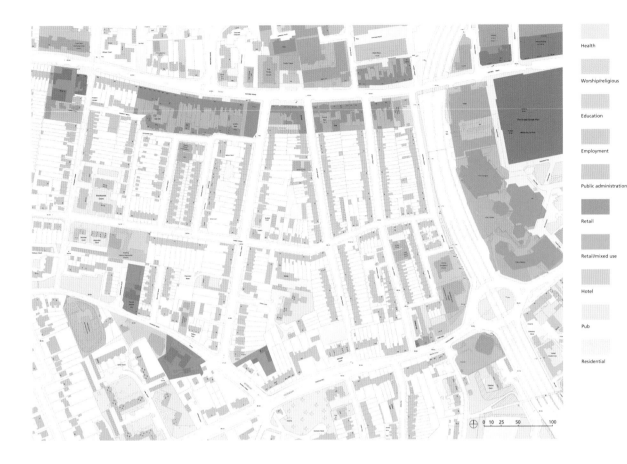

Health

Worship/religious

Education

Employment

Public administration

Retail

Retail/mixed use

Hotel

Pub

Residential

0 10 25 50 100

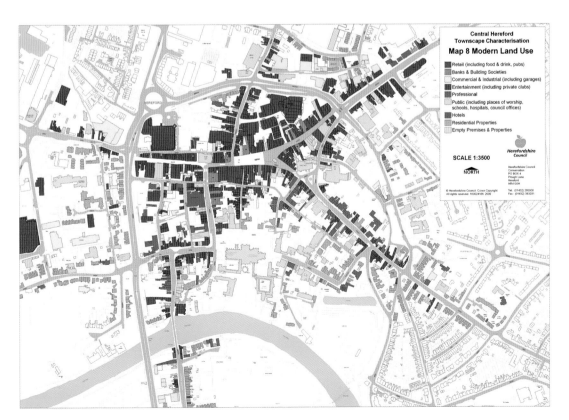

Central Hereford
Townscape Characterisation

Map 8 Modern Land Use

Retail (including food & drink, pubs)
Banks & Building Societies
Commercial & Industrial (including garages)
Entertainment (including private clubs)
Professional
Public (including places of worship, schools, hospitals, council offices)
Hotels
Residential Properties
Empty Premises & Properties

SCALE 1:3500

NORTH

Herefordshire Council

Herefordshire Council
Conservation
PO BOX 4
Plough Lane
Hereford
HR4 0XH

© Herefordshire Council: Crown Copyright
All rights reserved 100024168. 2009

Tel: (01432) 260000
Fax: (01432) 383031

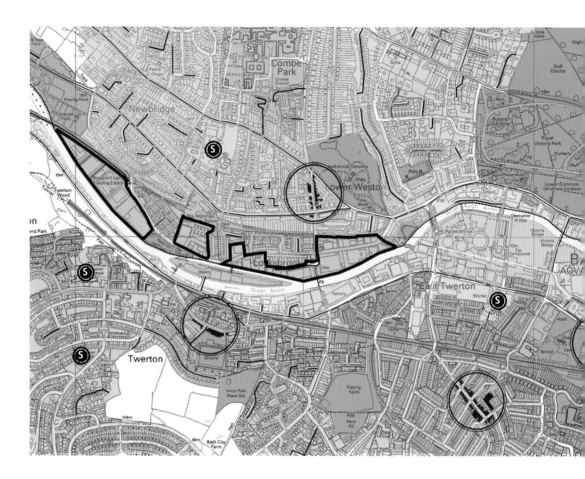

The result of the tendency is the general pattern of functional and physical centres found even in areas of dispersed development. For the purposes of analysis, a single use or shared resource that is a destination for people in the surrounding area can be referred to as a **pole**. An external space that is the confluence of routes and is a destination is a **node**. Clusters of similar and/or associated uses are **centres** of various rank.

Looking at a pole or centre on its own, the principal features to take into account are:

- Position within a wider pattern of centres
- Relative size and concentration
- Predominant uses and mix of elements
- Relative positions of elements and particular associations of different use types

Of equal importance to note are the associations between centres and other aspects and elements, in particular:

- Routes and route type (including different modes)
- Types of urban tissue
- Specific built features (buildings, open space, monuments, vegetation)
- Natural features

Many settlements, even smaller towns, show a relatively consistently spaced pattern of local centres – clusters of mainly retail and service uses. The pattern of local centres forms part of the framework of elements around which **neighbourhoods** in the social sense might form – allowing for the necessarily loose nature of a neighbourhood. The pattern of local centres can thus be taken as a partial indicator of **neighbourhood structure**.

PROCESS AND OUTPUTS
The basic process is to compile the data, transcribe it onto a plan, check and supplement the desktop work with the field survey and undertake analysis.

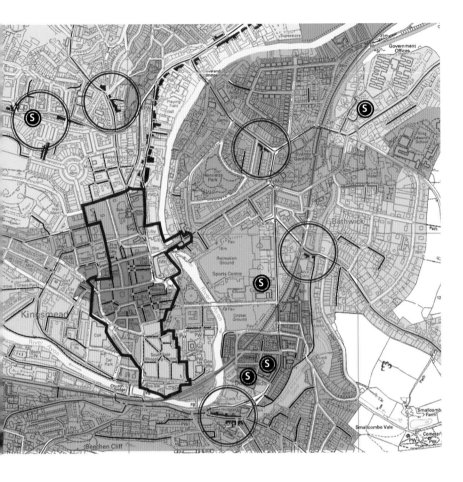

Figure 6.43
Plan showing the location
of retail clusters and
schools in Bath. The
pattern emerged over
time with the growth of
the city and coalescence
with surrounding
villages. The contents
and distribution of the
sub-centres provide an
initial basis for identifying
neighbourhoods.

The output of use analysis in many cases will be an overlay showing the land-use pattern within the study area. Because of the potential number of different use classes or zones, each use is typically designated by a different colour, tone or hatch pattern. For colour selection it is often best to follow conventions used in official planning documents for land-use maps, or a similar range, to avoid confusion. There is also some sense in using colours in a quasi-representational way, for example, using greens for open space and recreation.

As stated in Section 1, the aim of the distinctions identified in looking at use should be to capture the pattern of relationships and structure of activities within a settlement and their associations with different specific forms.

The analysis of the data may include identifying:

- Clusters of the same or similar uses
- Patterns, spatial arrangement and associations of different uses

- Associations between use and other aspects including built form, control, city image elements
- Patterns of spatial interaction

If the study includes investigating the patterns of use through time, the outputs will include a chronological sequence of overlays and analysis may include:

- Changes or continuity of location and association over time
- Changes in patterns of spatial interaction

CITY IMAGE, TOWNSCAPE AND OPEN SPACE NETWORK

While the perceptual aspects of city image and townscape are by definition experienced from the ground, it is still possible to undertake some desktop analysis of the aspects based on interpretation and inference from plans. If city image elements and serial vision can be mapped, then it is possible to follow the logic in reverse and identify on a map where the elements and routes are *likely* to be.

The concepts and analytical methods recommended here are set out in much more detail in the source texts of *The Image of the City* (Lynch), *The View from the Road* (Appleyard, Lynch and Myer), *Townscape* (Cullen) as well as extended methods developed by others including Reeve et al.[22]

The general process involves three main steps:

- Identify elements in plan based on principles, general experience or known examples
- Record the different elements on an overlay using a consistent set of plan symbols
- Check the desktop analysis and revise as necessary as part of the field survey.

The principal city image elements include:

- Nodes
- Landmarks
- Edges
- Paths
- Districts

Paths correspond broadly with routes, and districts with tissues. The correspondence can be checked and the perceptual prominence placed on specific instances determined on the field survey.

Other core elements of image and townscape include:

- Gateways
- Views and vistas
- Barriers
- Spatial definition/enclosure/frontage
- Key spatial sequences

OPEN SPACE NETWORK

The combination of principal open spaces within a built-up area can contribute significantly to its perceptual structure, in terms of both a navigational image and a distinct, tangible experience. A further, general method is therefore to outline all the principal open spaces in the study area and the connections allowing movement between them, if any. Types of spaces include:

- Principal squares and other nodes
- Parks, gardens and large archaeological sites
- Tree-lined avenues and boulevards
- River corridors and other natural open areas within the built-up area

Connecting elements might be streets, avenues and boulevards with street trees, green corridors and footpaths.

OUTPUTS

The principal output should be one or more plans with symbols and annotations. Ideally the plan should be produced in a way that it can easily be taken on the field survey for checking and *in situ* revision.

Figure 6.44
Plan highlighting the distribution of the main green spaces within San Francisco, including interconnecting tree-lined avenues.

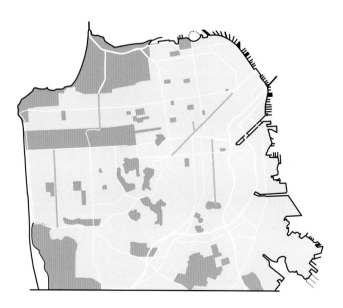

References

1 Anne Vernez Moudon, *Built for Change*, MIT Press (Cambridge, MA), 1986. Print.

2 Gustavo Giovannoni, 'Il "Diradamento Edilizio" dei Vecchi Centri', *Nuova Antologia* 997 (1913): 53–76. Print.

- Gustavo Giovannoni, *Vecchie Città ed Edilizia Nuova*, Unione Tipografico – Editrice Torinese (Turin), 1931. Print.

- Pierre Lavedan, *Qu'est-ce que l'Urbanisme?,* Henri Laurens (Paris), 1926. Print.

3 Sandrine Robert, 'Comment les formes se transmettent-elles?', Études Rurales, EHESS, 2004, pp 115–32. <hal-00371092>

4 GK Zipf, *Human Behaviour and the Principle of Least Effort*, Addison-Wesley (Cambridge, MA), 1949. Print.

5 Bill Hillier and Julienne Hanson, *The Social Logic of Space*, Cambridge University Press (Cambridge), 1984. Print.

6 N John Habraken, *The Structure of the Ordinary*, MIT Press (Cambridge, MA), 1998. Print.

7 Fernand Braudel, *The Mediterranean and the Mediterranean World in the Age of Philip II*, Fontana (London), 1990, p 277. Print.

8 Stephen Marshall, *Streets and Patterns*, Spon (London), 2005. Print.

9 Bill Hillier, *Space Is the Machine*, Cambridge University Press (Cambridge), 1996. Print.

10 A Ståhle, L Marcus, and A Karlström, 'Place Syntax: Geographic Accessibility with Axial Lines in GIS', Proceedings of the 5th Space Syntax Symposium, Delft, n. pag., 2005. Web.

11 Gianfranco Caniggia and Gian Luigi Maffei, *Architectural Composition and Building Typology: Interpreting Basic Buildings*, Alinea (Florence), 2001. Print.

- Giancarlo Cataldi, *Lezioni di Architettura, Biblioteca di Architettura*, Saggi e Documenti 26, Alinea (Florence). Print.

- Saverio Muratori, 'Studi per Una Operante Storia Urbana Di Venezia', *Palladio*, Istituto Poligrafico dello Stato (Rome), 1959. Print.

- Attilio Petruccioli, *After Amnesia: Learning from the Islamic Mediterranean Urban Fabric*, Dipartimento di Ingegneria Civile e Architettura Politecnico di Bari (Bari), 2007. Print.

12 Jean Castex, Patrick Céleste and Philippe Panerai, *Lecture d'une Ville: Versailles*, Éditions du Moniteur (Paris), 1980. Print.

- Philippe Panerai, Jean-Charles Depaule and Marcelle Demorgon, *Analyse Urbaine*, Éditions Parenthèses (Marseille), 1999. Print.

13 Brenda Case Scheer, *The Evolution of Urban Form: Typology for Planners and Architects*, American Planning Association (Chicago), 2010. Print.

14 MRG Conzen, *Alnwick, Northumberland: A Study in Town Plan Analysis*, Institute of British Geographers (London), 1969. Print.

15 Natalya Boujenko, Stephen Marshall and Peter Jones, *Link and Place*, Local Transport Today (London), 2007. Print.

16 Jürgen Lafrenz, 'The Metrological Analysis of Early Modern Planned Towns', *Urban Historical Geography: Recent Progress in Britain and Germany*, Dietrich Denecke and Gareth Shaw (eds), Cambridge University Press (Cambridge), 1988. Print.

- June A Sheppard, 'Metrological Analysis of Regular Village Plans in Yorkshire', *Agricultural History Review* 22 (1974): 118–35. Print.

- Terry Slater, 'English Medieval Town Planning', *Urban Historical Geography: Recent Progress in Britain and Germany*, Dietrich Denecke and Gareth Shaw (eds), Cambridge University Press (Cambridge), 1988. Print.

17 Jacob Dibble et al, 'Urban Morphometrics: Towards a Science of Urban Evolution', *arXiv:1506.04875 [physics]* (2015): n. pag., *arXiv.org*. Web. Accessed 25 Mar 2016.

18 Pierre Gauthier, 'On Street Networks, Spatial Configurations and Morphogenesis: A Case Study in the Greater Montreal Region', 2015, Rome: conference paper delivered to the 22nd ISUF Conference: *City as Organism. New Visions for Urban Life.*

19 Michael Voltersen et al, 'Object-Based Land Cover Mapping and Comprehensive Feature Calculation for an Automated Derivation of Urban Structure Types at Block Level', *Remote Sensing of Environment* 154 (2014): 192–201. Web.

- Irene Walde et al, 'From Land Cover-Graphs to Urban Structure Types', *International Journal of Geographical Information Science* 28.3 (2014): 584–609, *Taylor and Francis+NEJM*. Web.

20 Paul Osmond, 'The Urban Structural Unit: Towards a Descriptive Framework to Support Urban Analysis and Planning', *Urban Morphology* 14.1 (2010): 5–20. Print.

- Paul Osmond, 'An Enquiry into New Methodologies for Evaluating Sustainable Urban Form', unpublished PhD thesis, Faculty of the Built Environment, University of New South Wales, 2008. Print.

21 Meta Berghauser Pont and Per Haupt, 'The Relation between Urban Form and Density', *Urban Morphology* 11.1 (2007): 62–66. Print.

- Meta Berghauser Pont and Per Haupt, 'Space, Density and Urban Form', Technische Universiteit Delft, 2009. Web.

22 Donald Appleyard, Kevin Lynch and John R Myer, *The View from the Road*, MIT Press (Cambridge, MA), 1965. Print.

- Gordon Cullen, *Townscape*, Architectural Press (Oxford), 1961. Print.

- Kevin Lynch, *The Image of the City*, MIT Press (Cambridge, MA), 1960. Print.

- Alan Reeve, Brian Goodey and Robert Shipley, 'Townscape Assessment: The Development of a Practical Tool for Monitoring and Assessing Visual Quality in the Built Environment', *Urban Morphology* 11.1 (2007): 25–41. Print.

Field Survey

In most cases the field survey is a necessary part of the overall process and an essential complement to desktop analysis. It is often through direct investigation from the ground that the analysis begins to make sense and demonstrates its value.

The field survey has a number of purposes, including:

- Checking and refining the results of the desktop analysis
- Collecting additional information about the fabric not available from other sources, particularly the third dimension as well as access, movement and use
- Recording perceptual aspects, townscape and the more subjective responses and judgements

A further benefit should be to discover new things.

As set out in more detail in this section, the field survey should be undertaken using systematic methods of recording data and interpretations to capture the results as fully and accurately as possible. Steps in the process should therefore include:

- Planning the survey
- Designing and putting together recording methods
- Undertaking the survey
- Processing the results

More specifically, the tasks include the following:

- Identify and record specific types of physical form at the lower levels of scale
  - plot/block boundaries
  - buildings[1]
  - details and materials
- Identify frontage types and access points
- Record and/or check uses by plot and within the street
- Check and add to identification of perceptual structure, townscape and city image elements
- Check and refine tissue boundaries

Because the field survey can be very time intensive, one of the most important steps in the process is the planning. It is essential to be very clear what information is needed and to establish the best format for recording the data to ensure that processing the results is as efficient as possible. Planning of the survey therefore needs to take into account the way results fit into the overall process of analysis.

The extent of the field survey will depend on the purpose and scope of the study and can range from a rapid walk-through of selected areas to a building-by-building survey. If a site visit or field survey is not possible either because the place no longer exists or access is restricted, the scope of the study should be adjusted accordingly and a combination of other sources used to acquire the necessary information. Even when the scope does not strictly require a field survey, a visit can provide insights of significant value not available by any other means.

Some of the primary recording methods include:

- Structured text notes
- Annotation of plans
- Filling in and annotating *pro forma* survey sheets or 'fiches'
- Photography and video
- Measured surveys
- Laser point cloud surveys

As in the desktop stage, not all of the methods set out for this stage will be appropriate for every project. The methods used will depend on the purpose of the study. It is also worth noting that an increasing amount of information, including street level photography, is available through the Internet. For projects with limited resources, shifting field survey onto the desktop can allow much more to be done for less. Care obviously needs to be taken regarding the currency and completeness of online sources. There is also no substitute for the direct experience of walking through the study area.

If the project only requires a relatively low level of resolution or resources are limited, the field study can be run as a rapid check of boundaries by a walk-through with minimal recording using photographs for further desktop analysis. More extensive and systematic methods should be used for projects requiring greater detail at higher levels of resolution, such as design and conservation-based studies.

SURVEY PLANNING AND DESIGN

The main steps in organising the survey include the following:

- Identify sample areas (if appropriate)
- Plan the survey route
- Prepare recording sheets
- Gather the necessary materials and equipment
- Brief the team

RECORDING SHEETS

Recording sheets of some kind are essential in order to maintain the accuracy and integrity of the information gathered. Recording sheets also make the process much quicker and more efficient. Sheets are best if broken down by aspect, generic type of form and component elements. That way, the information can be fed directly into the descriptions of the tissues and component types.

The underlying principle of the sheet is that it anticipates the range of likely forms on the one hand and, on the other, allows for adding new forms/types/variants encountered in the field. The task is then to select from a list/menu the forms found in a particular place or write in a brief description of a new or unfamiliar type. Ideally the lists make use of a controlled vocabulary compiled from commonly used sources or previous studies, both general and specific, as well as the initial work done at the desktop stage. Clearly if there is little information on the types likely to be found, the lists will be short and most of the recording will be written descriptions. In that case it is helpful to begin to identify and name types, so if a given type is found in more than one place all that is necessary is to refer to the name once it has been described. A sample recording sheet is included as Appendix 1.

SAMPLING

With a large study area and/or limited resources, it may be necessary to use a sampling approach to the field survey. Samples are best selected in advance using the following steps:

- Identify the larger, more uniform tissues as defined in the desktop assessment
- Select a part of the tissue that is representative of the whole as far as can be determined from the information available
- Include only the selected area in the survey route

The more uniform the area, the smaller the sample can be while still providing robust representative information (surveying every single street of a large, uniform development is very unlikely to yield any more information pertinent to the study than a survey of a few, representative streets).

In general, there is likely to be less variation in more recent large-scale developments while older areas are likely to have experienced more change resulting in more variation. This trend justifies an overall bias in the selection of samples toward larger samples for older areas and/or those that show more variation on plan.

WORKING TIPS

The survey route should be planned out in advance, ideally to cover the study area/samples in a comprehensive and systematic way while limiting the amount of doubling back.

The aim of the organisation for the field survey should be to maintain consistent recording throughout. To this end, the basic materials should include the following:

- A plan of the survey route
- A copy of the study area map showing the draft boundaries of the tissues/character areas and city image/townscape/open space elements
- Several clean copies of the map of the study area for recording
- Pre-printed recording sheets (bound if possible)
- Pens/pencils
- Clipboard
- Camera

The copies of the map should be large enough to be able to read the annotations made in the field. The number of clean copies needed will depend on the range of aspects being covered. There is a balance to be struck between the workability of the survey process and the readability of the annotated plans. Too many plans can be awkward to deal with, too few can lead to illegible maps. There might potentially be up to six or more plans:

- Draft tissue boundaries
- Access points
- Land use
- Behaviour traces
- Perceptual aspects and features, including views
- Photo location recording

Several of these might be recorded on a single map depending on the scale of the map and the density and intensity of development.

- Draft tissue boundaries and photo locations
- Land use, access points, behaviour traces
- Perceptual aspects and features, including views

PHOTOGRAPHY

Photography is an essential means of recording a wide range of features in an efficient way, in particular street scenes and sections, frontage features, buildings, details and materials. Colour can also be recorded by matching material and paint colours to standard colour-system swatches and including the swatch in the photograph.

In addition to its recording function, photography is a central means of communicating the specific features and character of urban tissue and its constituent forms. If possible the day or days for the survey should be chosen for their quality of light, ideally sunny but avoiding the long shadows of early morning or late afternoon.

Depending on the nature of the study, the extent of the photography might range from taking a selection of general views to undertaking full, structured photographic surveys of streets and specific buildings.

In all cases the location of each shot should be recorded on a key map or geotagged with the camera or GPS device.

OTHER DIGITAL AIDS

A range of digital tools is available to aid and enhance the collection of data in the field. As just noted, GPS is now routinely used to geotag photographs but can also be used to record the location of a range of different elements such as unmapped physical features, land use and city image elements. As detailed by Osmond in his Enquiry,[2] fisheye photography is employed to record and assess vegetation cover as well as the characteristics of the skyline (see also the ViewCue method discussed below). A further technique that is becoming increasingly common is the point cloud survey. The method is particularly well suited to recording details of physical form but, because it can be resource intensive, is likely to be most appropriate either for small areas or selected elements.

BUILT FORM

As suggested above, the task of describing the internal structure of urban tissue is to a large extent a matter of identifying its component parts, as types, and their arrangement. The general concepts of generic and specific types apply equally to the various components. Building up a description of internal structure is therefore a recursive process, each iteration moving down the hierarchy of generic structure increasing the resolution of the description. The common use of the three structural perspectives of position, outline and internal structure for all generic types gives consistent descriptions that clearly identify the relationships between the elements in a coherent way.

The field survey provides the opportunity to view the place directly, rather than by way of other representations. This is particularly important in studies concerned with character and local identity and understanding how places are used. The level of detail and resolution will therefore depend significantly on the aims of the study. It is likely, for example, that a higher level of resolution and detail would be used in areas with high cultural and heritage value where the aim is to maintain those values through conservation and planning controls. Lower – or selective – levels of detail are likely to be sufficient for investigations into environmental performance or strategic planning. The range of elements included in the survey will ideally have been set at the outset by defining the level of resolution of the study. The elements included in the field survey will also depend on the information available from sources used in the desktop stage. Where there is an overlap, the field survey can be used as an opportunity to check the information and interpretations from the desktop stage.

THE DETAILED COMPONENTS OF URBAN TISSUE

The following lists set out the key elements of built form most commonly recorded in a field survey. Depending on the generic configuration of the tissues in the area, some elements, for example plot series, may not be present.

Streets
- Components (section), eg, pavement, carriageway, verge, island/median/reservation
- Tree and plant species
- Surface materials
- Street furniture

Plots series
- Position/orientation of access points common to the series
- Location, number and type of common spaces (parking, garden/landscape spaces)
- Position, type and materials of common boundary features
- Location and type of common vegetation

Plots
- Position, orientation and number of access points: vehicular and pedestrian
- Location, number and type of external spaces (parking, garden/landscape spaces, with reference to plot type)
- Position, type and materials of boundary features
- Location, extent and type of vegetation

Buildings
- Storey height (including basements, if any)
- Roof form
- Location, number and type of chimneys or other 'vertical features'
- Location of principal access points
- Period/style

Roofs
- Type/form
- Principal roof material
- Ridge (details and materials)
- Eaves, parapet, verge (details and materials)
- Dormers and/or rooflights (location, number, type, details and materials)
- Chimneys and other features (details and materials)
- Green roof species

Facades (walls)
- Position on building
- Principal wall materials
- Composition (eg, formal, informal, blank/blind)
- Number, type and arrangement of openings/details
- Corner details, material patterns
- Supplementary features

Openings/windows and doors
- Location within facade
- Shape, size and proportions
- Surround (details and materials)
- Frame/subframe/support (details and materials)
- Glazing or door leaf (details and materials: number, type and arrangement of elements)

OUTPUTS

The principal means of recording these elements is through survey sheets or photography or both. The material from the sheets can then be transferred into text descriptions and tables or, alternatively, into illustrative diagrams of types. By their nature, photographs are 'non-judgemental' and it may be necessary to use captions or manipulation of the image to isolate the features that are of most importance. Another technique is to selectively draw over only the elements of interest.

ACCESS, FRONTAGE AND BOUNDARY TYPES

One of the most significant features of built form is the interface or boundary between street spaces and occupation spaces, in particular in terms of access and openings. As the boundary between the public and private realms, it forms a nexus of aspects: form, movement, occupation, control and perception. Analysis and understanding of the nature of the boundary is crucial in many applications.

Graphically illustrating and/or quantifying access points provides significant information for assessing levels of activity and surveillance that contribute to vitality, security and character. The overall pattern and orientation of access points is also important in seeking to understand the configurational logic of aggregation of urban tissue.

FRONTS AND BACKS

The simplest method is to distinguish fronts, which contain the principal access points, from backs and sides, marking up a plan with a dashed line for fronts and a solid line for the backs and sides. This method can be used at different levels of scale, from a whole settlement to individual structured spaces. At the level of the settlement the 'fronts' are located where a route runs along the outer boundary of the built-up area and plots take their primary access from the route.

ACCESS AND ACTIVE FRONTAGE

At the level of the plot series and block, the method can be elaborated by distinguishing different types of frontage, again annotating the types on a plan. The principal interest is the location of primary access points, which establish the internal orientation of the plot/building and the way it relates to other elements in making up urban tissue as well as indicating the location of movement activity. Degrees of activity are introduced by further considering windows and secondary access points.

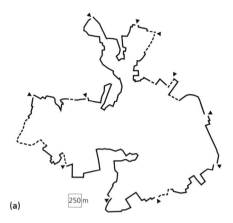

(a)

(b)

Figure 7.1
The outer boundary of a
settlement as a whole (a)
can present either a front
(b; shown as a dashed line
on the plan) or a back or
side (c; shown as a solid
line on the plan). The front
is essentially a single-
sided tissue with the
street space on the outer
edge. This kind of diagram
is helpful in assessing
possible configurations
for outward growth.

(c)

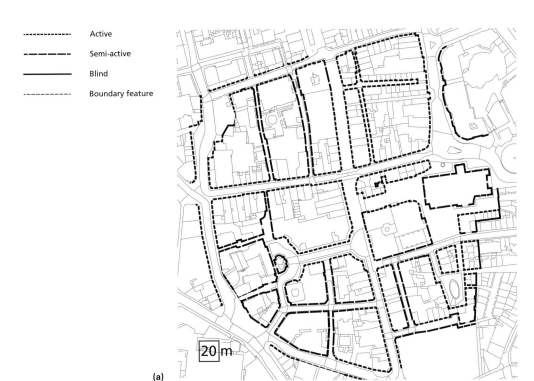

--------------- Active

— — — — — Semi-active

—————— Blind

- - - - - - - - - Boundary feature

20 m

(a)

The basis for identifying different types of frontage is the amount of openings within a given distance of frontage. The specific definitions used will depend on the nature of the study. Figure 7.2 shows an example with four types of frontage.

- Active (higher density of doors and windows)
- Semi-active (lower density of doors and windows)
- Blind (no doors or windows)
- Boundary feature (free-standing wall or fence)

ACCESS POINTS

At higher levels of resolution a more detailed method of analysis is to identify all the access points to the plots (buildings) along each frontage and note them on a plan. Access points can be indicated by a tick or the standard architectural symbol of a small black triangle.

To get a full picture, it is helpful to distinguish between two or three main types of entrance:

- Vehicular
- Pedestrian
- Service

A finer level of detail can be added by indicating whether the access to buildings is set back from the plot boundary and whether there are a number of access points within the plot.

The pattern of access can then be characterised in terms of:

- Density
- Distribution
- Orientation

Depending on the nature of the study, the results can either be left as a manuscript map and generalised with a description such as active or inactive frontage, or the notation can be transcribed and included in the final outputs. While this method can be started at the desktop stage using plans and aerial photography, it is best done during the field survey.

The results indicate the intensity of movement in and out along the frontage and to and from the locality. Importantly, mapping the access points and frontage types shows the relative position of the access point on the boundary and so the internal orientation of the plots, plot series or block

above and overleaf

Figure 7.2

The density of access points (physical and visual) can be generalised by identifying types of frontage based on the relative number of doors and windows per linear unit. The diagram (a) shows four types: active, semi-active, blind and boundary feature, where there is no building directly on the boundary. The photographs show an active frontage (b) and semi-active frontage (c).

(b)

(c)

Figure 7.2 *(cont.)*

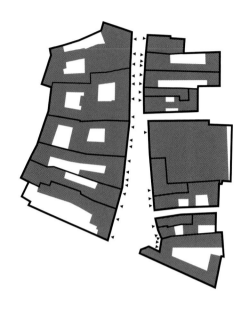

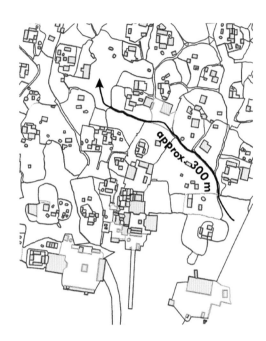

as a whole. This allows for configurational analysis (access graphs) of street/plot series/block patterns. The higher resolution detail also extends the information provided by desktop methods such as Place Syntax[3] and Space Syntax.[4]

BOUNDARY LINE TYPE ANALYSIS
As set out in Section 4, the configuration of space is fundamentally made manifest by the creation of boundaries. They constitute a significant part of our experience of places and can be a powerful basis for the interpretation and analysis of spatial structure and social interaction. Boundaries can be particularly useful in cases where the forms involved are unfamiliar and when other physical evidence of the built form is limited or missing. An obvious case in this respect is the interpretation of archaeological evidence. Boundaries also provide a robust reference feature for comparative analysis. A method that brings these two concerns together has been developed by archaeologist and geographer Benjamin Vis.[5] The methodology has been applied to the pre-Columbian Maya city of Chunchucmil, as represented by the survey of standing archaeological features produced by the Pakbeh Regional Economy Project.

The core of the method is the morphological principle of defining elements by their position relative to each other and within the pattern as a whole. Different types of boundaries are defined in terms of their relative position, shape, material and physical characteristics and all articulating a type of control in how they seclude spatial subdivisions, including distinctions between physical and implied boundaries.

The aim of the analysis is to establish a clear and comparative picture of the socio-spatial structure of a settlement with inferences drawn from the material presence of different types of boundary about, among other things, the experience of and opportunities for social interaction of particular locations.

The starting point of the analysis is the building, which is taken as a 'solid' (without internal divisions). This is referred to as a 'dominant' because it implies full control and seclusion of the enclosed surface. The procedure is then to identify all the dominants (termed Closing Boundaries) in the study area, annotating the plan outline of the building with a colour-coded line (dark brown). Openings for access (Facing Boundaries, exclusively applicable to dominants) are coded light green. The next step is to identify the Associative

above left **Figure 7.3 Identifying each individual access point provides further detail and allows for quantitative assessments.**

above right **Figure 7.4 Plan of Chunchucmil, Yucatán, Mexico, showing different boundary line types as described in the text**

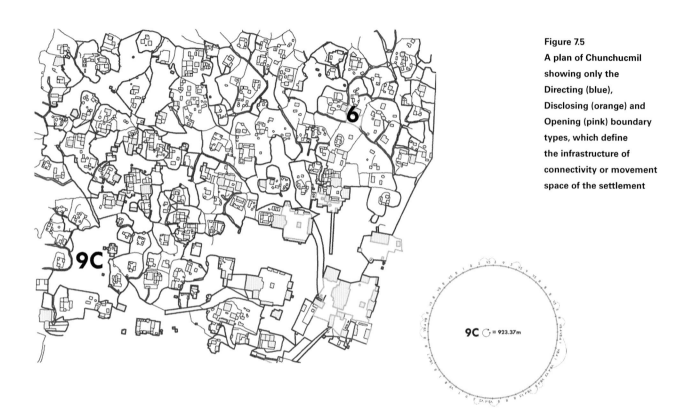

Figure 7.5
A plan of Chunchucmil showing only the Directing (blue), Disclosing (orange) and Opening (pink) boundary types, which define the infrastructure of connectivity or movement space of the settlement

Boundaries attached to single buildings (red), which are akin to the boundaries of a curtilage or pertinent area, along with their openings (Extended Facing Boundaries, dark green).

Two further types of boundary directly associated with buildings are: Enclosing Boundaries (yellow), which enclose one or more buildings with a high degree of seclusion, and Mutual Boundaries (purple), which connect distinct configurations of several buildings, creating a shared surface. Taking a further step outward, there are three boundary types that can be coincident with or adjoin any of the previous boundary types (and allow access to them). These differ from one another mainly in terms of the shape of the resulting surface and contextual relation to each other. The three together define the infrastructure of spaces allowing interconnections through the settlement and opportunities for interaction. They include Directing Boundaries (blue), which are linear and connect any number of spaces; Disclosing Boundaries (orange), which have multiple access points that are associated with buildings; and Opening Boundaries (pink), which have multiple connections to any type

of boundary and are varied in shape and size. The alignment, orientation and juxtaposition of material boundaries can imply their extension across a space such as at route junctions. The implied boundary is referred to as Virtual.

Finally, there is a group of three boundary line types that limit or prevent ordinary access either by a physical barrier or a change in surface. The three types are: Man-Made Boundaries of Unoccupiability such as railways or motorways; natural boundaries (termed Not Man-Made Boundaries of Unoccupiability) such as rivers or steep slopes; and the settlement Edge (termed Not Man-Made Negative Boundaries).

A further tool developed by Vis is the 'clock diagram', shown in figure 7.6, which maps the different combinations of boundary line types coincident with the boundary of a given space (termed topological segments). The diagram facilitates quantitative and qualitative analysis of the boundaries in terms of density and differentiation of the composition of the built environment structuring the potential for interaction. There are several variants of the clock

Figure 7.6
A clock diagram, used to visualise the topological relationships of coincident boundaries around a bounded space

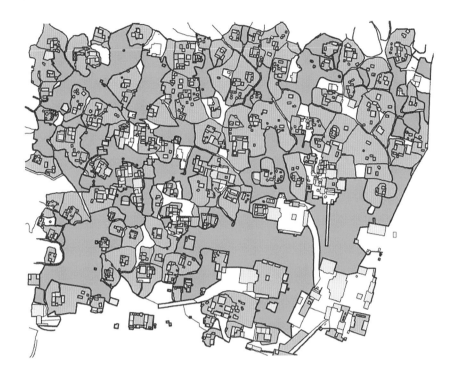

Figure 7.7
Plan showing the Mutual
(purple) and Opening
(pink) boundaries of
Chunchucmil. The Mutual
boundaries enclose
separate buildings in
shared space and Opening
boundaries define what
are effectively public
open spaces. Together the
spaces they define cover
most of the settlement.

diagram that serve to visualise the traversability of the space, surface size, frequencies, etc, facilitating further forms of analysis.

As shown in figures 7.5 and 7.7, the colour coding of the boundary line types clarifies the structure of the settlement and helps in identifying repeating patterns of features and the relationships between them. One of the aims of the method is to allow for better comparative analysis of examples from different cultures and over time. To that end, it has also been applied to a historical map sequence of Winchester, UK, which highlights how patterns of opportunities for interaction and occupiable space become structured in the development of built space over time.

OUTPUTS

The most common outputs for the survey of access, frontage and boundary types are plan diagrams that transpose the data collected in the field onto plans. The information is also generally incorporated into text descriptions and tables. Information on access points, particularly if collected by GPS, can also be used in quantitative analysis.

USE

USE OF PLOTS

The field survey of uses within plots involves the fairly straightforward task of recording on a plan or address list a use type or class for each plot, also indicating vacancies. This can be done directly on paper or tablet using a colour, letter or number designation from a menu as established in the desktop stage.

STREET SPACES AND PUBLIC REALM

In the same way that rooms in a building accommodate both a range of activities and local movement, street spaces accommodate a range of different kinds of occupation. Street spaces are not just for movement. As may be appropriate to the aims of the study, the field survey can include collection of information on the use of street spaces. The aim is to understand the relationship between the form of the street spaces and the ways they are used.

The fundamental flexibility in the use of street spaces means assigning specific activities to

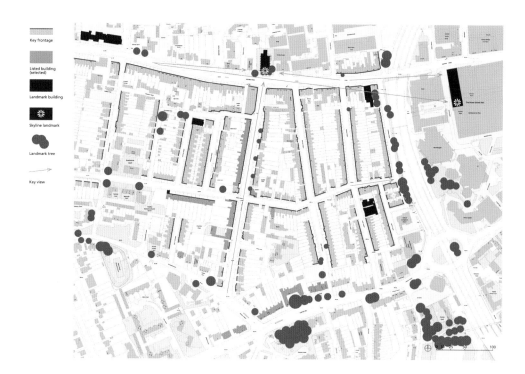

specific areas in any comprehensive way is neither practicable nor likely to yield accurate results. Many parts of the street are multi-functional and boundaries of activities overlap.

The start is to simply identify the activities accommodated without specifying a location within the space. This can be picked up on field survey forms. A simple but useful distinction is to identify **permissive** areas, where a range of activities is possible, and **restrictive** areas, where use is controlled, the obvious case being the carriageway of the street.

In looking at the public realm it may also be useful to distinguish between the different levels of what Stanford Anderson calls 'public claim'. This brings together the matters of access and use. Anderson notes in his 'Ecological Model'[6] that the boundary between street space and occupation space is not a hard and fast separation of public and private. Some buildings allow public access for part of the day and some open spaces that lie within a plot are publicly accessible. Some streets are not openly accessible to the public. It is also the case that some areas may be visually accessible and so constitute a part of the public realm.

The notation technique developed by Anderson is an extension of the principle of the Nolli Plan,

which shows the interior of public buildings as continuous with the street spaces. The method essentially applies a gradient to degrees of constraint on public access.

- Free access (street spaces)
- Free physical and visual access (plot spaces)
- Limited physical and visual access
- Limited physical access
- Visual access only
- No access

BEHAVIOUR TRACES

If the study includes a detailed analysis of the use of street spaces, an alternative or supplement to direct observation is to make inferences from the traces of activity within the street space. Examples of traces include:

- Conversions, alterations, personalisations
- Appropriation and occupation of public space
- Creation of 'outlaw' openings and paths
- Closing up of openings
- Unsanctioned parking (vehicles and bicycles)
- Physical repair of buildings and litter
- Graffiti
- Vandalism/damage (include probable cause)

Figure 7.8
Plan highlighting city image and townscape elements in the Russell Street area of Reading. Identifying city image and townscape elements is a fundamentally *selective* process. While some can be inferred from plans, these need to be checked and most will only be apparent from the ground.

(a)

OUTPUTS

As with access, frontage and boundaries, surveys of use – of both plots and street spaces – are most commonly transposed onto plans for analysis with other aspects and generation of composite images as discussed in Section 8.

PERCEPTUAL STRUCTURE, CITY IMAGE ELEMENTS AND TOWNSCAPE

As noted in the previous section, there is extensive literature that sets out methods for recording perceptual aspects and structure. Only a very brief summary is possible here. The principal tools for the task are the senses and perceptual capacity of the surveyor. The use of standard or common concepts and terms tempers the necessarily subjective nature of the results and makes them 'intersubjective'. The terms and methods developed by Appleyard, Lynch and Myer, Cullen and Reeve et al[7] remain current and very useful. The ViewCue method as summarised below makes a further step toward a more objective measure of perceptual qualities.

The core methods are to identify city image elements, townscape qualities and serial vision sequences. Again, the principal city image elements include:

- Nodes
- Landmarks
- Edges
- Paths
- Districts
- Gateways
- Views and vistas
- Barriers
- Spatial definition/enclosure/frontage
- Key spatial sequences

In general terms, the process involves walking along the routes selected in the planning stage and recording on maps and with sketches, photographs or video, as well as annotations on survey sheets describing the features appropriate to the method being applied. An ancillary technique in identifying city image elements that can be incorporated into the survey sheet is to identify the scale at which the elements operate (see the sample survey sheet in Appendix 1). A landmark, for example, might function at a local, neighbourhood or town-wide scale.

PERCEPTUAL DESCRIPTORS

A common method for identifying townscape qualities is to use binary text descriptors such as enclosed-open, isolated-connected or hard-

above and overleaf
Figure 7.9
Principal landmark buildings in Bath (a). Some buildings such as the Roman Baths function as landmarks not primarily for the visual prominence but for their social, cultural and historical role and meaning. Landmarks can be prominent for reasons other than height, such as position, form and detail (b) and their association with a nodal space (c). The nodal space is a crossing of routes, widened out to allow 'occupation' activities of various kinds.

Figure 7.9 *(cont.)*

(b)

(c)

soft. A particular space can then be described as occupying a position between the binary poles. This approach is best integrated into the survey sheet with the results transcribed into the text description.

VIEWCUE

As suggested above, the methods of analysis developed by Gordon Cullen in his *Townscape* provide a very strong and useful framework for describing and understanding the overall experience of a place. They also continue to have a significant contribution to make in seeking to ensure new development results in a positive experience through the design and regulatory process.

In practice – as well as design education – it can be difficult, however, to use the townscape methods in a systematic way. A major part of the challenge is the sheer visual complexity of settlements. Although we can appreciate that a place is complex – which may be positive – we struggle to decode and articulate that full complexity. This makes that task of achieving some control over the wider result of urban design proposals all the more difficult.

In an effort to overcome these problems, Jon Cooper at Oxford Brookes University has developed a set of tools called ViewCue. The tools build on the basic townscape principles of linear movement as the experiential reference for the perception of the configuration and material substance of a place.

The assessment is based on the objective analysis of photographic images. The overall process therefore involves taking photographs of the study area, analysing the images and mapping the results. At the core of the method is a composite index that provides an objective, standardised and consistent measurement of visual complexity, variety and intensity in the built and natural environment. The index helps to make sense of the true visual complexity of place by objectively measuring the composite character of place and allowing for a prediction of its aesthetic appeal.

The CVI index (for complexity, variety and intensity) collapses the visual effect of multiple individual elements – building size, mass, scale, plot width, enclosure, street width, landscape elements, amounts of open space, building materials, windows, doors, roof lines, street furniture and vegetation – into a single mappable index. Figure 7.10 illustrates the mapping of CVI values for a street in the Jewellery Quarter conservation area in Birmingham, UK.

Changes in the CVI index reflect changes in the physical character of places and so the index also reflects changes in the perceptions of visual diversity, attractiveness, beauty, order, coherence, preference, and interest – overall visual quality.

A significant part of Cooper's work has been to calibrate the results of CVI measurements from a large sample set with visual quality preferences of people from a range of cultures. The results of the calibration process show a significant degree of correlation between preference and CVI value across cultures. The calibration set thus provides the basis for using the index to predict visual preferences for specific locations and specific groups. Figure 7.11 shows an example where the CVI is calibrated with visual perception to construct a character and visual quality-mapping key.

Because the CVI index is generated by the analysis of photographic images, it is possible to use the method to assess proposals as represented by photorealistic renderings inserted into photographs of the site from a range of viewpoints. The method thus provides a tool for assessing the effect and impact of the proposals.

Similarly, a sequence of images representing movement through a site can be analysed to generate CVI values for the whole sequence. The results could be applied to existing locations to help to identify potential areas for intervention as well as provide evidence of visual improvement. This is a clear extension of Cullen's concept of serial vision. Mapping the sequence of CVI values offers an effective way of visualising the dynamic experience of place in an objective and consistent way.

OUTPUTS

As indicated in the previous subsections, the outputs of the field survey can take a number of different forms, singly or in combination, depending on the detail required for the study. The principal outputs are:

- Revisions to the draft tissue boundaries and descriptive text
- Transcription of survey sheets into additional descriptive text and tables
- Photographs
- Plan drawings
- Drawings or diagrams of selected characteristic types

If recording sheets are used, the information can be transferred direct to a table, supplemented by narrative text or summarised in the narrative text itself.

An output that is less tangible but of significant importance is the sense and understanding developed through direct experience of the place. This contributes more generally to the quality, coherence and insight of the final project outputs.

PARTICIPATION AND EVALUATION

COMMUNITY PARTICIPATION AND COLLABORATION

The inclusion of community participation and evaluation within a morphological study represents a large subject that can only be touched on very briefly here. There can be significant benefits to taking a collaborative or participatory approach to morphological studies, particularly for applications in planning, urban design and historic conservation. Most stages of a morphological study can benefit from the local knowledge residents or community members can bring to the work and, at the same time, participation in a structured analysis can help to break down preconceptions and fixed ideas about the nature and character of a place.

Collaboration can take many forms, from crowd-sourced collection of data, as exemplified by the OpenStreetMap project, to small-scale community workshops on character areas and photography days to collect images of the different areas. In virtually all cases, collaboration works most effectively when it is well structured, with clear tasks and procedures for collecting and transcribing the information. Survey sheets are particularly useful in this respect. It is also important to acknowledge that while collaboration can help to collect large amounts of information

that would take a smaller team a much longer time, the resources necessary to structure and organise the collaborative work can be significant.

EVALUATIVE ASSESSMENTS

A step on from collaborative analysis and collection of data is to undertake evaluative assessments of the areas identified in the analysis. As with collaboration, evaluation is a large field that can only be noted here. Evaluative assessments extend and build on the more objective description of a place in a morphological study to judgements about the value and condition of the place. They can be seen as the intermediate step in a three-stage process of description, evaluation and design. Clearly, moving into evaluation significantly opens out the range of possible issues. The principal foundation for the move is to acknowledge the range of values involved, which to a large extent reflect the different aspects of urban form. Thus any given place is ascribed value in terms of, among other things:

- Material and embodied energy
- Ecosystem services
- Use
- Market price
- Heritage
- Community identity
- Character and experience

In very basic terms, it can also be useful to set the evaluative process into the context of the three-way energy cost of the built environment for production, use and maintenance. This puts a pragmatic dimension into the evaluation and translates into concerns on the one hand, for which forms might meet the needs of a community, and on the other, for the condition of a place and its ongoing repair.

Figure 7.10
Plan interface of ViewCue software showing photograph locations and CVI values for each location as well as the mean value for the street

Figure 7.11
ViewCue calibration interface, which correlates CVI values with stated visual quality (VQ) preferences of a wide range of individuals. The calibration process is cumulative, with successive rounds of assessment and calibration added to the data set to broaden the basis for correlation between CVI value and preference.

References

1 Investigation of the internal arrangement of buildings is often problematic socially and culturally. One way or another, analysis of this level demands significant resources and so is often undertaken only at the desktop stage with available resources, or in the field with a small sample, or excluded.

2 Paul Osmond, 'An Enquiry into New Methodologies for Evaluating Sustainable Urban Form', unpublished PhD thesis, Faculty of the Built Environment, University of New South Wales, 2008. Print.

3 Lars Marcus, 'Plot Syntax: A Configurational Approach to Urban Diversity', Proceedings of the Fifth Space Syntax Symposium, Delft, 2005. Web.

- A Ståhle, L Marcus, and A Karlström, 'Place Syntax: Geographic Accessibility with Axial Lines in GIS', Proceedings of the Fifth Space Syntax Symposium, Delft, 2005. Web.

4 Bill Hillier, *Space Is the Machine*, Cambridge University Press (Cambridge), 1996. Print.

5 Benjamin Vis, 'Mapping the Inhabited Urban Built Environment: The Socio-Spatial Significance of the Material Presence of Boundaries through Time', unpublished PhD thesis, School of Geography, University of Leeds, 2013. Print.

6 Stanford Anderson, 'Ecological Model of the Urban Environment', in *On Streets*, Stanford Anderson (ed), MIT Press (Cambridge, MA), 1986. Print.

7 Donald Appleyard, Kevin Lynch and John R Myer, *The View from the Road*, MIT Press (Cambridge, MA), 1965. Print.

- Gordon Cullen, *Townscape*, Architectural Press (Oxford), 1961. Print.

- Kevin Lynch, *The Image of the City*, MIT Press (Cambridge, MA), 1960. Print.

- Alan Reeve, Brian Goodey and Robert Shipley, 'Townscape Assessment: The Development of a Practical Tool for Monitoring and Assessing Visual Quality in the Built Environment', *Urban Morphology* 11.1 (2007): 25–41. Print.

Synthesis

As emphasised in the introduction, urban morphology extends beyond a simple thematic analysis by bringing together the products of analysis and building up a number of different composite images. Synthesis is therefore an essential part of the overall process of most morphological investigations. The aim is to visualise and seek to understand the patterns of relationship between aspects and elements that make up a whole study area or settlement. The end product is not an array of disassembled parts but a number of views of an articulated whole. There is no one 'correct' view. Rather, the different views work together to give a sense of the greater whole. There are five principal composite views that might be produced as part of a study:

- **Settlement structure** (structural view): the structure of individual elements and the groupings of urban tissues that articulate the large-scale structure of a settlement
- **Composite character, relationships and associations** (overlay view): combinations of different aspects to illustrate the depth of complexity and identify relationships and associations
    - overlays or sequence of rectified views
    - character areas
    - multiple descriptions
    - diagrams
- **Experiential view**: serial vision, emotional response and interpretation
- **Interactions, development and evolution** (time and process view): sequential views to illustrate and articulate the process of formation, transformation and evolution of forms
- **Stocks and flows** (metabolic view): quantification of energy and material flows of production, maintenance and use

Each view emphasises a different aspect, dimension or combination of aspects of urban form and so a different sense of **depth**. These are by no means the only composite views. More generally, a study might combine two or more of these in a report that generates a greater sense of depth when seen together.

The study might also seek to explain the structure and characteristics of a place by combining descriptions in accordance with an explanatory logic. In essence this is done by 'mapping' the descriptions onto the structure of causal and inferential connections. Examples of some of the different forms of explanatory logic that might be used include:

- The general process of learning
- Persistence and the law of least effort/convenience
- Configurational and combinatorial logic of aggregation
- Cultural adaptive response to assets and constraints and the inflection of form
- The emergence of patterns at one level as a result of interactions between agents and elements at the level below
- The sequential processes of formation and transformation in relation to social, cultural and economic drivers and interactions (development)
- The typological process, involving cultural habits, interactions and the evolution of types
- Polymorphogenesis and the interrelation between development and evolution
- Material and energy flows
- Perception, interpretation and the process of unlimited semiosis

The composite views included in a given study will clearly depend on the purpose of the project. The following sets out some of the main considerations in taking forward the different kinds of synthesis.

SETTLEMENT STRUCTURE

A NOTE ON THE GENERIC FORM OF SETTLEMENTS

In terms of generic types of form, a settlement can be anything from a single building to a plot series, street or complex combination of tissues. There is no single generic type of form that corresponds to 'settlement' or any of the other terms we generally use to refer to settlements, such as 'village', 'town', 'city' or 'metropolitan region'. These entities are not defined primarily by physical form other than a fairly vague notion of size. As the word settlement itself suggests, each term is perhaps better seen as a different act (or stage in a process) of occupation rather than a physical form.

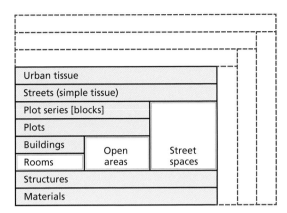

Much has been written on the definition and ranking of settlements that sheds light on the issue but which is not central to the main morphological consideration here, which is the physical structure of settlements. Also, within the scope of this book the interest is primarily on the internal structure, in particular the patterns of urban tissue. In principle, the multi-level diagram used to describe the generic structure of built form up to the level of complex tissue might be extended to encompass larger entities. What those entities might be remains an open question that is rightly the subject of further research.

TYPES OF SETTLEMENT BY POSITION, OUTLINE AND INTERNAL STRUCTURE

Whatever generic form it takes, a settlement as a whole can be seen in terms of the same three structural perspectives used with other elements of built form:

- The position of the settlement within the wider context
  - environment and countryside
  - pattern of settlements
- The overall shape and size of the settlement in outline, including points of access
- The internal arrangement (generic and specific types of form)

Types can be defined from all three points of view, separately or together. The position of settlements *relative to other features* is of particular importance in terms of understanding the extent to which the overall shape and size, access points and internal structure are part of a response to the position. Key features to consider in terms of relative position include:

- Topography
- Springs, watercourses and water bodies (hydrology)

- Habitat and plant and animal communities
- Routes
- Settlements (within a pattern of settlements and proximity to individual settlements)

SUCCESSIVE FRINGE FORMATION AND SETTLEMENT STRUCTURE

Setting aside the terminological issue, the growth of settlements by the successive addition of urban tissue, or **polymorphogenetic accretion**, tends to lead to a common emergent pattern rooted in the basic geometry of a nucleated settlement: centre, middle and edge. MRG Conzen refers to these three relative positions within a settlement as the kernel, integument and fringe.[1] What Conzen also recognised, building on the work of Otto Schlüter,[2] is that due to the necessarily outward direction of growth, the periodic variation in the rate of growth and the phenomenon of persistence, it is possible to identify a larger-scale structure within settlements based on **successive fringe formation**.

The process of fringe formation involves the tendency for a varied mix of predominantly non-residential uses, typically with requirements for large areas of land and lower rents, to locate at the edge of the current settlement, most often at times of general stasis in outward growth.[3] Such uses include mineral extraction, manufacturing, storage and distribution, large-scale retail and leisure, office parks, institutions such as military bases or installations, prisons, hospitals, religious houses, schools and universities as well as open areas such as cemeteries, recreation grounds, drainage retention areas and, increasingly, land set aside for habitat. Generally these can be referred to as **fringe features** because of their tendency to cluster around the outer edge of settlements. Typical fringe features are illustrated in figure 8.2.

Figure 8.1
The compositional hierarchy can, in principle, be extended beyond complex tissues. This points to the larger-scale structure of settlements and the idea of typical combinations of tissues served by strategic routes. Identifying these larger-scale patterns is the subject of ongoing research.

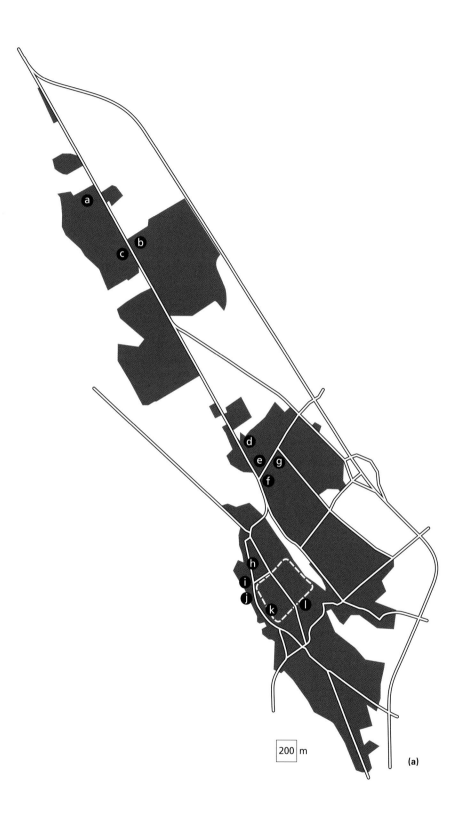

200 m

(a)

left, opposite and overleaf

Figure 8.2
Plan of Sulmona, Italy,
indicating the location of
various typical fringe
features (a). A sample of
specific fringe features in
Sulmona includes:
b) open storage; c) large
floor-plate buildings
for manufacturing;
d) electricity substation;
e) large floor-plate 'out of
town' retail; f) building
supply/merchants;
g) bus and other vehicle
depots; h) isolated open
field; i) filling station;
j) fire station; k) vehicle
parking and landscape
park. Typical of older
settlements, particularly
those initially enclosed
within city walls, are
persistent features that
once occupied the
periphery at an earlier
stage of development. The
smaller buildings on the
right (l) once sat just
inside the wall. The open
space (m), now a main
piazza, was a field just
outside the wall.

(b)

(c)

(d)

(e)

(f)

(g)

Figure 8.2 *(cont.)*

(h)

(i)

(j)

(k)

Figure 8.2 *(cont.)*

(l)

(m)

What is important to note is that in addition to the difference in position – centre or periphery – there tends to be a general difference in the internal structure of fringe tissue and 'central' tissue corresponding to Scheer's distinction between more uniform static and heterogeneous elastic tissue. Fringe tissue tends to be elastic because it is generally the product of relatively ad hoc development over time for a wide range of different uses. Central tissue tends to be static because it is predominantly for residential use and designed specifically to accommodate the current or leading types of residential plot and building.

The general tendency for the clustering of uses reinforces the concentration of fringe features into loose **belts** or **corridors**. Frequently they are associated with elements of infrastructure such as roads, railways, canals and fortifications, as well as natural features such as rivers and shorelines. The specific geometry of the fringe belts and corridors can vary considerably and may be either contiguous or dispersed depending on patterns of ownership, the presence and geometry of the natural features and infrastructure, and the development process (see Michael Conzen's survey for examples[4]).

The association between fringe features and infrastructure such as fortifications, canals, railways and motorways, or natural features such as rivers, tends to occur because the latter often form a barrier to outward growth. The effect is to fix the outward edge of the settlement. The infrastructure or natural feature forms a **fixation line** that acts as a **matrix** around which fringe features tend to cluster both inside and outside.

A consequence of the clustering of fringe tissue at the periphery, combined with the general tendency for periodic cycles of growth and stasis and the general principle of persistence, is **successive fringe formation**. With persistence, once outward growth of the settlement begins again and the edge of the settlement moves outward, the fringe features become **embedded** in the urban fabric. In time these sites are often redeveloped (and **absorbed** into the fabric), but

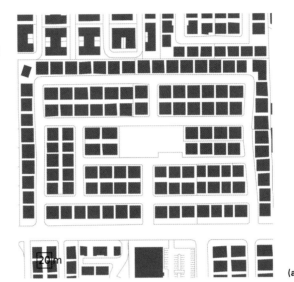

(a)

Figure 8.3
Examples of central (a)
and fringe tissue (b)
from St George, Utah.
Fringe tissue is typically
coarser grained and more
heterogeneous.

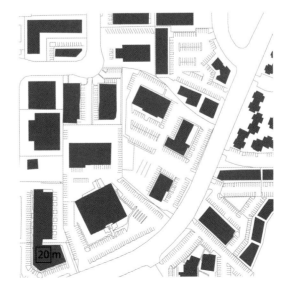

(b)

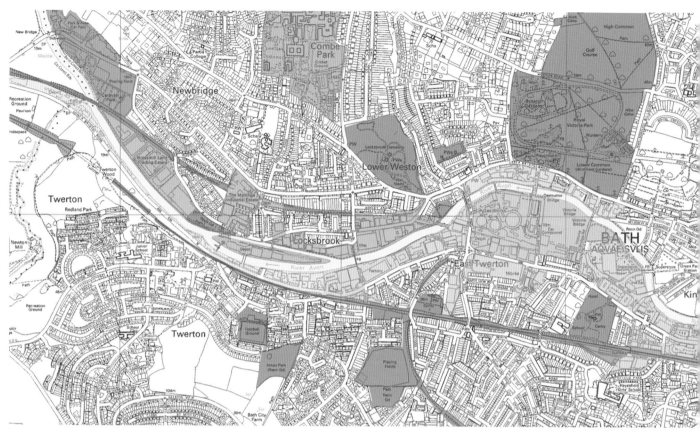

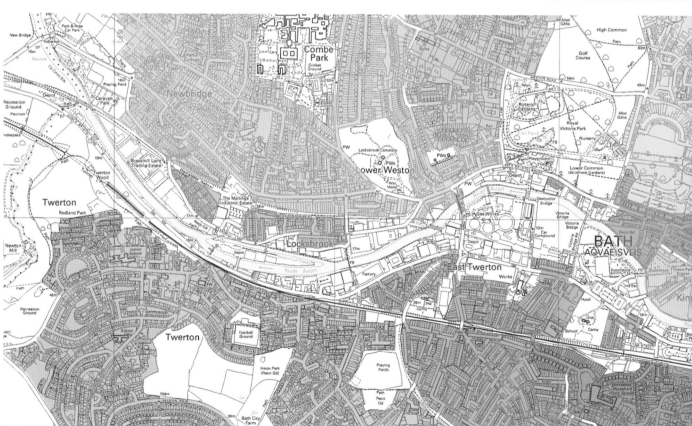

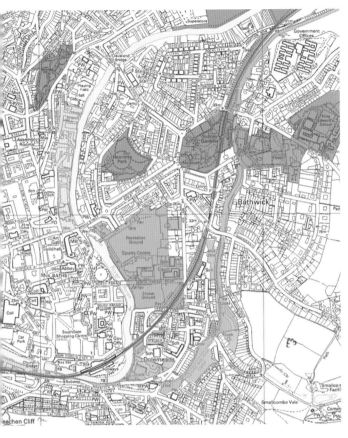

(a)

Figure 8.4
Two plans separating out fringe tissue (a) and central tissue (b) in Bath. While close analysis shows there are inner fringe elements around the Roman/medieval core and a middle fringe around the 18th-century extensions, the main fringe features form a corridor along the river.

(b)

again because of persistence the structures of street patterns, plot boundaries and open spaces remain as the traces (material, substitution and inflection) of the earlier, initial fringe tissue at the edge of the settlement. These traces along with the differences in tissues from different periods of growth are physical evidence of the development process and give shape to the large-scale structures of settlements. The sequence of plans in figure 8.5 illustrates an example of the process.

Another tendency or **developmental regularity** that contributes to large-scale structure is the formation of sub-centres. This can occur through the transformation of existing fabric, the creation of new sub-centres with outward growth, or the merging of two or more outwardly extending settlements. Sub-centres are primarily clusters of non-residential uses. While the use clusters or poles can occur without differences in physical form, they tend to emerge where physical features such as street pattern and network centrality are conducive to the vitality of the uses. When the uses persist, they can lead to transformation and inflection of the fabric and the creation of a distinct physical sub-centre. The transformation can take different forms in different periods and places. Historically, in Europe and the US, for example, the high value of retail frontage led to the subdivision of land and buildings and a finer-grained tissue within centres. More recently, with the tendency for large

retail operations, the opposite is occurring, leading to a coarser grain within centres.

The basic structure of centre, middle and fringe provides an initial distinction of tissues by position that can in turn be applied to successive, persistent fringe features as inner, middle and outer. Taking a very general, simplified view, this leads to a pattern as follows:

- Historical/initial core
- Inner fringe
- Intermediate extensions and sub-centres
- Middle fringe
- Outer extensions and sub-centres
- Outer fringe

The practical task in taking forward the synthesis involves the following steps:

- Review the analysis of growth and transformation (and map sequence)
- If possible, identify cycles of growth and stasis
- Review and compare the tissues identified
- Identify the traces of fringe formation – or successive formations as appropriate
- Group the tissues in terms of position, outline and internal structure into combinations that correspond to the historical development of the settlement as a whole

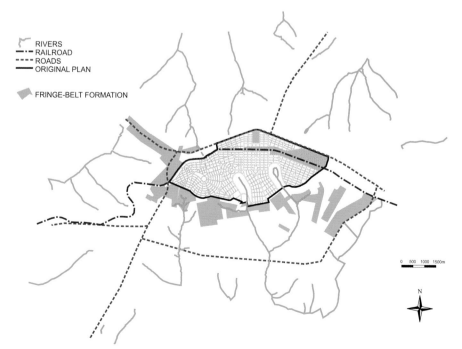

RIVERS
RAILROAD
ROADS
ORIGINAL PLAN

FRINGE-BELT FORMATION

0 500 1000 1500m

N

Figure 8.5-a
The planned new town of Maringá, Paraná, Brazil, founded in 1947. The plan shows the state of the town *c* 1950. This and the following series of maps were produced by Karin Schwabe Meneguetti and Staël de Alvarenga Pereira Costa.

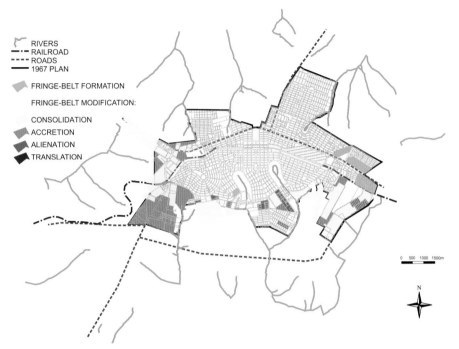

RIVERS
RAILROAD
ROADS
1967 PLAN

FRINGE-BELT FORMATION

FRINGE-BELT MODIFICATION:

CONSOLIDATION
ACCRETION
ALIENATION
TRANSLATION

0 500 1000 1500m

N

Figure 8.5-b
Maringá in 1965 with residential extensions to the north and east and fringe extensions to the south-west

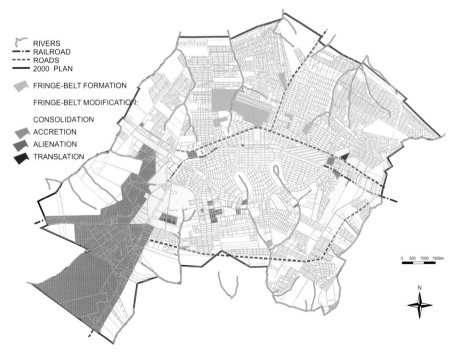

RIVERS
RAILROAD
ROADS
2000 PLAN

FRINGE-BELT FORMATION

FRINGE-BELT MODIFICATION:

CONSOLIDATION
ACCRETION
ALIENATION
TRANSLATION

0 500 1000 1500m

N

Figure 8.5-c
Maringá, 1980. Residential extensions have jumped the original fringe and embedded it within the body of central tissue except in the west, where the fringe has extended outward as well.

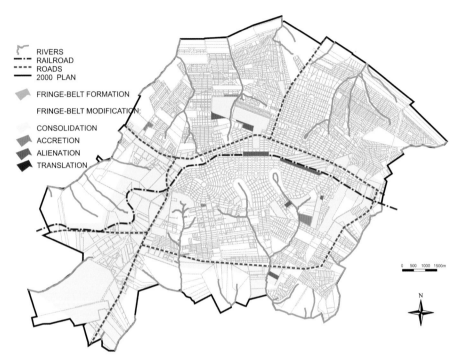

Figure 8.5-d
Maringá, 1995, indicating
a period of relative stasis
with a consolidation of
the fringe features

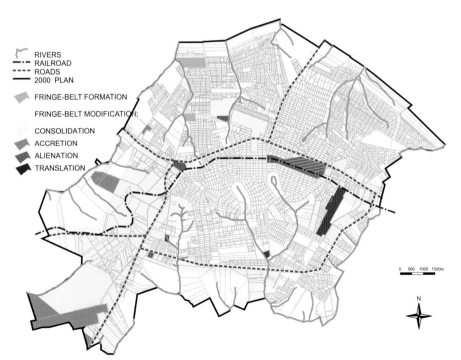

Figure 8.5-e
Maringá in 2010 showing
further consolidation and
some transformation of
fringe features

RIVERS
RAILROAD
ROADS
2000 PLAN
FRINGE BELTS:
1950
1965
1980
1995
2010

0 500 1000 1500m

N

Figure 8.5-f
The fringe features of
Maringá distinguished by
the date of their formation

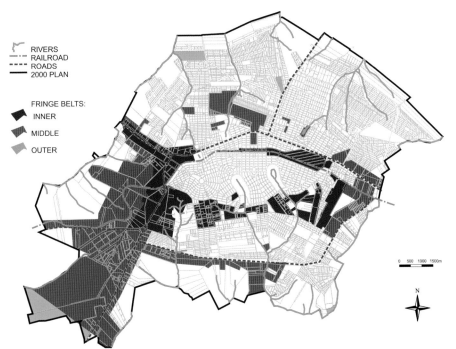

RIVERS
RAILROAD
ROADS
2000 PLAN

FRINGE BELTS:
INNER
MIDDLE
OUTER

0 500 1000 1500m

N

Figure 8.5-g
Distinction of the inner,
middle and outer fringe
belts of Maringá, defined
as, inner: forming around
the periphery of the
initial settlement; middle:
forming at the edge of
later extensions but
subsequently embedded
in further extensions;
outer: on the current edge
of the settlement.

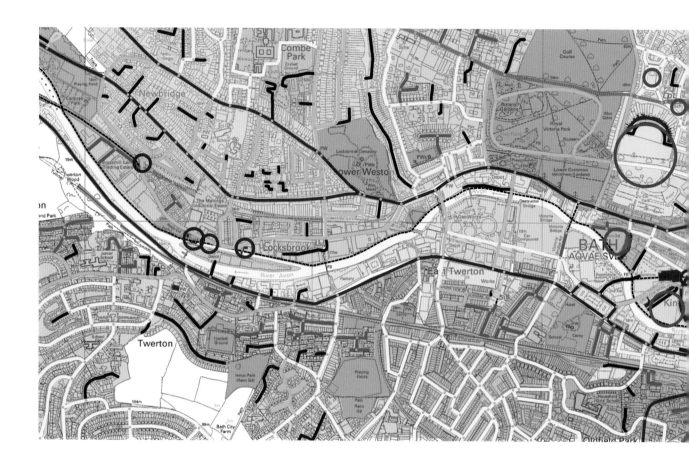

PLAN SEAMS AND TRANSFORMATIONS

In cases where there are very few or no obvious traces of historical fringes, the aim of the synthesis is still to capture the process of formation resulting from polymorphogenetic accretion. One of the principal signs of growth where there are no obvious fringe features is likely to be a **plan seam**, which is more extended boundary between distinct tissues originating from different periods.

At the same time, the synthesis should seek to capture the **transformations** of initial tissues that tend to occur over time with changing patterns of land value, use and control as well as innovations in technology. An obvious example of the former is the increase of building density and intensity by changes of building type and plot pattern with increasing land value. An example of transformations with technological innovation is the insertion (or removal) of railways, trams, relief roads and motorways. These can lead to direct changes and longer-term transformation in response to knock-on changes in other patterns such as movement, land use and control.

OUTPUTS

The primary output at this stage is a plan that identifies the groups of tissues to illustrate and highlight the larger-scale structure of the settlement and its process of formation and transformation. Several plans may be necessary to fully illustrate historical fringes.

It sometimes helps to use separate plans for the central and middle tissues on the one hand, and fringe tissues on the other. It can also be helpful to use a colour and/or density gradient to distinguish both the chronological sequence and differences between central, middle and fringe tissues. Commonly the gradient runs from darker-older to lighter-more recent with one group of hues or patterns used for central and middle tissues and another for fringe tissues.

COMPOSITE CHARACTER, RELATIONSHIPS AND ASSOCIATIONS

As noted at the beginning of this section, the principal objectives in creating a composite image of the different aspects of form are to:

Figure 8.6
Composite view of Bath, combining route structure, tissues, nodes and landmarks. Showing the elements from the different aspects together facilitates the identification of characteristic associations or combinations features. Typical combinations in Bath include nodes on the boundaries of tissues, in a number of cases also associated with landmarks; nodes defined/enclosed by landmark buildings within the centre of tissues; green nodes in relatively peripheral positions.

- Identify character areas or geographical regions
- Identify diagrammatic structures and associations of elements
- Communicate the nature and characteristics of the place

REGIONS AND CHARACTER AREAS

The most commonly produced composite view is the combination of plan units, land use and building fabric (type, materials and period of origin) as originally developed by MRG Conzen.[5] From this combination, Conzen identified what he termed **plan divisions** or **morphogenetic regions**. As developed further, particularly within the UK, the resulting regions are also referred to as **character areas** and are sometimes defined using additional aspects such as historical land uses, perceptual qualities and physical condition.

The technique for identifying character areas and regions is essentially the same as for urban tissue:

- Compile and overlay semi-transparent plans showing the analysis of each aspect to be included in the definition of the character area or region (that is, areas of different tissues, land use, control and perceptual qualities)
- Identify unique combinations of the different aspects
- Outline and label the distinct areas
- Group and/or split the areas as appropriate to the purposes of the study to form a nested hierarchy of regions that highlights both general commonalities and specific differences

Bringing together and overlaying the different aspects of a study area clearly multiplies the potential complexity of the resulting image. In broad terms, the purpose of the composite image is to improve our understanding of the still more complex experience of the place itself. The resulting character areas or regions should help to clarify the structure and gives us insights into – and begin to help us predict – the process of diversification and the way places work in terms of regularities of processes, behaviours, responses and interactions. The distinction between fringe and central tissue in figure 8.6 is an example of a grouping into two broad morphogenetic regions.

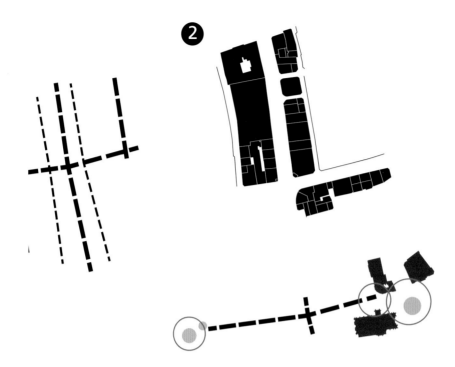

ASSOCIATIONS

One of the principal reasons for combining views of selected aspects is to visualise and investigate possible relationships between them. The questions are not just, what is the pattern of tissues, what is the structure of the route network or where are the nodes and landmarks but, are there consistent or characteristic relationships between, for example, nodes in relation to routes and tissues, landmarks in relation to tissues or between structural/configurational characteristics and quantitative measures such areas and densities?

For the synthesis of associations to contribute to improving our insights and understanding, it is essential to identify the specific kind of relationship involved. The nature of the association might be general or specific, loose or tightly bound. Kinds of association include the following:

- Co-location
- Specific relative orientation or arrangement
- Inflection of form in response to the presence of other elements
- Consistent covariance
- Causal mechanism

The following are some of the combinations of aspects and elements that are most commonly investigated:

- Urban tissue and patterns of control
- Urban tissue and route structure
- Routes, topography and views
- Routes and functional centres
- Plot series and orientation to route hierarchy
- Building type and position within a plot series or block
- Plot series and topography
- Urban tissue, land use, centres and polarity
- Route structure, city image elements and land use
- Urban tissue and city image elements
- Methods of construction and plot pattern

The inference to be drawn from consistent associations and relationships is that they may be the result of an underlying generative principle and general repeating processes of formation and transformation.

COMBINING AND TOGGLING PLANS

A specific method of developing a composite image that provides insights into particular relationships and associations between aspects at a more local level is to select two or three aspects, for example, urban tissue, route structure and city image elements, and either **combine** them in the same image or **toggle** between views of separate plans in quick succession. Both methods require that the information about the different aspects is drawn

Figure 8.7
Diagrams can be helpful tools to focus on typical associations and combinations of elements. The diagram is fundamentally an abstraction, so isolates and highlights the elements but at the same time clearly presents the relationships between elements. The diagrams shown, from the Bath study, include, 1) a tartan grid – alternating major (active frontage) and minor (semi-active frontage) streets; 2) single plot depth blocks either side of a major street; 3) axial compositions of streets with terminal and intermediate nodes, some associated with landmarks.

up using the same base map, at the same size and scale and, for toggling, registered to the same position on the page.

Combining plans or toggling screen images make it much easier to see where the elements of each plan correspond, or not, in terms of position, extent and internal structure. Where the different elements are geometrically distinct, such as the areas of urban tissue, lines of route structure or point features of city image elements, combining or toggling the image make it possible to identify composite patterns or associations of elements. The results might be the identification of unique patterns characteristic of a particular place or repeating patterns that suggest a common interaction or developmental regularity that warrants further investigation.

DIAGRAMS

The combination or pattern of different aspects and elements can be captured and communicated through the medium of graphic diagrams. Similarly, diagrams can be used to summarise the key characteristics of individual component patterns. The aim of a diagram is to isolate the essential elements and relationships that make up a given entity, be it a whole settlement, urban tissue or distinct combination of different types of element. The role of the diagram is to abstract a **pattern of relationships** that is significant for some purpose and present the pattern visually.

To a large extent, producing diagrams is a graphic exercise and the main task is to identify the most effective way to represent the elements and relationships. One example would be a diagram that illustrates the successive historical fringes of a whole settlement by consolidating the central, middle and fringe tissues and simplifying their shape. Another might show in abstract form a characteristic compositional 'figure' such as a combination of nodes, landmarks, routes, views and building frontage.

EXPERIENTIAL VIEW

Methods that adopt the experiential perspective such as those developed by Lynch, Cullen[6] and others provide a range of tools for putting together, viewing and communicating composite images. These include:

- Diagrammatic plan symbols
- Plan diagrams of experiential routes
- Image sequences of experiential routes

- Video of movement through or time lapse of single location
- Composite measures such as ViewCue

While frequently used in the context of design and management of the built environment, there is also scope to use these methods and the resulting composite images to explore the effect our experience of places may have on the process of formation and transformation. The experiential view is also a crucial part of spatial interactions, development and the evolution of form as set out below.

INTERACTIONS, DEVELOPMENT AND EVOLUTION

Of the different modes of synthesis, the one most commonly considered the 'signature' method of urban morphology is the time series or chronological sequence. This follows from the underlying morphological principle that form is the product of a generative process and we seek to understand form by understanding that process. The deep interconnection between the two is already evident in the method used above for grouping urban tissue to generate the composite image of settlement structure. The process of development is used as the principal point of reference. In this respect, settlement structure is a snapshot of a particular stage in the process. The further step in generating time depth is to visualise the process as a whole.

To refer to a 'time view' as a composite image may perhaps appear to over-articulate what is generally considered a common experience: watching a film or video. The obvious point is that the time scale for the 'movement' of urban form is very long. Urban development is a slow process. The closer equivalent is therefore a film made from time-lapse photography or animation.

There are three principal time views or 'animations' that are most commonly compiled in a morphological study:

- Descriptions, models and visualisations of spatial interactions
- Sequential views of development – the formation and transformation of urban form
- Sequential views of the evolution of types

As will be explored briefly in the following section, these three are interrelated but each is revealing on its own.

SPATIAL INTERACTIONS

Descriptions of spatial interactions, whether a narrative account or an abstract mathematical model with or without visualisations, involve a time series of different states of a system in which agents respond to specific conditions by making decisions and carrying out actions that change the state of the system. The aim is to generate a picture of human interactions within the built environment over time. The task is therefore to compile and order the necessary information and/or choose or develop a model that best describes the states and dynamics of the interactions over time.

There is a significant and extensive body of work that sets out the principles and methods for describing and understanding spatial interactions (see, for example, Batty and Wilson[7]). The aim here is to highlight how that work fits in with other methods to generate the composite images that shed more light on the whole process. In this respect, the central point is that spatial interactions principally involve the activities, uses and decisions that generate the need for changes in physical form, with those changes often represented in more general, abstract ways. The principal interest from a morphological perspective is the specific nature of the relationship between spatial interactions and changes in physical form and the role played by the structure of built form.

DEVELOPMENT

In simple visual terms a time view of development is constructed with map or diagram sequences, usually supplemented with a narrative account highlighting the changes at each stage and describing their characteristics as well as identifying the drivers of change. It is essentially a rudimentary form of stop-frame animation, usually viewed as a sequence of single frames rather than a fully animated 'moving picture'. It is possible with maps and plan diagrams, however, to use the toggling method to move quickly through a sequence to simulate animation. As set out above, the map sequencing may be undertaken within the desktop stage of the study. The time view of development is therefore not necessarily an end product but an interim synthesis used in an iterative process of analysis. In many cases, having compiled and separated out the steps in the sequence, putting it back together and comparing the steps can be a trigger to asking more searching questions about the processes underlying the development.

There are three main types of developmental time view, which differ mainly in terms of the extent and level of resolution of the view:

- Outline growth (extent and shape)
- Emergence of internal structure
- Transformation of internal structure

A simple growth sequence usually shows a whole settlement (figure 6.10) or individual element such as a building (figure 8.8). The level of resolution tends to be low, showing only the outline of the element; in the case of a settlement, for example, showing the extent of the built-up area and perhaps primary routes, with the extent of the view expanding with outward growth.

A sequence showing the emergence of internal structure is essentially a growth sequence shown at a higher level of resolution, usually including primary routes and groups of tissues (figure 8.5). The view might also include plots and buildings.

A transformational sequence looking at changes in internal structure tends to maintain a fixed extent and focuses on a particular generic type of form such as plots in a tissue or rooms in a building. In some cases the level of resolution will be low, using a single element separation to focus on a particular generic type; in others the resolution will be higher, for tissue typically including streets, plots and buildings.

EVOLUTION

As set out in the Introduction, the evolution of form starts to occur when people begin to reproduce objects according to a particular idea, actively use those objects in a specific context and, as circumstances change (including associated technologies), assess the object and modify and reinterpret the idea, often by recombination with other ideas, to form a new generating idea leading to the reproduction of a new version of the object.

Representing evolution as a time series therefore involves two types of composite image. One is a 'typical' or representative example of each type in the series. The type example, which might be represented diagrammatically, is 'composite' in the sense that it represents in a single image the abstracted characteristics of all the examples that make up and define the type. As a composite of the shared characteristics, the example or diagram can then be taken as a representation of the generating idea rather than a particular example.

Figure 8.8
A time sequence diagram illustrating the development of a house. In this case the diagram shows only the outline growth of the building though some inferences can be made about internal structure.

Figure 8.9
Sequence showing the evolution of tissue types from Isfahan, Iran as identified in a study by Yones Changalvaiee: a) historic centre, characterised mainly by courtyard types; b) the extended, transformed centre, characterised by a combination of courtyard and multi-storey front court types; c) informal extensions characterised by single and multi-storey front court types; d) peripheral planned development with a formalised version of the multi-storey front court type.

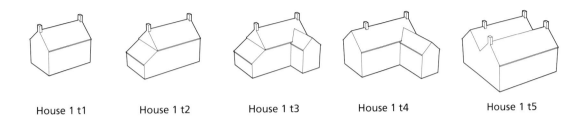

House 1 t1   House 1 t2   House 1 t3   House 1 t4   House 1 t5

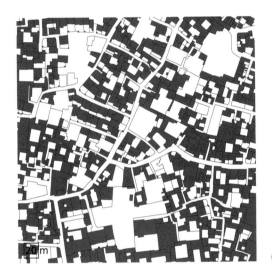

(a)

(b)

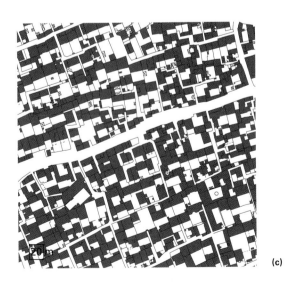

(c)

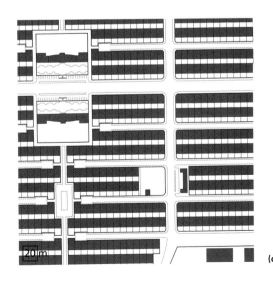

(d)

The other composite image is then the sequence of types related one to the next by derivation. The task of representing the evolution of types therefore involves two main steps. The first is to identify types at different points in time and abstract the defining pertinent characteristics in order to compile the diagrams. The second is to identify the similarities and differences between the types to establish the relationships of both continuity and change over time. The fundamental basis of this process is, again, analysis, comparison and synthesis.

Detailed studies of evolutionary change might focus on any one of the primary generic types of built form, from materials and details through to urban tissue. Probably the most commonly undertaken study is of the building type. One of the benefits of a focus on building types is that it can help to understand and explain changes in urban tissue due to the interrelationship between building types and tissue.

An area of current interest and investigation is the relationship and interplay between intentional and emergent structure at the levels above urban tissue (see for example Marshall's *Cities, Design*

and Evolution and Kropf's 'Agents and Agency'[8]). It is unclear, for example, whether there is a common generating idea for large complex settlements. On the other hand, can patterns emerge that are then observed and come into consciousness as a generating idea?

A full account of the evolution of form should also include the physical circumstances and social and economic context in which the changes occur. Setting aside the possibility of a general drift in ideas and forms, the underlying logic of evolution is that changes in form are a response to changes in circumstances. If the context and circumstances remain constant, there is unlikely to be any change in form. Establishing positive evidence for the connection between changes in circumstance and form is, however, not always easy or possible. Rather, it is often the case that changes in form are used as a basis for inferring changes in circumstances. The underlying assumption is that if a sufficient body of examples is found of the same type, the generating idea must have become a common, shared idea in response to some change in circumstances. The task is then to find the most plausible candidate change in circumstances.

below, opposite and overleaf
Figure 8.10
Examples of the typological process in which modifications to existing buildings are taken as the basis for a new building: a) a barn conversion; b–c) a 'new-build barn conversion'; d) insertion of garage with a side entrance on a corner plot; e) new-build side entrance garage; f) porch extension; g) new house with integral porch extension

(a)

(b)

8.10-c.TIF

(c)

(d)

(e)

Figure 8.10 *(cont.)*

(f)

(g)

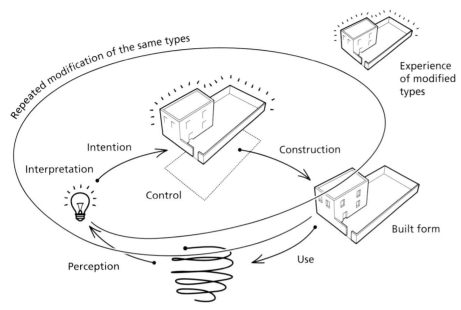

Repeated modification of the same types

Experience of modified types

Intention

Interpretation

Construction

Control

Built form

Perception

Use

Repeated use over time in the context of changing needs and environment

Environment

Flows of energy and materials

There is a large body of work that explores the evolution of built form that can help to make the connections of continuity, change and derivation, (see, for example, Steadman, Kropf, Muratori, Caniggia and Maffei, Scheer, Marshall, and more generally, Weinstock and Arthur[9]). Here, the aim is to set out the basic means of communicating the time view of evolution and establish how it relates to the others.

In summary, the time view of evolution involves the following elements:

- Composite diagrams of types at successive steps (illustrating the common features of all examples at each step)
- Chronological sequence of type diagrams
- Text identifying the similarities and differences between steps
- Text account of physical circumstances and social and economic context
- Evidence or inferences identifying the changes of form as a response to changes in circumstances

STOCKS AND FLOWS
Urban metabolism is an emerging field in its own right and can only be dealt with briefly

here. Research in this area includes the work of Kennedy, Salat et al, Ratti and Steemers, Rode and Keim,[10] among an increasing number). Like experience, spatial interaction, development and evolution, the metabolic view is necessarily a time view but focuses on the quantitative differences in rates of flow from one point in time to the next. As a quantity, a rate incorporates the time dimension (for example kilowatt/hours or tons/year) and an average or comparative rate is a composite of several samples.

Within the context of a morphological approach, an account of the stocks and flows involved in the formation, transformation, use and maintenance of built form might either be the principal focus of a study or part of a wider investigation. At its most basic, the metabolic view involves an input-output analysis and calculation of average rates of flow and stocks held for a given time period. There are many different specific inputs and outputs that might be selected for analysis depending on the aims of the study. Recent studies have tended to focus on the comparative energy use of different forms and configurations.

As suggested in the Introduction, a basic distinction can be made between local and external inputs (based on a defined boundary for the local

Figure 8.11
Diagram of the interconnected processes of development and evolution highlighting the modified type as the source for the new building. The status of 'type' comes with repeated reproduction.

system) and between beneficial use and waste outputs. Waste outputs can in turn be divided between those with and without further potential use.

Within such a basic framework, a metabolic view is likely to take the form of data tables or geo-spatial visualisations supported by explanatory text. The steps necessary to generate the view include:

- Identify the generic form and process to be assessed
  - formation/transformation
  - use
  - maintenance
- Identify the specific inputs and outputs of interest
- Select or devise the appropriate measures
- Undertake the assessment
- Select or devise a means of communicating the results

INTEGRATION

In the end, the more general task of synthesis in urban morphology is to improve our understanding of urban form, that is, to explain it. At a very general level, explanatory value is delivered by putting together our descriptions of the built environment following some internal logic that links one description to another. On the one hand, the internal logic provides us with a story to tell that makes the results much easier to communicate. On the other hand, the logic makes it possible to make more predictive statements about urban form and the processes of formation and transformation.

A first step is to recognise that the different aspects of urban form are essentially different views of the same 'thing'. It thus follows that each aspect is most effectively described by a different analytical view. A core argument of this book is that there is significant benefit in combining those views with reference to the principal aspect of physical form. At a broad philosophical level this is a necessity because we have no direct access to urban form *in itself*. It is only by comparing different views that we can gain a rigorous conception of it one way or the other. Understanding what the different views reveal is crucial to that effort.

The task of tying together our descriptions of urban form using internal logic is in effect to map the descriptions onto some coherent structure that links the descriptions together. There is, however, no one single internal logic, but many logics or logical structures that are used and have been suggested

and tested within urban morphology over the years. Each logical structure is a set of relationships (spatial, temporal, causal and inferential). Some are simple and obvious, others more complex. In essence, the logical structures constitute some of the concepts and logical tools we use to make sense of our experience and the evidence we find.

What becomes evident in considering the role of synthesis in morphological studies and the logic of the composite views is that the *views* are, themselves, mappings of descriptions onto logical structures. The composite views are not random collections of data but structured perspectives, first and foremost in terms of the basic foundations of:

- Spatial dimension, continuity and extent
- Chronology and sequence
- Conservation of energy, entropy, momentum and inertia
- Least effort/greatest convenience

The aspects of urban form and generic structure of built form are distinguished both in terms of basic relations and in terms of their role in a general, evolutionary process of learning. Each of the composite views – structural, overlay, experiential, time/process and metabolic – have their own internal logic, or complementary and competing logics, in various states of articulation and coherence. So, for example, one of the logics of the structural view is the process of successive fringe formation, which is a complex mechanism involving a range of developmental regularities including, among others:

- Persistence of material, form and relationship
- Differential rates of change of different generic types of form
- Periodic variation in rates of growth
- Periodic variation in land value
- Clustering of uses
- Urban allometry and scaling

As with all interpretations of sense perception, the composite views are imbued with theory, which is what helps them to clarify what we see. The composite views are in effect a form of explanation.

COMPARISON

In order to *improve* our explanations and understanding we involve ourselves in the general circuit of learning: making hypotheses (a suggested mapping of descriptions onto a particular internal

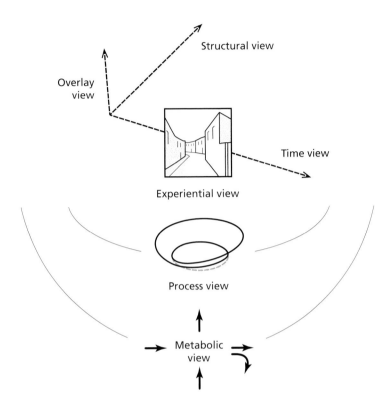

structure), deducing the implications and testing the results against a number of specific cases. As argued throughout the book, an essential element of the testing is comparison: on the one hand, comparison of the examples we investigate with the logical structures and, on the other, comparison of a number of examples with each other. One of the principal aims of comparing a number of different examples is to identify developmental regularities – recurring forms and processes. Comparative analysis to find regularities is the foundation for testing our existing explanatory logical structures and identifying new ones.

COMBINING LOGICAL STRUCTURES
A further step is to try to integrate the different logical structures by finding the relationships between them and how they fit together. This is in effect to see if we can link different concepts or show that one is a transform of another. An intriguing question here is whether any two logical structures that accord with experience, for example spatial interactions and successive fringe

formation, can be mutually exclusive or whether there will always be some transform by which one structure can be converted to, embedded within or mapped onto the other. That is to say, what might appear to be mutually exclusive may just be different parts of the same structure. An example of this is the way in which the different aspects of urban form can be tied together by the typological process illustrated as a process diagram (see figures 3.15 and 8.11 above). Another example is to map the different methods and approaches to morphology onto the multi-level diagram of generic structure (see figure 8.12). One way or the other, a long-term goal of urban morphological investigation should be to discover the links and transforms between the various logical structures – and the disciplines that develop them.

FINAL OUTPUTS
Because urban morphology has a role both as an independent and as an auxiliary discipline, there are different levels of output. When urban morphology is used as an auxiliary support for another field or

Figure 8.12
Diagram illustrating the relative positions of the different composite views as a basis for understanding how the different views and approaches can be integrated

Figure 8.13
The multi-level diagram of generic structure proves to be a useful basis for integration and understanding the roles and domains of the different approaches to urban morphology that have developed over time, often in isolation. In this capacity, the diagram of generic structure is a kind of 'projection' onto which we can map the different approaches.

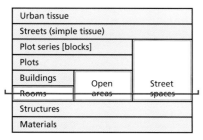

The Nolli Section

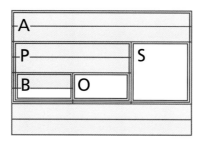

Area measures

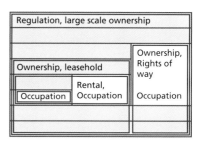

Control/use

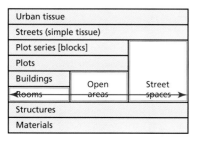

Territorial Depth

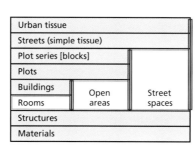

Boundary analysis

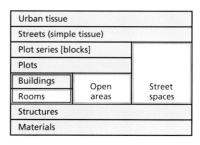

Architectural morphology
Social logic of space

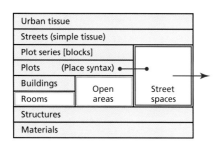

Place syntax, Space syntax,
network analysis

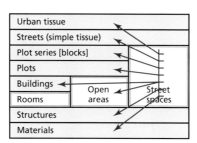

Townscape, city image

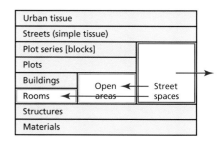

Spatial interaction

discipline, the analysis required may only be the minimum necessary to identify the basic structural units: urban tissue, plan units or character areas or types at other levels such as streets, blocks or plots, depending on the application.

The basic, minimum outputs might include:

- Plan drawings of tissues or types
- Tables of dimensions and measures
- Elevation, section and/or 3D drawings and/or photographs

The final output of more self-contained studies will likely take the form of a report including:

- A map set with single aspect and composite views
- Tables of dimensions and measures
- Text descriptions of the elements and process of development
- Photographs
- Diagrams and drawings of detailed elements
- Explanatory text

As an example, if the aim of the study is to investigate a single settlement – in part or whole – the principal output in terms of content might include:

Single aspect views
(plans, diagrams, photographs and text)

- The geology, topography and hydrology of the site and broad patterns of surrounding vegetation
- Social and economic drivers and general historical background
- Route structure
- Patterns of control
- Specific types of constituent elements such as tissues, blocks, plot series, plots, buildings and methods of construction
- Patterns of land use
- Patterns of city image elements, townscape and open space networks

Composite views
(plans, diagrams, photographs and text)

- The sequence of development, transformations and evolution of types
- Groupings or associations of tissues that form distinct, larger-scale patterns

- Aspect overlays, defined character areas or morphogenetic regions
- Diagrams of aspect and element combinations
- Serial vision diagrams or animations
- Input-output tables of resource flows
- Explanatory and interpretative texts

Intermediate levels of output would include selected single aspect and composite views to suit the aims and objectives of the study.

The extent to which a study makes reference to explanatory structures and seeks to actively explain specific examples will clearly depend on the purposes of the study. One way or another, the act of putting together the material generated by a study to communicate the results represents another form of composite view. The way in which the information is presented can have a significant effect on the way it is absorbed and the composite image it generates. As discussed in the Introduction, multiple descriptions can provide additional information that makes things easier to understand.

When compiling a final document for an urban morphological study, it is extremely beneficial to include a number of different types of information that all describe the same thing – the study area.

An example illustrated in figure 8.14 (from *The City of Bath Morphological Study*[11]) shows that the structure and character of urban tissue can be very effectively conveyed by combining:

- Plan drawings
- Brief descriptive and narrative text
- Tables of quantitative and qualitative attributes
- Photographs
- Diagrams of elements, associations and processes

Juxtaposing the different types of information on the same page, in particular, plans, text and photos, can help enormously in generating the sense of depth that comes with the composite view. For studies that go beyond just identifying types of form, there is significant value in tying together the descriptions with even a brief narrative and explanatory text, even if the purpose of the study is not explicitly explanation. The structure of a story makes the information much more accessible and memorable.

The following section illustrates with specific examples the various ways morphological studies and information can be applied and communicated.

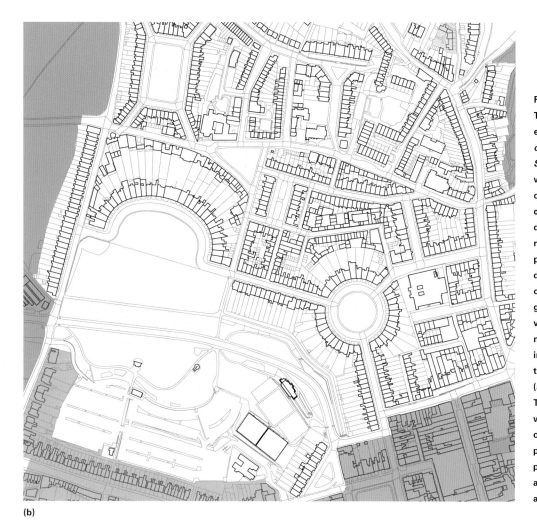

(b)

Figure 8.14-a and b
The following pages are
excerpted from *The City
of Bath Morphological
Study* and illustrate the
way that different kinds
of information can be
combined in a 'multiple
description' to generate a
rich understanding of a
place with a sense of
depth similar to that
of depth perception
generated by binocular
vision. Using a single
medium such as text or
images on its own is in
this sense, flat. The map
(a) shows the location of
The Circus and Crescent
within the wider pattern
of tissues. The detailed
plan view (b) shows the
pattern of streets, plots
and buildings with
adjacent tissues in colour.

CIRCUS AND CRESCENT

HISTORICAL DEVELOPMENT
The Circus and Royal Crescent are central elements
of this tissue that extended the northward growth
of the city from the 1750s into the 19th century.
Starting with The Circus and completion of George
Street, growth continued north, filling in the frame
established by John Wood's (Elder and Younger)
plans as well as existing roads and boundaries.
North of what is now Julian Road, the development
occurred in a more piecemeal fashion with
Lansdown, Somerset and Camden crescents first
appearing as isolated features in the landscape.

Figure 8.14-c
Image of The Circus
showing how the plots
and buildings shape the
central space

(a)

(c)

GENERAL	
LOCATION	ST 7462 6562
PERIOD OF ORIGIN	MID- TO LATE GEORGIAN 1760–1800
SIZE	55 HECTARES
POSITION	NORTHERN EXTENSION TO EARLY GEORGIAN EXTENSION
USES AND ACTIVITIES	MAINLY RESIDENTIAL WITH SOME RETAIL, FOOD, HOTEL, OFFICE, PUBLIC AND INSTITUTIONAL USES

(d)

**Figure 8.14-d
Image showing plots
and buildings on
Rivers Street which are
truncated and vary in
depth because they back
on to Julian Road, to
the right**

SUMMARY DESCRIPTION
The clear geometrical order of The Circus and Royal
Crescent give way to a more irregular connected
grid of streets, inflected in response to the steep
slopes and pre-existing roads and boundaries.
There are main streets, side streets and mews,
the streets very well enclosed by townhouses
on individual plots along both sides of the street
space. In some cases a unified facade is applied
to a series of individual plots and there are many
corner sub-series to keep all sides of a block active.
Buildings are mostly three-storey with flat fronts in
a Classically inspired style faced in Bath stone.

(e)

Figure 8.14-e
Plan highlighting the elements that existed prior to the development of the Circus and Crescent tissue and remain as persistent features: Julian Road, Lansdown Road, George Street, Gay Street and field boundaries. The plots forming the eastern side of The Circus are inflected to adapt to the field boundary.

Figure 8.14-f
View south along Lansdown Road, one of the persistent features and a primary route connecting Bath with the settlements of Lansdown and Wick

ALIGNMENTS AND SPACES

This tissue was essentially greenfield development and the distinct line along the east side of The Circus is the trace of a previous boundary between what were kitchen gardens and orchard (to the east) and open fields (to the west). The other key pre-existing features were a further field boundary to the east, George Street, Lansdown Road, Walcot Street/London Road and the road to Weston.

(f)

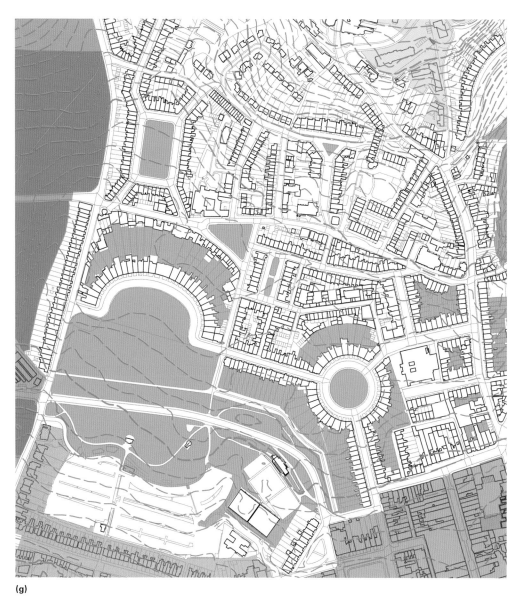

(g)

Figure 8.14-g
Composite plan with overlays of contour lines and green spaces. Despite forming clear geometric shapes, the street pattern is inflected to adapt to the topography with streets running predominantly at right angles or parallel to the contours. The public green spaces are shaped and enclosed by the buildings and plots.

(h)

Figure 8.14-h
View from the central green space within The Circus looking west to Brock Street

TOPOGRAPHY	
UNDERLYING FORM	SOUTH-FACING PROMONTORY RISING FROM A MEANDER IN THE RIVER AVON TO A PLATEAU AT LANSDOWN
SITUATION	SOUTH-FACING SLOPE WITH UNDULATIONS ON HIGHER REACHES
SLOPE	STEEPLY SLOPED, 8.3%, INCREASING FROM SOUTH TO NORTH

VEGETATION	
TYPE AND LOCATION	EXTENSIVE AREAS OF GRASS AND LARGE STATURE DECIDUOUS TREES IN SPACES ASSOCIATED WITH THE CIRCUS, SQUARES AND CRESCENTS; TREES AND OTHER ORNAMENTAL PLANTS IN GARDENS AND CAR PARKS

STREETS	
ACCESS POINTS	PRIMARY ACCESS FROM A4/ROMAN ROAD, LANSDOWN ROAD, GAY STREET, WESTON ROAD
ROUTE TYPE	PRIMARY STRATEGIC ROUTES, ROMAN ROAD AND LANSDOWN ROAD NORTH; SECONDARY STRATEGIC ROUTE, WESTON ROAD WEST; THOROUGHFARES AND PEDESTRIAN ROUTES AND SOME CUL-DE-SACS
PATTERN	THREE DISTINCT SUB-TYPES OF THOROUGHFARE GRID INCLUDING COORDINATED AND UNCOORDINATED ISOLATED GEOMETRIC COMPOSITIONS. SUB-TYPES INCLUDE: COMPOSITE PATCHWORK OF ORTHOGRAPHIC GRIDS WITH CIRCUS AND CRESCENT; SEMI-IRREGULAR LADDER-FORM GRID WITH VARIOUS SYMMETRICAL COMPOSITIONS; AND IRREGULAR NETWORK INFLECTED IN RESPONSE TO TOPOGRAPHY; THESE BEING THE PRODUCT OF SEVERAL STAGES OF DEVELOPMENT AND TRANSFORMATION
HIERARCHY	HIERARCHY EVIDENT FROM CONTINUITY OF ROUTE AND STREET WIDTH
ALIGNMENT/ORIENTATION	STRAIGHT, CRANKED AND SINUOUS; MOST STREETS PARALLEL OR AT RIGHT ANGLES TO CONTOURS
CHARACTER	MAINLY ACTIVE FRONTS ON BOTH SIDES WITH DIFFERENT METHODS OF TURNING CORNERS (EG, DOOR ON GABLE END, WINDOWS ON FRONT), SOME SEMI-ACTIVE FRONTS AT CORNERS

Figure 8.14-i
View east across the green to the eastern side of the Royal Crescent and Brock Street

(i)

(j)

Figure 8.14-j
Route structure analysis
showing a network of
thoroughfares within a
frame of primary routes.
The cul-de-sacs and
pedestrian links were
added later or created by
excluding vehicular traffic.

(k)

Figure 8.14-k
View south down Gay
Street to Beechen Cliff.
The Circus tissue is
integrated with the Queen
Square tissue to the south
by incorporating the
extended line of
Gay Street

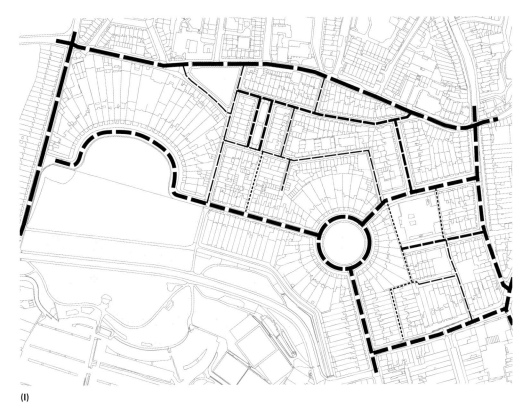

(l)

Figure 8.14-l
Route hierarchy diagram showing the pre-existing routes and those connecting the main public spaces occupying the highest level, and routes connecting minor spaces and higher level routes at the intermediate level

Figure 8.14-m
View south along Catharine Place, a minor space treated as a central garden square with a street space proportionate to the level of the position of the street and space in the hierarchy

Junction spacing
Long: 70–240m
Short: 40–66m
Street section
Main:
Frontage-to-frontage: 13–18m
Facade-to-facade: 17–21m
Side:
Frontage-to-frontage: 10–14m
Facade-to-facade: 12–18m
Lane/mews:
Frontage-to-frontage: 5–9m
Facade-to-facade: same as frontage or + 1m

(m)

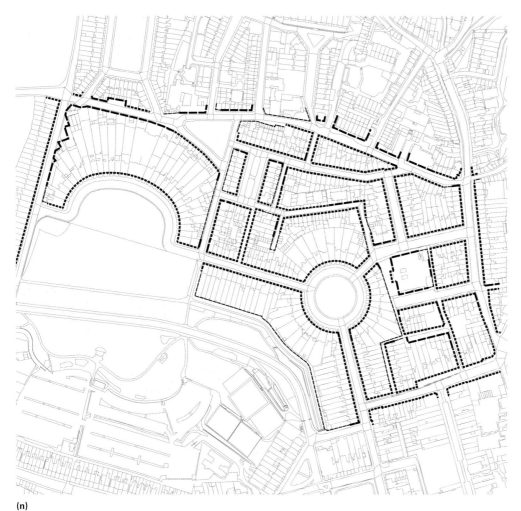

Frontage
······· Active
▬ ▬ ▬ Semi-active
▬▬▬ Side/back
▬ ▬ ▬ Boundary feature

Figure 8.14-n
Diagram of frontage types showing a general predominance of street spaces with active frontages on both sides. There are a number of exceptions, however, where the back of the plot series creates a semi-active or back boundary along a public street.

(n)

HIGHWAYS	
COMPONENTS	VEHICULAR: CARRIAGEWAY WITH A FOOTWAY ON BOTH SIDES; PEDESTRIAN: LEVEL SURFACE
PARKING	ON-STREET PARKING ON ONE AND BOTH SIDES MAINLY ON WIDER SIDE STREETS
PLANTING	NO STREET TREES IN THE HIGHWAY
MATERIALS	CARRIAGEWAY PREDOMINANTLY TARMAC; FOOTWAYS AND LEVEL SURFACES PREDOMINANTLY STONE AND CONCRETE PENNANT SLAB

BLOCKS	
TYPES	PREDOMINANTLY PERIMETER BLOCKS, SOME HALF PERIMETER WITH MAIN BUILDING ON THE FRONT AND IN SOME CASES MEWS BUILDING AT THE BACK; ALSO BLOCKS CONTAINING PLANTING (EG, THE CIRCUS, ROYAL CRESCENT, ST JAMES'S SQUARE)
SHAPE	RECTANGULAR OR POLYGONAL, SOME INFLECTED TO CREATE 'SHAPED SPACE', EG, THE CIRCUS, ROYAL AND OTHER CRESCENTS, ALSO SINUOUS SHAPES ASSOCIATED WITH MAIN HISTORICAL ROUTES, EG, LANSDOWN ROAD
ARRANGEMENTS	PLOT SERIES BACK-TO-BACK AND BACK-TO-SIDE, SUB-SERIES IN CORNER ZONES

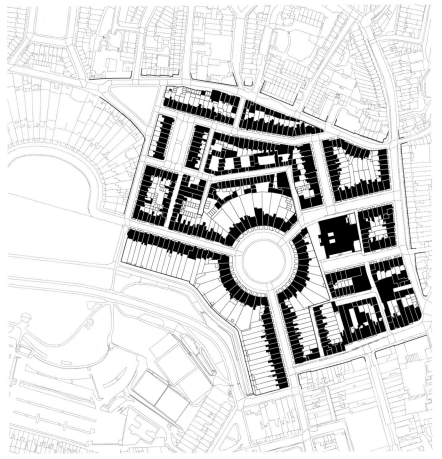

Block dimensions
Rectangular blocks
Long side: 10–20 plots,
The Paragon, 50+,
Short side: 2–8 plots
Square and small blocks
5–8 plots per side

Figure 8.14-o
Diagram highlighting
the building footprint
and plot boundaries – a
more detailed version
of the figure-ground
diagram. The plot series
and blocks are inflected
to adapt to the existing
streets and the main
composed spaces
while the consistent
building position on the
frontage maintains the
enclosed street spaces.
The resulting pattern is
irregular with isolated
regularities.

(o)

PLOT SERIES	
TYPES	PREDOMINANTLY REGULAR WITH MANY VARIETIES OF CORNER SUB-SERIES
SHAPE	PREDOMINANTLY REGULAR RECTANGULAR, SOME SPLAYED SERIES TO ACCOMMODATE CRESCENTS AND CIRCUS
ORIENTATION	PREDOMINANTLY ACTIVE FRONT ON STREET FRONTAGE, SOME SEMI-ACTIVE FRONTS IN CASES OF HALF BLOCKS AND MEWS
BUILDING LINE	PREDOMINANTLY CONTINUOUS ALONG FRONTAGE, OR CONTINUOUS SET-BACK WITH FRONT BASEMENT ACCESS, SOME CONTINUOUS SET-BACK WITH GARDEN
SERIES FRONTAGE	CONTINUOUS BUILDING LINE OR RAILINGS TO FRONT BASEMENT ACCESS, SOME LOW STONE WALLS, HIGH STONE WALLS ON BACKS OF HALF BLOCKS
VERTICAL ALIGNMENT	STEPPED, PREDOMINANTLY WITH A SINGLE PLOT BEING THE UNIT OF STEPPING, MORE VARIATION LOWER DOWN SLOPE WITH DIFFERENT BUILDING HEIGHTS OBSCURING THE STEPPING
SKYLINE	PREDOMINANTLY STEPPED PARAPET LINE OR HORIZONTAL PARAPET LINE, PUNCTUATED BY CHIMNEYS, DORMERS AND VIEWS SOUTH TO OPPOSITE SIDE OF VALLEY; VIEWS NORTH UP THE HILL GENERALLY TERMINATED WITH BUILDING OR TREES

(p)   (r)

(q)

Figure 8.14-p and q
A moderate-sized block
with four straight series,
one (p) inflected in
response to the diagonal,
and three corner series.
Corner building (q) with
principal windows on
one side and door on
adjacent side

Figure 8.14-r
Blocks with corner zones
and shared internal
parking areas

(s)

Plot dimensions

Plot width: Large plots: predominantly 7–8m,
   some 9–14m; small and corner zones: 5–6m

Plot depth: Large plot, small and corner
   zones: 7–18m

Built area: Large plots: 10–15m; small: 8–10m

Back-to-back: 20–57m

Back-to-side: 6–13m

(t)

Figure 8.14-s and t
Small block (s) with a
corner zone sub-series on
each corner. Single bay
(t) width corner building
with doors on side street

(u)

Figure 8.14-u
The Circus with its radially splayed plots, stepped in to meet with the straight series of Gay Street, Brock Street and Bennett Street and truncated along the eastern edge in response to the field boundary that lay to the east when the tissue was laid out

Plots	
Type	Predominantly attached dominant frontage building, some outbuildings and mews buildings
Shape	Predominantly rectangular, narrow frontage, some splayed to accommodate The Circus and crescents
Size and location	Widths vary, a few amalgamations to form larger multiples, smaller plots at corners, in mews and plot tails
Access	Front pedestrian access, some carriageway entrances to shared internal parking plots
Components	Main building (dominant) outbuildings/extensions, mews buildings, back gardens, some front gardens
Planting/vegetation	Trees and ornamental planting in back gardens, front gardens
Frontage	Building, iron railings, enclosure wall

Buildings	
Types	Attached town houses, a few amalgamated
Overall form	Predominantly rectangular/polygonal in plan, flat front, rear projection
Height	Predominantly 3 to 4 storey, 2 storey on mews and lanes
Style	Predominantly Georgian and later Classical or Classically inspired
Materials	Walls predominantly in Bath stone; roofs predominantly slate, some clay tile and infrequent flat roofs

References

1 MRG Conzen, *Alnwick, Northumberland: A Study in Town-Plan Analysis*, Institute of British Geographers (London), 1969. Print.

2 Otto Schlüter, *Die Ziele der Geographie des Menschen*, Antrittsrede (Munich), 1906. Print.

3 JWR Whitehand, 'Building Cycles and the Spatial Pattern of Urban Growth', Transactions of the Institute of British Geographers 56 (1972): 39–55. Print.

- JWR Whitehand and NJ Morton, 'Fringe Belts and the Recycling of Urban Land: An Academic Concept and Planning Practice', *Environment and Planning B: Planning and Design* 30 (2003): 819–39. Print.

- JWR Whitehand and NJ Morton, 'The Fringe-Belt Phenomenon and Socio-Economic Change', *Urban Studies* 43 (2006): 2047–66. Print.

4 MP Conzen, 'How Cities Internalize Their Former Urban Fringes: A Cross-Cultural Comparison', *Urban Morphology* 13.1 (2009): 29–54. Print.

5 MRG Conzen, *Alnwick, Northumberland*.

6 Gordon Cullen, *Townscape*, Architectural Press (Oxford), 1961. Print.

- Kevin Lynch, *The Image of the City*, MIT Press (Cambridge, MA), 1960. Print.

7 Michael Batty, *The New Science of Cities,* MIT Press (Cambridge, MA), 2013. Print.

- Alan Wilson, *Urban Modelling: Critical Concepts in Urban Studies*, Routledge (Abingdon), 2012. Print.

8 Stephen Marshall, *Cities, Design and Evolution*, Routledge (London), 2008. Print.

- Karl Kropf, 'Agents and Agency, Learning and Emergence in the Built Environment: A Theoretical Excursion', *Shapers of Urban Form*, Peter Larkham and Michael P Conzen (eds), Routledge (London), 2014. Print.

9 W Brian Arthur, *The Nature of Technology: What It Is and How It Evolves*, reprint edition, Free Press (New York), 2011. Print.

- Gianfranco Caniggia and Gian Luigi Maffei, *Architectural Composition and Building Typology: Interpreting Basic Buildings*, Alinea (Florence), 2001. Print.

- Karl Kropf, 'Evolution and Urban Form: Staking Out the Ground for a More Mature Theory', *Urban Morphology* 17.2, 136–49. Print.

- Karl Kropf, 'Conceptions of Change in the Built Environment', *Urban Morphology* 5.1 (2001): 29–42. Print.

- Marshall, *Cities, Design and Evolution*.

- Saverio Muratori, 'Studi per una Operante Storia Urbana di Venezia', *Palladio*, Istituto Poligrafico dello Stato (Rome), 1959. Print.

- Brenda Case Scheer, *The Evolution of Urban Form: Typology for Planners and Architects*, American Planning Association (Chicago), 2010. Print.

- Philip Steadman, *The Evolution of Designs,* revised edition, Routledge (London), 2008. Print.

- Michael Weinstock, *The Architecture of Emergence*, John Wiley & Sons (Chichester), 2010. Print.

10 Christopher Kennedy, 'A Mathematical Description of Urban Metabolism', *Sustainability Science: The Emerging Paradigm and the Urban Environment*, MP Weinstein and RE Turner (eds), Springer Science & Business Media (Berlin), 2012. Print.

- C Ratti, N Baker and K Steemers, 'Energy Consumption and Urban Texture', *Energy and Buildings*, 37.7, 762–76. Print.

- Philipp Rode, Christian Keim et al, *Cities and Energy: Urban Morphology and Heat Energy Demand*, LSE Cities, London School of Economics and European Institute for Energy Research (London and Karlsruhe), 2014. Web.

- Serge Salat, Françoise Labbé and Caroline Nowacki, *Cities and Forms: On Sustainable Urbanism*, Éditions Hermann (Paris), 2011. Print.

11 Karl Kropf, *The City of Bath Morphological Study*, Bath and North East Somerset Council (Bath), 2014. Web.

PART 3

Applications

Case Studies

This section includes a selective survey of different applications of urban morphology. The aim is to illustrate the ways in which the concepts and methods of the discipline are being actively used to investigate different aspects and properties of urban form. Comparing the different applications and taking them together reinforces the general characterisation of morphology as an independent and as an auxiliary discipline. Urban morphology draws on the work of allied fields to assemble a range of methods and techniques to identify regularities and build up more general theories of urban form. The allied fields in turn are applying the resulting concepts and techniques to find further, more detailed regularities as well as to inform the creation, transformation and management of the built environment. As detailed in Section 1, the allied fields include urban geography, urban and architectural history, archaeology and anthropology as well as architecture, historic conservation, urban design and planning.

POSSIBLE FORMS: ALLOMETRY, MORPHOSPACE AND COMBINATORICS

The act of building is fundamentally one of composition. We create objects by putting together smaller parts. Every time anyone embarks on that process he or she necessarily poses the question, consciously or not: which parts should be used and how should they be put together? There are three broad ways to approach this question. One is to refer to previous attempts and follow the patterns established in the objects already created. Another is to experiment by picking parts and trying out arrangements to suit a particular purpose. The third is to identify the minimum constituent parts and explore all the possible ways they might be put together and then select the form most suited to the need. There are any number of variations and blendings of these approaches and in simple terms they could be said to lie on a continuum from empirical to theoretical.

The theoretical approach has been developed by a number of different authors and applied both in the generation of designs and in a broader effort to understand what factors might limit the range of *workable* or *useful* forms out of the wider range of the possible. To a large extent the work is rooted in concepts borrowed from biological morphology such as the pioneering work of D'Arcy Wentworth

Thompson and later developments by David Raup and George R McGhee Jr, among others.[1]

Taking these precedents as a basic foundation, theoretical morphology of the built environment can be characterised as, 1) the mathematical and geometric simulation of form; 2) the representation and comparison of possible forms with actual forms; 3) the investigation into why certain forms tend to predominate, identification of the limits on actual forms, if any, and the sources of those limits. The steps in the process are thus:

- Modelling/parameterisation
- Comparison of possible and actual forms
- Identification and interpretation of limits

There are a number of different specific approaches to theoretical morphology based on the specific parameters that are taken into account. This very brief introduction will look at:

- Allometry
- Morphospace
- Combinatorics

ALLOMETRY

The feature that distinguishes allometry is the focus on **size** as the key independent variable. The aim is to examine the effect of changing or varying the size of a built form on other parameters such as its shape, proportions, internal arrangement and resource use (metabolism) at different scales, usually buildings, urban tissue and whole settlements.

Allometry therefore deals specifically with the **dimensional** limits dividing possible and actual built form. At the level of the building, Steadman, in his *Architectural Morphology,*[2] provides a very good explanation of basic techniques and considerations using studies of residential buildings. One example looks at the changes in wall surface area with increasing total volume and another looks at the amount of linear circulation space with increasing floor area. The procedure involves taking measurements of the parameters from a sample of cases and plotting them on a coordinate grid to determine if they fall on or near a distinct line. The line for the actual cases is then compared with a slope based on the isometric scaling of some ideal form to determine whether the actual line

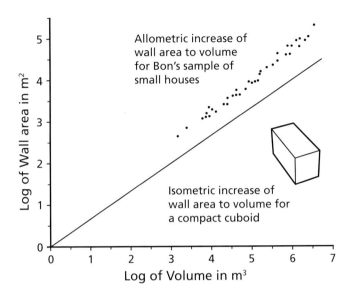

Allometric increase of wall area to volume for Bon's sample of small houses

Isometric increase of wall area to volume for a compact cuboid

Figure 9.1
Graph showing the covariation between wall surface and volume of residential buildings with increase in size. The surface area tends to increase at a faster rate because of the desire for daylight and natural ventilation.

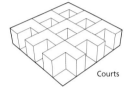

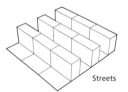

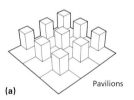

(a)

Figure 9.2-a
Diagram of the development types – or tissues – investigated by Martin and March: the court, street and pavilion

sits above or below the isometric line (positive or negative allometry).

The further step is then to explain why the cases show a negative or positive allometry. With wall surface to volume in residential buildings, the faster increase in surface area with an increase in volume (positive allometry) is explained by the general desire for daylighting, views and natural ventilation which tends to result in elongated forms or projecting wings.

Martin and March's seminal study of different types of built form[3] also takes a fundamentally allometric approach. Aggregates (or tissues) of three different basic types of building – the pavilion, slab or street and courtyard – are examined using storey number as the independent variable, and floor space index (FSI or FAR) as the dependent variable with floor-to-floor height, plan depth and cut-off angle fixed. Martin and March's analysis shows that for each form the FSI reaches a limit, with the courtyard form achieving the highest total and the pavilion the lowest – the FSI of the pavilion in fact decreasing with higher storey numbers because of the constraint of the cut-off angle. The value of the analysis is that it clearly shows that the limits are imposed by the choice to constrain built form for particular purposes rooted in human needs and values – access to light, air and open space.

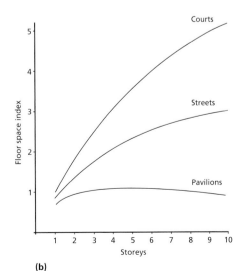

(b)

Figure 9.2-b
Graph showing the covariation in floor area with increasing height (storey number), keeping other aspects constant. All flatten out but, importantly, the pavilion decreases with greater storey number

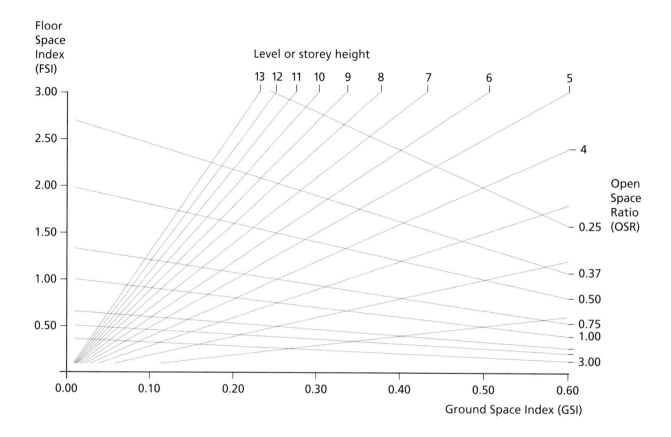

URBAN ALLOMETRY AND SCALING LAWS

A long-standing interest at the level of the whole settlement or urban system is the relation between the size of a city and other parameters such as population density, rent, average income and energy use. This is in effect **urban allometry**, examining the effects of urban growth on some feature with reference to a mathematical model of the relation. As pointed out by Batty in his *New Science of Cities*, these are generally non-linear, scaling relations. While hesitating to give them the full status of laws, Batty sets out what he calls a casual list of seven scaling regularities of cities.[4]

- **Frequency of cities:** decreases with size – there are fewer large cities than smaller towns and villages (rank-size rule/Zipf's Law)
- **Interactions between cities:** increase with size at a greater than proportionate rate (but decrease with distance) (Alonso-Wilson Law)
- **Population density/land rent:** decrease with growth away from the centre – negative allometry (von Thünen's Law)
- **Population density profile:** flattens, decreasing in the centre as the city grows (Bussière's Law)

- **Potential connections between people:** increase as the square of the population as the city grows (Metcalfe's Law/Moore's Law)
- **Average income** (also productivity, innovation and violent crime): increases at a greater than proportionate rate with population growth (Bettencourt-West Law/Marshall's Law)
- **Sustainable solutions:** increase in viability and cost-effectiveness with greater density (Brand's Law).

As Batty points out there is as yet no formal synthesis of scaling in city systems but there are strong interrelationships between the regularities that bear further investigation. A key area for investigation – and perhaps a source of Batty's hesitance in calling these laws – is identifying the 'expected' relations between size and the other variables in question, not least because there are different ways of measuring size and density. Another issue pointed out by Arcaute et al [5] is the variability in the scaling exponent in different specific situations such as when there is a dominant 'king city' in a country or region.

Figure 9.3
The Spacemate graph of Berghauser Pont and Haupt provides a richer definition of density by combining ratio measures and so adding dimensions to the two-dimensional graphic representation.

SPACEMATE

An extremely useful tool that provides a more general view of the key parameters used to measure the density of urban tissue has been developed by Berghauser Pont and Haupt.[6] The method was devised as a means of overcoming the limitations and bluntness of the common single measures of density such as dwellings per unit of land area or floor area per unit of land area. As with allometric studies, the parameters are set as variables on the x and y axes of a two-dimensional coordinate grid. In this case, because the two principal parameters are related ratios, the Floor Space Index (Building Footprint*Floor Height/Total Area) and Ground Space Index (Building Footprint/Total Area), it is possible to plot reference lines for two further, related parameters on the same grid, namely the building height and Open Space Ratio (GSI-1/FSI). The result is a space that lays out all the possible combinations of the parameters in which actual examples can be placed. Different types of tissue cluster in different locations on the coordinate grid allow a more effective comparison and visualisation of differences.

MORPHOSPACE

Spacemate is a variety of what is termed a *morphospace* in theoretical morphology. In simple terms, morphospace is a phase space in which the axes take the values of selected morphological parameters. Each point in the space represents a possible form with a unique combination of values for the selected parameters. Developed for use in evolutionary and developmental biology (see Raup, McGhee, Mitteroecker and Huttegger[7]), morphospace provides a framework for comparing possible forms with actual forms. As with Spacemate, it can be used to help visualise quantitative and formal differences, locating actual examples within the space. When actual forms only occupy limited areas of the morphospace, it is a prompt to investigate what phenomena or interactions constitute the limits and why some forms are more prevalent than others. Philip Steadman applies morphospace to the built environment in his book *Building Types and Built Forms*.[8] He develops and explains the application of the concept to built form and examines a range of historical examples, asking, are there limits to the different ways we might possibly put built form together? What are the limits and where do they come from? Do some forms arise not by habit or choice but because of physical/formal constraints or correlations?

COMBINATORICS AND EMERGENCE

Another question to ask in this vein is, do some forms arise not by conscious choice but through the combined activities of many people over time? The pattern of plots in a tissue, for example, can emerge from years of subdivision and amalgamation of individual plots undertaken by individual owners without any intention of creating a particular pattern. One also finds that some of the patterns are repeated, not in exact form but in what Marshall calls 'characteristic' order.[9]

One of the ways of investigating how and why this happens is by exploring all possible combinations or configurations of the constituent elements, a variety of **combinatorics**. Steadman sets out some of the basic techniques in *Architectural Morphology*,[10] focusing on two basic methods of generating combinations. One is by the **dissection** of a simple **rectangular plan**, the other by progressive **aggregation** of cells in a **polyomino.**

Figure 9.4
Examples of a dissection and polyomino as used in morphological analysis of built form. Both are 'dimensionless' representations of buildings – and other forms – that allow a focus on configurational relationships.

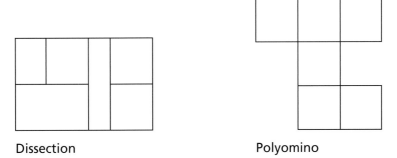

Dissection   Polyomino

One example given by Marshall[11] is a generic settlement using polyomino squares to represent the initial settlement and successive extensions. He presents a matrix of all possible configurations up to x squares.

One of his principal points is that of all the possible configurations, there are far more generally compact shapes (tending toward circular) than there are linear or spider-form. This suggests on the one hand that, all other things being equal, there is a general tendency, in terms of statistical likelihood, toward the emergence of compact or near circular settlement form. On the other hand, when we find actual cases that are not compact, it is a clue that other things are not equal and there are other tendencies at work – or specific intentions on the part of the agents – that warrant investigation.

A key point in using combinatorics to investigate actual built form is that the reference to statistical likelihood applies when there is an aggregate or series of independent or quasi-independent acts of building. This is much more likely at or above the **level of the plots series** because control of the elements above the plot is distributed over a number of different agents and/or points in time. The separation of the acts allows in the element of chance.

As Marshall shows, one of the principal reasons for exploring all possible configurations is to identify which specific forms are statistically most common when individual acts of building are uncoordinated and so effectively 'random'.

MICROCLIMATE

The general concept of urban tissue is being used in a widening range of research focusing on **environmental performance**. A significant amount of this work has come out of the field of urban ecology, in particular studies making use of satellite imagery, remote sensing and land-cover mapping. In broad terms, the research tends to focus on performance measures such as energy and resource use and indicators of environmental conditions that arise with different types and constituents of urban form.

Within the field of urban ecology, a number of specific methods have been developed for defining distinct types of built development making use of remote sensing data to cover large study areas. The resulting types of built development, referred to variously as **urban structural types** (UST) or **urban structural units** (USU), are then subject to

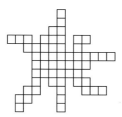

left **Figure 9.5 Polyomino representations of settlements as might be generated in a combinatorial analysis of possible forms. As indicated by Marshall, there are statistically a greater number of generally compact forms; therefore, given a more or less random process of growth over the long term, compact forms are more likely to occur.**

USU types

- Open space with significant tree cover
- Open space, sparse or no tree cover, no or few buildings
- Low intensity built form: small low- to medium-rise buildings
- Low intensity: large low-rise buildings
- Low intensity: medium- to high-rise buildings
- Medium intensity: small low-rise buildings
- Medium intensity: mid-scale low-rise buildings
- Medium intensity: large low-rise buildings
- Medium intensity: mid- to high-rise
- High intensity: low- to mid-rise, extensive impervious surfaces
- High intensity: mid- to high-rise, extensive impervious surfaces
- Sea

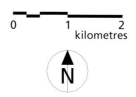

0 1 2 kilometres

N

left and opposite **Figure 9.6-a Plan of the Urban Structural Unit (USU) types in the Randwick Local Government Area, in which the University of New South Wales Kensington campus is located. The blue line represents the municipal boundary. The USUs are essentially equivalent to urban tissue.**

measurement by various means and comparison to determine the relative performance of the different types.

The concept of the UST/USU is rooted in the ecological patch and, as shown by Osmond (in his *Enquiry into New Methodologies for Evaluating Sustainable Urban Form* and other papers[12]), is very similar if not strictly equivalent to urban tissue. Following through that equivalence, Osmond explores the potential of combining methods from urban ecology, space syntax and general descriptive urban morphology to generate tools for assessing the more general sustainability of different forms of urban development at a more local level in terms of urban metabolism and ambience.

The overarching aim is to generate feedback that allows us to assess the potential impact of different forms of development, in particular to identify which forms help to reduce energy and resource consumption while still maintaining acceptable living conditions. It is worth noting that the concepts of *performance* and *feedback* necessarily involve the aspect of perception, first and foremost through our own role as sensory agents, directly in the construction and use of forms and indirectly through research and assessment. The perceptions can then be formalised as objective **measures** and normative **standards**, **benchmarks** or **targets**.

Osmond suggests a combination of methods to formulate a composite, synergistic assessment of sustainability based on seven meta-properties:

- Diversity
- Efficiency
- Resilience
- Permeability
- Legibility
- Stimulance
- Intensity

The principal methods of analysis include:

- Material accounting
- Microclimatic simulation
- Convex space analysis
- Isovist analysis
- Fractal analysis
- Leaf area index and green plot ratio analysis

Figures 9.6 a to e show the results of some of the methods.

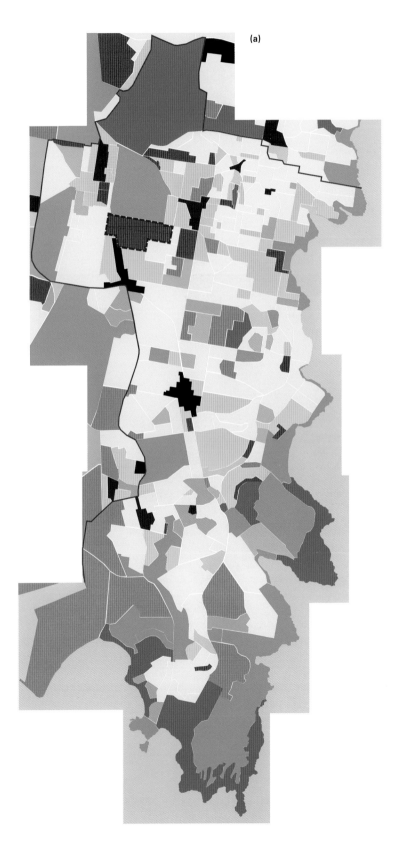

(a)

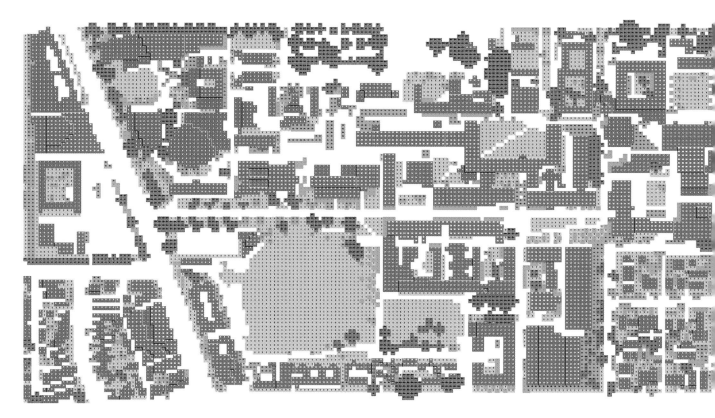

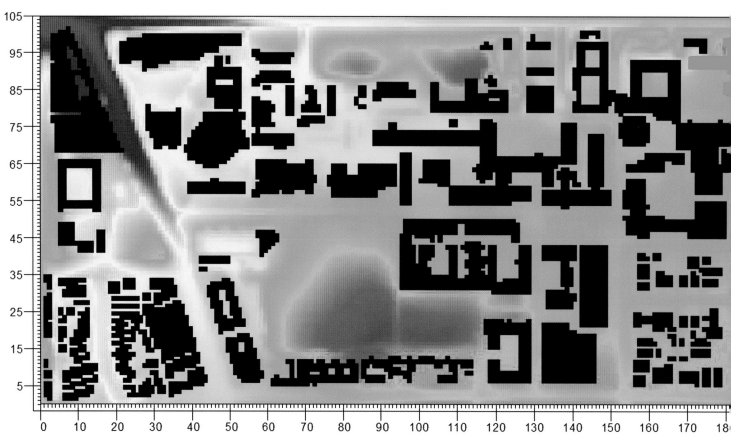

(b)

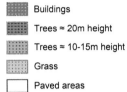

Buildings

Trees ≈ 20m height

Trees ≈ 10-15m height

Grass

Paved areas

Figure 9.6-b
Plan view of the 3D model of University of New South Wales Kensington campus tissue as of January 2008. The model was used for the key microclimate assessments of the tissue with ENVI-met simulation software at a resolution of 5m x 5m cells.

(c)

Potential Temperature

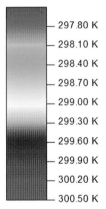

— 297.80 K

— 298.10 K

— 298.40 K

— 298.70 K

— 299.00 K

— 299.30 K

— 299.60 K

— 299.90 K

— 300.20 K

— 300.50 K

Figure 9.6-c
Heat map of potential ambient temperature for the Kensington campus tissue generated by the ENVI-met simulation software, with units in degrees Kelvin. The map shows the contrast between the 'heat trap' associated with a main road and the cooler, shaded campus and residential area, which is a different type of tissue included in the model.

200   210   220   230

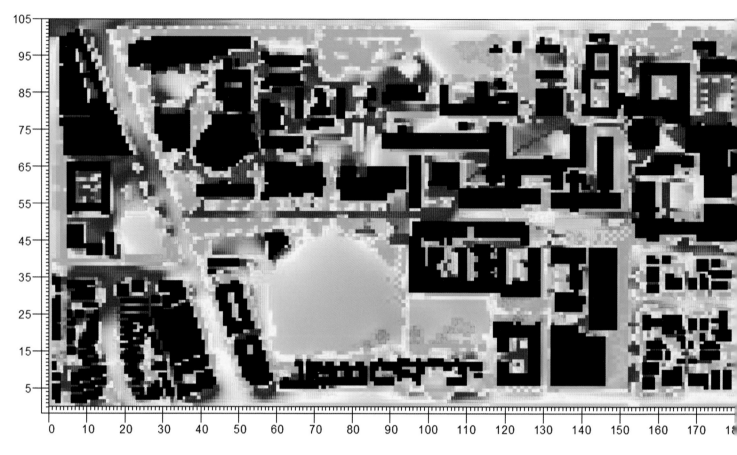

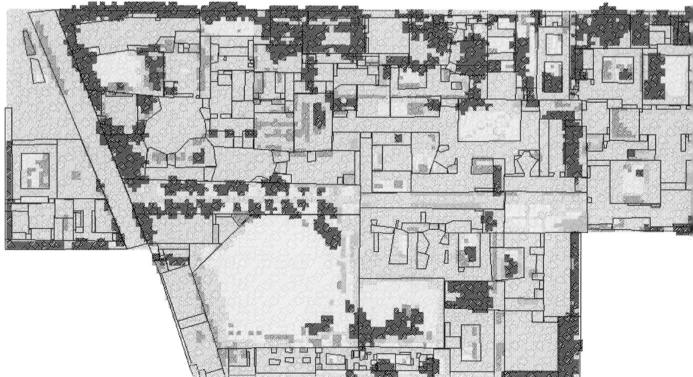

(d)

PMV Value

— 0.30
— 0.60
— 0.90
— 1.20
— 1.50
— 1.80
— 2.10
— 2.40
— 2.70
— 3.00

200   210   220   230

Figure 9.6-d
Heat map of Predicted
Mean Vote (PMV) for
the Kensington campus
tissue from the ENVI-
met model. PMV is a
measure of thermal
comfort combining air
temperature, radiant
temperature, relative
humidity, air speed,
metabolic rate and
clothing insulation. The
relative differences show,
among other things,
the impact of the wider
spacing of larger buildings
within the main campus.

(e)

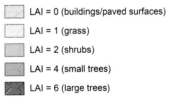

LAI = 0 (buildings/paved surfaces)
LAI = 1 (grass)
LAI = 2 (shrubs)
LAI = 4 (small trees)
LAI = 6 (large trees)

Figure 9.6-e
Leaf Area Index (LAI)
map of the Kensington
campus, using
standardised vegetation
data. Red boundaries
indicate convex spaces,
which serve as a basic
sub-unit of the tissue. LAI
is used as a comparative
indicator of ecological
function primarily in
terms of photosynthesis,
transpiration and
energy exchange.

ENERGY USE: CITIES AND ENERGY STUDY

An example of a more tightly focused assessment of environmental performance using urban tissue as a research tool is the study titled *Cities and Energy: Urban Morphology and Heat Energy Demand* undertaken by the LSE Cities group at the London School of Economic and the European Institute for Energy Research (EIFER).[13]

The principal aim of the research, led by Philipp Rode and Christian Keim, was to determine whether the physical form of built development *at the level of urban tissue* has an effect on passive solar heat gain. This is set in the wider context of the question, if we are searching for more sustainable forms of urban development, which are the most efficient? A range of different specific types of tissue from London, Paris, Berlin and Istanbul – as well as idealised versions – were analysed in detail to determine the level of passive solar heat gains associated with each type as well as which specific characteristics of urban tissue make the most difference. As stated in the report, 'this allowed an investigation of trade-offs between design, density and energy demand at the neighbourhood level'.[14]

The principal features used in defining the different types of tissue included:

- Building type (size, volume and shape of the single unit)
- Number of floors
- Plot shape and proportion
- Alignments
- Street layout/pattern
- Street width
- Street/facade proportion
- Aggregation principles of parts
- Size, volume, shape and proportions of blocks (the aggregation of the single units)
- Built-up density
- Coverage ratio

The main analysis involved calculating the heat energy demand for the different types, taking into account:

- External temperature in relation to a constant internal temperature of 19 degrees
- Heat loss
  - transmission
  - ventilation
- Heat gain
  - orientation

- transparent area
- ratio of frame
- shading

Demand is calculated as the difference between heat losses and gains.

Figure 9.7 shows a graphic representation of the primary heat energy demand per square metre of floor space per year for the actual examples from London, Paris, Berlin and Istanbul. A bivariate analysis was also undertaken to understand the effect of four specific attributes on heat demand: floor area ratio, surface to volume ratio, building coverage and average building height.

Table 9.1 shows the results of the analysis by type and city.

The results confirm the study's hypothesis that different specific types of tissue have different energy demands and that higher density tissues lead to greater heat energy efficiency. It also showed that along with density, average building height and surface to volume ratio are good indicators of heat energy efficiency. In terms of types, detached housing is consistently less efficient and compact urban blocks consistently more efficient. Surprisingly, tissues with high-rise apartments generally perform well and terraced housing in London performs poorly.

The LSE/EIFER research supports the work of the Urban Morphology Laboratory in Paris led by Serge Salat within the Centre Scientifique et Technique du Bâtiment (CSTB). An example of Salat's work is the 2009 paper 'Energy Loads, CO_2 Emissions and Building Stocks: Morphologies, Typologies, Energy Systems and Behaviour'.[15] A much more extended elaboration of morphological principles and methods that incorporates the assessment of energy use can be found in *Cities and Forms: On Sustainable Urbanism*.[16]

ACOUSTICS

Another example of research making use of urban tissue in assessing environmental performance is the work of Jian Kang at the University of Sheffield School of Architecture. Kang's research focuses on the effect of urban morphology on the acoustic environment or 'soundscape' of a place. A specific study that illustrates the principle is set out in the paper 'Integrated Effects of Urban Morphology on Birdsong Loudness and Visibility of Green Areas'.[17] The paper is of particular interest because it combines an assessment of both the mechanical characteristics of sound propagation within different

LONDON

DETACHED HOUSING
© C.Keim - EIFER

HIGH-RISE APARTMENT
© C.Keim - EIFER

SLAB HOUSING
© C.Keim - EIFER

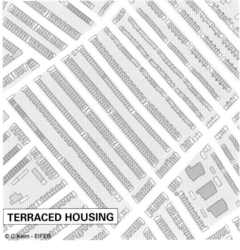

TERRACED HOUSING
© C.Keim - EIFER

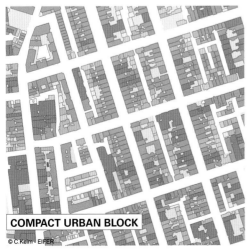

COMPACT URBAN BLOCK
© C.Keim - EIFER

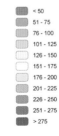

Figure 9.7
Tissue samples from London, Paris, Berlin and Istanbul used for the analysis and visualisation of primary heat energy demand (kWh/m²/year). The diagrams illustrate both the different types of tissue analysed and the specific results.

< 50
51 - 75
76 - 100
101 - 125
126 - 150
151 - 175
176 - 200
201 - 225
226 - 250
251 - 275
> 275

PARIS

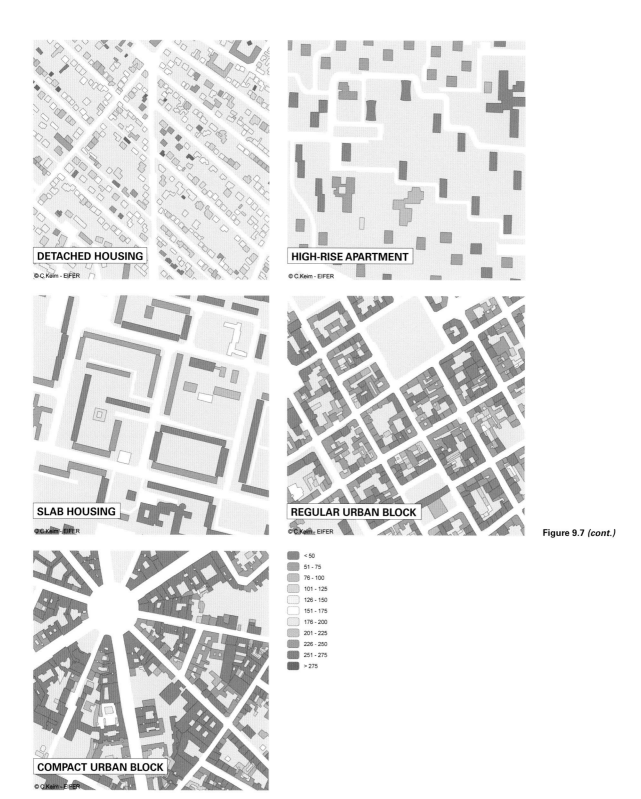

Figure 9.7 *(cont.)*

BERLIN

Figure 9.7 *(cont.)*

ISTANBUL

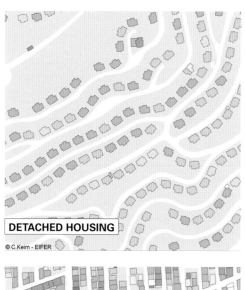

Figure 9.7 *(cont.)*

	DENSITY	SURFACE TO VOLUME	BUILDING HEIGHT	SURFACE COVERAGE
COMPACT URBAN BLOCK	−0.80	0.69	−0.80	−0.24
DETACHED HOUSING	−0.36	0.62	−0.70	−0.13
HIGH-RISE APARTMENT	−0.94	0.44	−0.54	−0.50
SLAB HOUSING	−0.76	0.64	−0.86	−0.21
ALL SAMPLES	−0.75	0.79	−0.86	−0.35

Table 9.1-a
Correlations by typology
between the main
typological parameters
and heat energy demand.
Source: LSE Cities and
EIFER research

	DENSITY	SURFACE TO VOLUME	BUILDING HEIGHT	SURFACE COVERAGE
LONDON	−0.70	0.63	−0.73	−0.46
PARIS	−0.84	0.93	−0.88	−0.51
BERLIN	−0.86	0.90	−0.90	−0.49
ISTANBUL	−0.65	0.70	−0.86	−0.16
ALL SAMPLES	−0.75	0.79	−0.86	−0.35

Table 9.1-b
Correlations by city
between the main
typological parameters
and heat energy demand.
Source: LSE Cities and
EIFER research

urban tissues as well as the inferential masking of sounds induced by the context in which the sound is perceived. In this case, the masking is enhanced by the visibility of green space.

On the basis that buildings can mask noise physically and the visibility of green space can mask noise by modifying our perception of it, the aim of the research was to assess the effects of urban morphological parameters on birdsong loudness and the visibility of green areas in low-density residential areas.

In broad terms, the research involved selecting different types of urban tissue to assess, modelling the spatial distribution of birdsong using noise mapping software, calculating visibility using Depthmap and correlating the results of both with various morphological parameters.

The parameters chosen included:

- Ground Space Index (total building footprint/ total area)
- Complete Aspect Ratio (exposed ground+wall+roof/total area)
- Building Surface Area Ratio (wall+roof/total area)
- Building Frontage Index (length of frontage onto green space/total building footprint)
- Building Frontage Distance (mean distance of frontage to green space)
- Green Area Perimeter (sum of green space perimeters)
- Green Area Dispersion (variance of the distances between the centre of the study area and each vertex of green areas divided by the mean value of the linear distances)

The results show that in low-density residential development the geometry of green areas has the largest influence on birdsong propagation. The loudness increases with both perimeter and dispersion and, interestingly, with building coverage. In quiet areas, higher ratios of building footprint to total study area are correlated with greater birdsong propagation due to the fact the buildings reflect sound and so increase the loudness. With regard to visibility, in areas close to open spaces, loudness increases with visibility but, further from the green spaces, loudness decreases with visibility.

In terms of environmental quality, other research has shown that both birdsong and visibility of green space help to mask the perception of traffic noise. The result that, in some circumstances, birdsong loudness increases where visibility of green space is lower, suggests that the birdsong and visibility of green space can work together in a complementary way to achieve a more natural and pleasant soundscape overall.

FLOOR SPACE ACCESS

Movement is fundamental to the functioning and success of retail environments. Various methods of network analysis have been used to investigate how different configurations affect the success and vitality of retail activity. An extension of those methods developed by Pete Ferguson at the Centre for Advanced Spatial Analysis at University College London works on the continuity of the three basic types of void in built form. Rather than looking at just the street spaces, the method increases the level of resolution of the analysis, extending the network to include internal spaces. This is in effect to use the Nolli section, taking the building footprint as a proxy for the internal ground floor space.

Figure 9.8-a shows the structure of such a network for an area of central London. Every building is connected to its adjacent street at the access point to form a continuous network across the boundary between street space and building spaces. The aim of the analysis is to generate information about the cost of travelling from any building to any other through the street network and so determine the relative advantage each site holds for accessing the rest of the urban environment. As with street-based network analyses, a wide range of measures can be used to calculate the cost and benefit of undertaking a journey, such as the metric distance, route continuity or simplicity, as well as estimated time cost or environmental conditions.

In the area of central London investigated, the costs lie principally in the physical characteristics of the route network. Two appropriate measures in this case are therefore closeness centrality (integration) and betweenness centrality (choice). Figure 9.8-b and figure 9.8-c show the results respectively of using these two measures of building level accessibility for the study area.

The figures use a heat map gradient to visualise the variation in the accessibility of buildings to each other through the street network. The most accessible buildings are in the red range through to blue for the least accessible. In terms of closeness (figure 9.8-b), the West End and Soho are highlighted as the most inter-accessible parts of inner London

with the urban 'village' centres of Mayfair and Marylebone also identified. 9.8-c represents the relative likelihood of each building being passed while travelling on the shortest path between any origin or destination, which can be thought of as a measure of 'passing trade' potential. This property highlights a very different pattern of relative advantage with Oxford Street, Bond Street and Tottenham Court Road containing many buildings that benefit greatly from this property. These images highlight the strong influence of the physical configuration of the built environment on the potential any building has to access different resources and under what conditions.

Calculating and overlaying a number of these properties for an individual location can help build an accessibility profile for each site. Some buildings emerge as less inter-accessible but are subject to higher levels of passing trade, some have an inverse set of benefits, some are accessible in both respects and some in neither. Comparisons with the location decisions of retailers show how commercial activities more dependent on selling a large number of inexpensive products are attracted to less accessible, but more frequently passed sites where a high level of passing trade can be enjoyed for comparatively less expensive rents while, at the other end of the spectrum, high-end boutiques selling a small number of expensive comparison items are found in accessible but less frequently passed sites.

Figure 9.8-a
Plan of the study area
showing the connections
between the street space
and internal space

Figure 9.8-b
Plan using the heat map
convention to represent
closeness centrality (or
integration). The red end
of the spectrum indicates
spaces that are the most
inter-accessible.

Figure 9.8-c
Plan representing the
betweenness centrality
(or choice) of floor space
in the study area, the
red indicating locations
that are most likely to be
passed because they are
on the highest number of
shortest routes

HISTORICAL SIGNIFICANCE AND UNDERSTANDING: URBAN CHARACTERISATION OF CENTRAL HEREFORD

A common application of urban morphological methods in the United Kingdom is an urban characterisation study. Usually commissioned by the local authority and carried out either by archaeologists, landscape architects, urban designers or conservation professionals, the general purpose of the studies is to provide an evidence base to inform planning policy, development control decisions, conservation initiatives, townscape management and improvement or regeneration schemes. In many cases, the underlying theme and concern is the historical structure and fabric of the settlement. Working from a detailed morphological description, the studies provide a basis for assessing the distinct patterns and elements that constitute the place and their significance as heritage assets, among other values.

An excellent example is the urban characterisation study of Hereford carried out by archaeologist Nigel Baker for the County of Herefordshire and English Heritage. As stated in the introduction, the purpose of the study is to:

examine the townscape of central Hereford from an archaeological perspective, in order to determine what its historical components are, their state of preservation and their significance – both from the point of view of their historical importance and for their contribution to local distinctiveness and sense of place.[18]

The study examines the aspects of environment, built form, land use and development, which are combined and summarised in the identification of Townscape Character Areas. In terms of specific methods, the study makes use of Lidar to generate an image of the underlying topography, which aided in identifying earthworks from earlier stages in the development of the settlement. Similarly, the earlier street and plot patterns were inferred from the 1888 Ordnance Survey maps working on the principle of persistence and differential rates of change between street, plot and building patterns. The working assumption is that a high proportion of the original medieval street and plot boundaries will have persisted through the pre-industrial period.

Analysis of the patterns along with archaeological and archival evidence helps to identify a sequence for the stages in the development of the city, from the initial

Figure 9.9-a
Plan analysis drawing of the historic centre of Hereford, UK showing the plot boundaries, street lines and main buildings from the 1888 Ordnance Survey plan and likely to have persisted as originally laid out. The distinct street and plot pattern of the area north of the pre-Conquest defences and its position outside the defences supports the inference that it is a significant early extension to the settlement.

Figure 9.9-b
Detailed plan analysis drawing of central Hereford, outlining the plan units that reflect the smaller-scale process of development

Figure 9.9-c
The Townscape Character Areas of Hereford as of 2010. The areas represent distinct combinations of street and plot pattern, building type and land use. The broad division between the Commercial and Cathedral cities is expressed in all three aspects with finer distinctions drawn between the sub-areas.

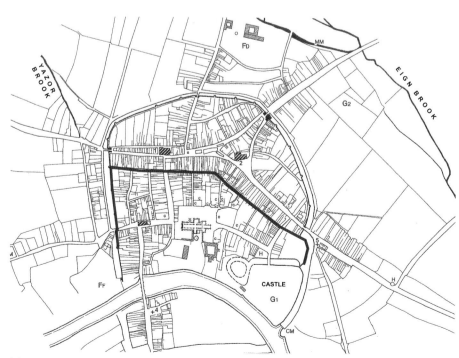

(a)

morphological frame through distinct episodes of planned and piecemeal growth. Detailed interpretation of the street and plot pattern helps to clarify uncertainties and fill gaps in other sources of historical information and build up a more detailed and comprehensive picture of the historical structure of the city. The result is a pattern of historical plan units which were then combined with surveys of the standing building types (including height and age) and current land use to identify the Townscape Character Areas.

The Townscape Character Areas become the tangible tools for both understanding and working with the fabric of the city. For each area, the study sets out a character description, a statement of its distinctiveness and historical significance, as well as the opportunities each area presents for the future. The interpretation of the morphological analysis thus becomes the foundation for further action, from targeted archaeological investigations to informed conservation, public realm improvements, regeneration and new development. For Hereford in particular, the study shows that the city is exceptional for the high degree of continuity in the street and plot patterns, the clear distinction between the Cathedral and Commercial cities and the integrity of the Cathedral Close as a sacred space.

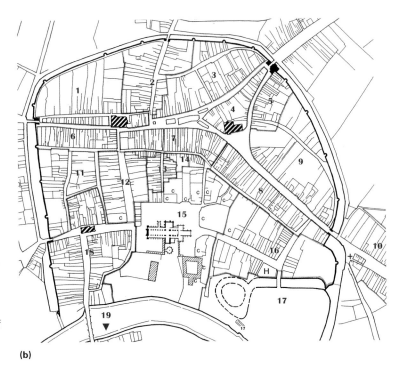

(b)

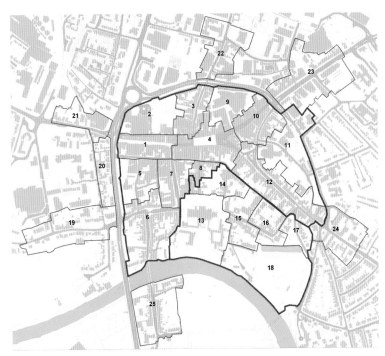

(c)

SOCIAL AND CULTURAL INVESTIGATION: AHMEDABAD

As set out in Section 1, a fundamental principle of urban morphology is that built form is the product of a socio-cultural process or, more accurately, a combination of interacting processes. In this respect, urban morphology can be seen as a supporting, service discipline to anthropology, archaeology and cultural geography. As practised in those fields, the clear connection between form and process allows inferences to be made about social and cultural groups from their material traces and productions. The detail and nuance that urban morphological analysis helps to reveal provides an equivalently detailed and nuanced capacity to interrogate the processes and activities that generate and make use of the physical forms. In particular, the minimum elements of surface, boundary, structure and opening make it possible to progressively build up a picture of distinct assemblages of structured spaces, how they fit together and how they are used.

Acknowledging that any analytical method is itself culturally rooted and not 'universal', urban morphology can be used as a tool in the allied fields for a range of specific purposes including:

- Understanding cultural structure, values and practice
- Recording cultural diversity
- Comparative studies
- Undertaking cultural critique

A study that helps to illustrate this kind of application of urban morphology is an analysis of the urban structure and tissues of Ahmedabad, India.[19] The analysis of the Aka-Sheth-Kuwa-Ni-Pol, undertaken by Nicola Scardigno and Marco Maretto, helps to elucidate the concept and workings of the Pol, a distinct type of social unit and urban tissue within the historical centre of the city. Taking a two-way view, the study focuses on the interrelated structure of routes and poles within the tissue on the one hand, and the configuration and evolution of the local building types on the other. The combined view helps to clarify the interrelations between configurational constraints and the logic of socio-cultural practice operating at the two levels as well as identified intermediate assemblages.

The socio-cultural dimension has been a significant component of the work of French architects and urban morphologists such as Roncayolo, Castex and Panerai.[20] The seminal

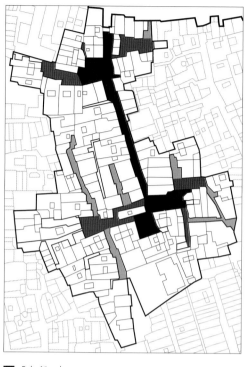

Figure 9.10-a
Plan of the Aka-Sheth-Kuwa-Ni-Pol highlighting the hierarchy of routes within the Pol

- ▮ Pol - 1st order
- ▨ Sheri - 2nd order
- ▨ Khadki - 3rd order

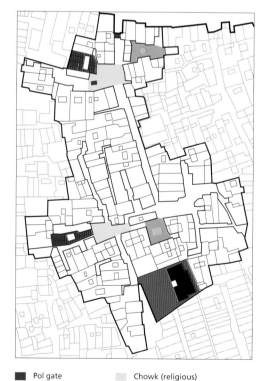

Figure 9.10-b
Plan identifying the poles or focal points within the Aka-Sheth-Kuwa-Ni-Pol. Together the route structure and poles illustrate the general framework that has emerged out of and continues to structure interaction between the social group and built form.

- ▨ Pol gate
- ▨ Chowk (domestic)
- ▨ Public well
- ▨ School
- ▨ Chowk (religious)
- ▮ Hindu temple
- ▨ Mahalla Mata

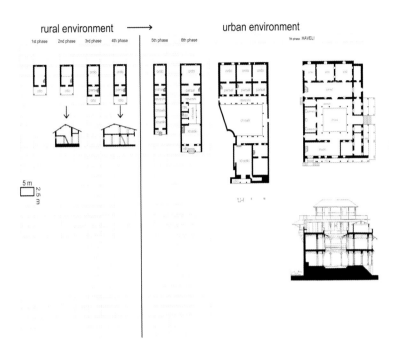

rural environment ⟶   urban environment

Figure 9.10-c
Projection of the
evolution of the building
type characteristic of
Ahmedabad and the
surrounding region. Based
on a range of sources,
the projected evolution
gives an understanding
of the development of
the Pol by providing a
basis for interpreting the
transformations it
has undergone.

study *De l'Îlot à la Barre* is one of the most notable examples, extending the morphological investigation into a social critique.

Similar but not specifically morphological approaches to the socio-cultural interpretation and critique of built form and the 'ordinary landscape' include the work of geographers such as Michael Conzen, JB Jackson and Paul Groth, among others.[21]

A further potential application is in the recording of ethno-diversity as expressed through built form, particularly in the face of large-scale redevelopment in many countries.

URBAN CHARACTER AND NEIGHBOURHOODS: BRIGHTON AND HOVE URBAN CHARACTERISATION STUDY

Within the discretionary planning system in the United Kingdom, the physical form of proposed development is not directly controlled as it can be through the *règlements* and ordinances of zoning systems such as in France or the United States. The latter can regulate such features as plot size, plot coverage, building position and height. Over the past twenty years in the UK, efforts have been made to develop tools that do provide a greater degree of control over form within the discretionary system. The efforts have been made in response to a number of factors including a perceived loss of local distinctiveness because of homogeneous new development. One of the ways in which this

concern has been addressed is through the use of characterisation studies.

An example is the *Brighton and Hove Urban Characterisation Study* by Eline Hansen and Gill Thompson for Brighton & Hove City Council.[22] The range of issues the study seeks to address include heritage protection, urban regeneration, local distinctiveness and sustainable development.

The aim of the study is to provide a clear understanding of the city's urban character and the pressures it faces through an analysis of the city's physical and neighbourhood structure. The purpose of the study is to:

> help guide decisions about the location,
> form and type of future development, and
> more particularly inform the Core Strategy
> component of the City Council's Local
> Development Framework.

The study combines Landscape Character Assessment (see Swanwick[23]) with urban analysis to differentiate areas at a range of scales. It starts with the identification of landscape character areas and within them neighbourhoods defined on the basis of residents' perceptions of how they use the parts of the town in which they live, among other factors. A further step is to combine physical and social aspects by correlating census data with each of the physical areas. As stated in the study,

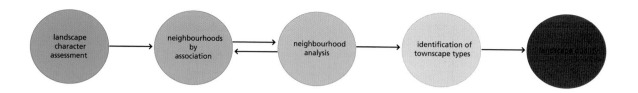

above **Figure 9.11
Diagram of the Brighton
and Hove study
methodology. The
urban characterisation
is an element within
a wider landscape
study combined with
the complementary
identification of
neighbourhoods as
perceived by residents
based on their association
with particular areas.**

*to obtain an understanding of relationships
between topography, settlement patterns
and developments in human activity each
neighbourhood has been analysed against the
following criteria*

- *Historic influences*
- *Settlement typology*
- *Topography and microclimate*
- *Land use*
- *Scale and density*
- *Architecture*
- *Socio-economic characteristics*
- *Movement*
- *Open space*

The study is thus an example of applying the idea
of the composite view, combining different kinds
of information in order to provide greater insights
into the kinds of interventions that might be most
appropriate to deal with the physical characteristics
of the place and its social and cultural issues. In this
context, urban tissue provides a common physical
frame of reference for dealing with different
aspects in different areas.

MEASURES AND QUALITATIVE EVALUATION: MORPHO

One of the main attractions of urban morphology
in the design fields is its capacity to assist in the
evaluation of places and prospective proposals
either comparatively or against identified standards
or benchmarks. A widening range of measures
is being developed to assess the environmental
performance of different types of built form.
Another example is the 'Morpho' method
developed by Vítor Oliviera from the University
of Porto.[24] Focusing on the principle of **urbanity**,
the method is fundamentally composite and, like
Osmond's work,[25] seeks to integrate methods from
the different approaches to urban morphology.

The aspects that are brought together to
assess (and by inference, to define) the degree of
urbanity include seven key measures:

- Accessibility of the street network
  (connectivity, global integration and
  local integration)
- Plot density (plots per street block)
- Building age
- Street block dimensions (area)

above left **Figure 9.12
The neighbourhoods of
Brighton and Hove as
identified by residents'
perceived associations.
The shape and size of the
neighbourhoods relate
to a number of factors in
addition to associations
including topography,
roads and urban tissue.**

7 hanover & elm grove neighbourhood

open space

character areas

(a)

Figure 9.13-a
Open space and character
diagrams from the
Brighton and Hove
Urban Characterisation

Study. In some cases
the neighbourhoods
correspond with a single
urban tissue, in others it
is a mix of several tissues.

Figure 9.13-b
Land use and movement
diagrams from the
Brighton and Hove Urban
Characterisation Study.
The composite view

generated by combining
the information from the
different plans gives a rich
correlated image of the
elements that make up
the neighbourhood.

7 hanover & elm grove neighbourhood

key characteristics

land use

movement

(b)

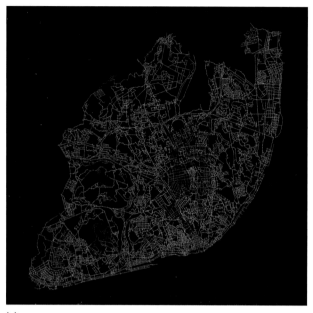

(a)

(b)

- Building alignment (dominant common orientation)
- Building height to street width ratio
- Land use (degree of residential to non-residential mix)

The rationale in selecting these measures is to balance the focus on objects and relationships. Three of the seven capture a fundamental characteristic of each of the three elements individually: streets, plots and buildings; three capture a crucial relation between pairs of elements and one captures the link between form and function.

The assessment process involves three main steps:

- Identify the aims and objectives of the assessment process, the data available and the suitability of the measures and techniques
- Undertake the assessment
- Evaluate the seven measures using tables and maps to identify the different degrees of urbanity in different parts of the territory

The differentiation provides both an evidence base and a set of indicators for making policy and design decisions to reinforce, increase or decrease degrees of urbanity depending on the overall objectives of the plan.

Morpho and the other applications of morphological measures underline the importance of the 'fact-value' distinction in urban morphology. If there is a legitimate claim for urban morphology to be a tool for *objective* research, the basic concepts and principles applied cannot be fundamentally *normative*. That is not to say urban morphology cannot be used to support normative aims. In that light, there are in principle two basic approaches that can be taken in developing measures to assist in design. One is to establish an *inherently* normative measure such as 'liveability' that may itself be a composite of other measures. The other approach is to take a 'neutral' measure such as height, density or centrality and identify the preferred values (or range of values) that correspond to a particular design objective.

To a large extent, the distinction lies in the way the measures are used. Even a normative measure can be used as a comparative indicator without saying a particular value is 'good' or 'bad'. The preferred value may depend on the specific context and circumstances.

Figure 9.14-a
Global integration map (closeness centrality) of Lisbon, indicating the accessibility across the whole study area – red to blue: higher to lower accessibility

Figure 9.14-b
Local integration map of Lisbon, representing accessibility within local areas

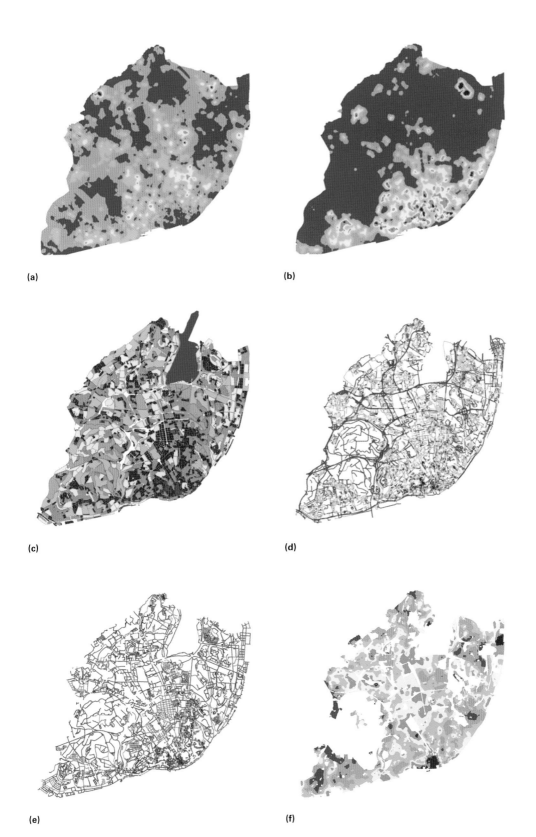

(a)

(b)

(c)

(d)

(e)

(f)

Figure 9.15-a
Heat map showing the density of plots in Lisbon in terms of the number of plots per unit area, denser areas in red

Figure 9.15-b
Plan showing the distribution of building age in Lisbon with concentrations of older buildings indicated on the red end of the scale and younger on the blue end

Figure 9.15-c
Map of street block size in Lisbon with areas of smaller blocks in red to orange, larger blocks in green to blue

Figure 9.15-d
Analysis of building alignments in Lisbon. Areas in red indicate common alignments or consistent 'building lines' and areas on the blue end indicate mixed alignments.

Figure 9.15-e
Enclosure ratio of streets in Lisbon, being the ratio of frontage height to front-to-front width. The red end of the spectrum indicates higher ratios and the blue end lower.

Figure 9.15-f
Heat map indicating the degree of mixing of land uses. The red end indicates areas of greater mix and the blue end single use zones.

URBAN STRUCTURE AND DEVELOPMENT PLANS: THE ANATOMY OF SPRAWL

A seminal article exploring the potential for more active application of urban morphology in planning is Brenda Case Scheer's *The Anatomy of Sprawl*.[26] The central argument is, first, that planners need a working knowledge of the 'body' they are seeking to treat in the same way that physicians need a working knowledge of human anatomy. In this respect, the urban morphologist is the anatomist of urban form. Secondly, Scheer argues that there are two fundamental regularities of urban form revealed by urban morphological analysis that open out a space for planning practice that has remained obscure to planners.

Crucially, Scheer emphasises the importance of not just the static internal structure of urban form, but also its dynamics. Specifically, the first regularity she highlights is the differential rates of change between elements at different levels in the hierarchy of generic structure: street patterns change more slowly than plot patterns, which change more slowly than the pattern of buildings. Reinforcing the argument by noting that similar principles of hierarchy, scale and differential rates of change are used in ecology, Scheer makes a finer distinction between the elements of urban form that change at different rates.

From the slowest to the most rapid, the elements are:

- Site (topography, hydrology)
- Superstructure (initial morphological frame of streets and parcels)
- Infill (subsequent additions of streets and plots to the frame)
- Buildings
- Objects (vegetation, materials and structures)

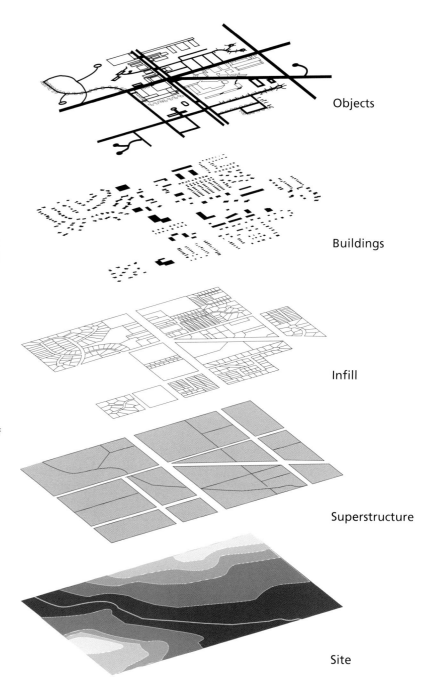

Objects

Buildings

Infill

Superstructure

Site

above **Figure 9.16 Diagram illustrating the separation of elements in terms of differential rates of change. The superstructure and infill layers combine both routes and plots (separate** elements in the hierarchy of generic structure) but are separated because the older routes and plot boundaries tend to change less frequently than the later infill.

opposite **Figure 9.17 Plan sequence showing the growth of Hudson, Ohio. The sequence, together with the layered element separation in** Figure 9.16, illustrates what Scheer calls the spatio-temporal model of urban form.

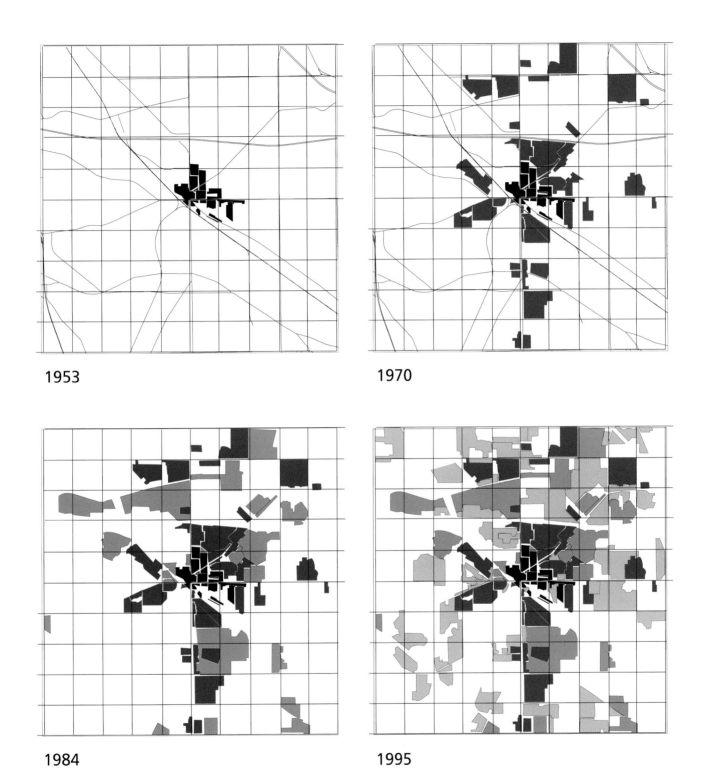

1953

1970

1984

1995

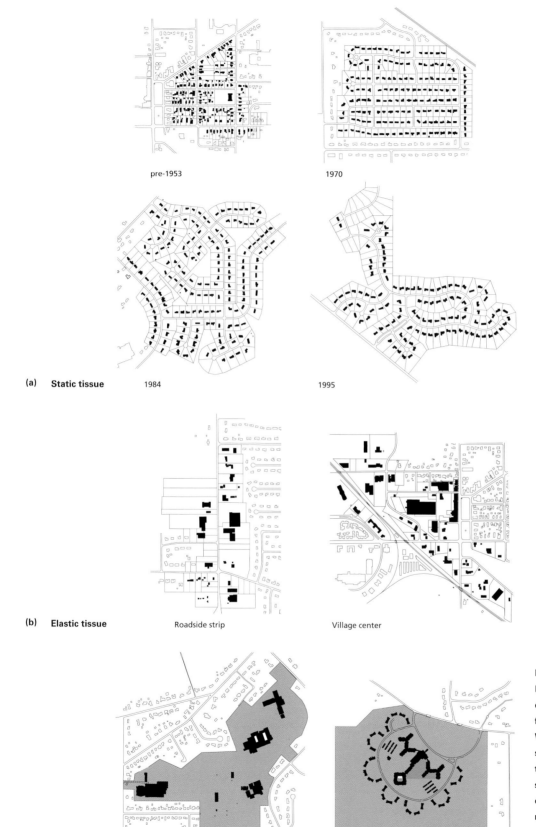

(a) **Static tissue**

pre-1953

1970

1984

1995

(b) **Elastic tissue**

Roadside strip

Village center

(c) **Campus tissue**

School complex

Apartment complex

Figure 9.18-a to -c
Examples of static,
campus and elastic tissue
from Hudson, Ohio.
Within the context of the
spatio-temporal model,
these examples represent
spatio-temporal types
of tissue. It is also worth
noting that fringe features
are commonly made up
of the faster-changing
campus and elastic tissue.

The second regularity identified by Scheer is that different general types of urban tissue show different degrees of resistance to change depending on the specific patterns of elements. This leads to Scheer's identification within the context of North American suburban development of three general types of urban tissue, which she terms static, campus and elastic.

Static tissue tends to be relatively uniform with small plots and a high density of routes. The plots and routes are generally designed to accommodate a specific range of building types. These characteristics contribute to the general stability of the tissue and its tendency to change relatively slowly.

Campus tissue is composed of a range of isolated buildings with a low density of routes within a single large plot, usually under the control of a single owner or occupant. Campus tissue tends to change more rapidly than static tissue.

Elastic tissue is generally a heterogeneous mix of plot and building types and sizes with a low density of routes. The heterogeneity and sparse routes allow for more rapid change.

The concluding point is that these dynamic regularities are in effect currents in the 'flow' of urban form. If we are ignorant of them, we will be carried where they take us. If we can plot them we might then be able to either let them run as they will or seek to channel and direct them – or change them at their source. One way or the other, to get that level of control requires a thorough understanding of both the depth of structural detail and long-term patterns provided by urban morphological analysis.

Figure 9.19
The distribution of static, campus and elastic tissue in Hudson, Ohio. As general indicators of likely rates of change, the spatio-temporal tissues together represent in two dimensions a four-dimensional surface on which planning decisions are made.

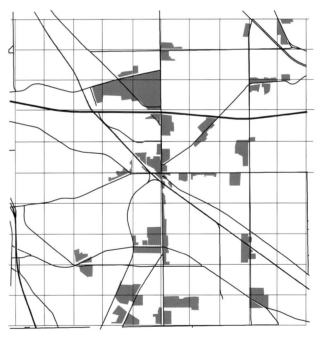

campus tissues

elastic tissues

static tissues

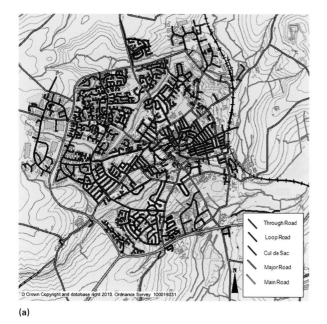

(a)

(b)

ROUTE STRUCTURE AND DEVELOPMENT PLANS: NORTH NORTHAMPTONSHIRE URBAN STRUCTURE STUDY

Within the planning system in the United Kingdom, local authorities are required to produce development plans to guide future development. The plans need to identify specific development sites and set out policies to assess the proposals that are put forward by landowners and developers for those and any other sites.

The process of identifying sites involves the collection of an evidence base of relevant data and the analysis of the evidence to inform the selection of sites and establish key principles of development and associated supporting infrastructure.

The North Northamptonshire Joint Planning Unit, which is a local partnership between a number of adjacent local authorities, has been tasked with preparing a joint development plan for the participating authorities. A key component of their evidence base is the Urban Structure Study looking in detail at the towns in Northamptonshire.[27]

The aim of the study is to:

understand the urban structure of the towns in North Northamptonshire, the framework of existing streets and open spaces, and how they function together. This will be used to inform policy development for the revised Core Spatial Strategy [Development Plan].

A central, underlying principle of the study is stated at the outset:

Movement, land use and character are woven together in each settlement. And therefore to achieve thriving towns that are economically and socially sustainable, we need to understand the role of the urban structure in promoting or inhibiting movement.

The structure of the study includes four main steps: undertake a theoretical review of best practice; identify the spatial principles of individual settlements; explore and select general development principles; apply principles to individual settlements.

Specific tasks in the second step are set out below, broadly following the methods set out in Section 2:

- Review historic maps of the town
- Create a series of walking and cycling isochrones for the town centre
- Undertake a route structure analysis
- Identify areas of different urban tissue or morphological character
- Create a movement map – axial line analysis
- Identify existing open spaces and green infrastructure
- Locate key facilities (schools, shops and services)

The results of the route structure and tissue analysis are shown in figures 9.20-a to -c.

These are then translated into a summary movement plan for the town (figure 9.20-c),

Figure 9.20-a
Route structure of Wellingborough, Northamptonshire. The method of analysis used is a modified version of that set out in Section 2. The aim of the analysis in this case is to provide a picture of the role of route types and patterns in the overall structure of the settlement in order to inform planning policy.

Figure 9.20-b
Character areas of Wellingborough based primarily on route types. The combination of route structure and character areas reinforces the importance of routes and movement to the structure of the settlement and how it works.

which in turn is translated into draft policies in the Development Plan. Importantly, the summary plan highlights the association between routes and green spaces. A further step is to use the summary plans and principles as part of more detailed policies on design and Place Shaping as well as Town Transport Strategies, which will follow on from the Development Plan.

The draft policy document notes that the results of the study show 'that many town centres are not as accessible as they could be, being disconnected from their immediate residential areas, transport interchanges or local open spaces'. In response, the relevant policy requires that proposed development should: connect the maximum number of local streets; integrate with the existing movement network; improve or create green spaces that tie in with the wider network of green spaces and routes; provide direct routes to local facilities.

ZONING PLANS AND REGULATIONS: RENNES AND PORTO

The urban morphological conception of urban tissue is being actively put to use within zoning systems of planning and development control as part of a move toward form-based rather than use-based zoning. The aim of the move is to increase the sensitivity of zoning systems to the nuances of a wider range of both specific urban forms and activities on the one hand, and increase the level of control in areas of particular historical or cultural significance on the other. Essentially, urban tissue provides an alternative means of defining zones and composing the regulations or ordinances that apply to them (see Kropf for more detail[28]). This approach takes advantage of the fact that at the abstract level, zoning systems are agnostic with respect to both use and form. The three basic elements of a zoning system are:

• A set of defined areas (zones) to which different rules, ordinances or regulations apply
• The specific rules, ordinances or regulations that apply to each zone
• A procedure for administering assessment and determination of proposals

In principle, the rules for a zone might include any number of options and need not be defined primarily in terms of use – as they have been historically.

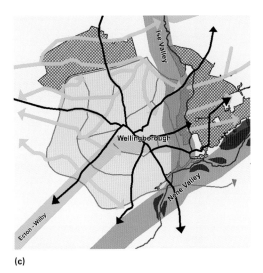

(c)

Figure 9.20-c
Policy diagram for Wellingborough derived from the analysis of the settlement in combination with agreed general principles. The diagram illustrates how policies for elements such as green corridors build directly on the understanding gained from the analysis of route structure and character areas.

below **Figure 9.21 Generalised morphological zoning plan forming part of the *Plan local d'urbanisme* (PLU) for the city of Rennes, in France. The colouring of the zones helps to accentuate the** process of development of the city, for example with the darker central historic core and radial avenues and pericentric routes – the result of transformation – just outside.

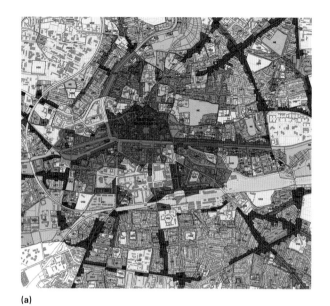

(a)

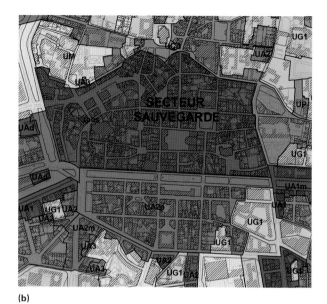

(b)

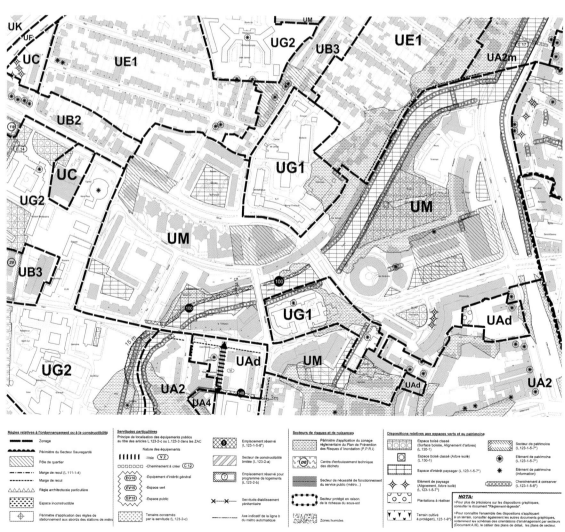

(d)

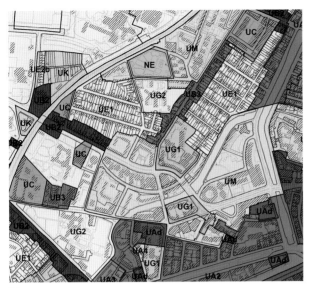

(c)

Figure 9.22-a
Detail of the zoning plan focusing on the centre. Note the redevelopment sites around the historic core (zones UG1 and UM), which constitute an inner fringe belt.

Figure 9.22-b
Detail of the zoning plan showing the relatively homogeneous historic core, treated as a conservation area (*secteur sauvegardé*).

Figure 9.22-c
Detail of the zoning plan illustrating the more heterogeneous inner fringe area. Some degree of grouping or lumping of areas would be possible to reduce the apparent sense of fragmentation.

Figure 9.22-d
Technical version of the zoning plan for the Rennes PLU, which includes various symbols representing different elements of the *règlement* (zoning regulations or ordinances) controlling such things as building height and set-back.

Morphological approaches to zoning plans have been developing over the last thirty years and two of the more mature examples illustrated here are the *Plan local d'urbanisme* for the city of Rennes in Brittany, France,[29] and the *Plano Diretor Municipal* for Porto in Portugal.[30] A fundamental principle underlying the morphological approach is that not only are the zones form-based, they are based on the existing urban tissue that constitutes the city. The aim is to maintain both the overall structure of the city in terms of the distinct pattern of different tissues making up the built area as a whole, and the character and identity of the individual tissues.

The process of formulating the plan involves three main steps:

- Undertake a morphological analysis to identify the distinct tissues making up the overall area to be zoned
- Select out the key characteristics that define the tissues – both form and use
- Define zone boundaries and transcribe the key characteristics into regulations that fit within the given legal framework, adding any further regulations as appropriate

In principle a zone based on an existing tissue can be used in three main ways:

- To maintain the character of the tissue
- To allow transformations of the tissue, within certain limits, with forms that are suited to the particular elements the make up the tissue
- To extend the tissue, as a type, into different areas

In the latter case, zones based on existing tissues can be used for:

- The directed transformation of similar tissues
- Redevelopment of different types
- Greenfield development

Because of the variation possible in the choice of regulations to be applied, the extension of a zone based on an existing tissue can allow for the evolution of elements within the tissue in order to respond to new and emerging needs while still maintaining valued characteristics. For example, an extended zone might only include regulations based on the existing street and plot pattern but allow for new building types.

URBANIZED LAND

▨ HISTORICAL CENTRE

▨ CONSOLIDATED CONTINUOUS URBAN FRONTAGE

▨ CONSOLIDATING CONTINUOUS URBAN FRONTAGE

▨ DETACHED HOUSING

   DETACHED MULTI-FAMILY HOUSING

▨ ACTION AREA

▨ BUSINESS PARK

▨ EXISTING PUBLIC FACILITIES AND INSTITUTIONS

▨ PROPOSED PUBLIC FACILITIES AND INSTITUTIONS

▨ TRANSPORT AND MOVEMENT INFRASTRUCTURE

GREEN INFRASTRUCTURE

▨ EXISTING PUBLIC FACILITIES INTEGRATED WITH GREEN INFRASTRUCTURE

▨ PROPOSED PUBLIC FACILITIES INTEGRATED WITH GREEN INFRASTRUCTURE

▨ PUBLIC GREEN SPACE

▨ MIXED GREEN SPACE

▨ PROTECTED PRIVATE GREEN SPACE

▨ GREEN CORRIDORS

▨ PROTECTION OF NATURAL RESOURCES

above **Figure 9.23
Overall plan for the *Plano Diretor Municipal* (PDM), technically, the *Carta de Qualificação do Solo* – the land-use plan – for the city of Porto, Portugal. Despite the name of the plan, the zones are defined primarily in terms of physical form.**

opposite **Figure 9.24-a
Detail of the Porto PDM plan. Note the zones tend to correspond to either simple or complex tissue. The red zone indicates an area for redevelopment, which follows the general arrangement for a simple tissue.**

opposite **Figure 9.24-b
Detail of the Porto PDM again highlighting the use of the simple tissue as the basic unit for zones**

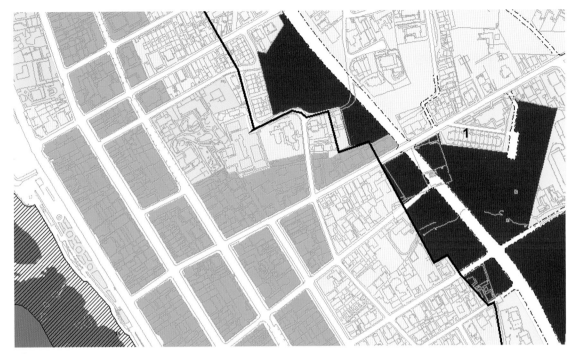

(a)

(b)

On the basis that the specific regulations applied within a given zone are always a matter of choice and not strictly fixed either by use or pre-existing form, a zoning system can allow for significant degrees of flexibility and variation while still controlling key characteristics.

The hierarchy of generic types of form and the distinction of position, outline and internal structure provide a consistent framework within which the range of variation can be systematically focused and controlled. The level of specificity of the regulations might be set quite high, for example for conservation purposes, controlling a wide range of characteristics, from street pattern to materials. Alternatively, the specificity could be left low, for example fixing only the building line and building height to maintain some continuity while allowing for flexibility and responsiveness to economic conditions.

TISSUE STUDIES: APPRAISAL, COLLABORATION AND EDUCATION

The basic principle of a 'tissue study' is to use existing urban tissues to explore the potential of a development site. Specific applications include site appraisals for development, collaborative and participatory design, inter-professional design development, negotiation and urban design education.

The methods set out here are compiled from those developed by Hayward, Kendall and Habraken.[31]

BASIC TECHNIQUE
Start with a base map of the site proposed for development at a scale of between 1:5000 and 1:200 (1:1000 or 1:1250 are ideal) and a range of sample tissues reproduced at the same scale as the base map. Samples should be large enough to fill the site or be copied and connected to extend the sample. Use copies of paper plans with scissors and glue or image files on a computer. It is also helpful to have larger-scale drawings of the component building types (1:100 or 1:50).

- All example tissues should have a clearly defined purpose or use
- Include examples from the locality
- As many as possible should be familiar to the participants
- Include one or more 'inappropriate' types to stimulate debate and question assumptions, particularly in educational settings

- Look beyond simple footprint – investigate/ interrogate relationships, dimensions and relationships between both similar and different types
- Dig into the forms to understand the underlying reasons for the dimensions and relationships – their potential and their limitations as a possible design solution for current practice, habits and activities
- Find out about and seek to understand the 'prejudices' and ideological content of tissues and their social and cultural roots

Round 1: Initial test Overlay a tissue on the plan of the site, without modifying the tissue and adjusting its position, trying as far as possible to make connections to existing access points and follow the logic of adjacencies. Once a position is agreed, the tissue is stuck down and the consequences of the 'intervention' are explored.

Round 2: Adjustment With a fresh site plan, overlay another copy of the tissue, this time allowing some minor modification or 'disaggregation' and rearrangement to fit the tissue into the site, while still preserving the internal structure, logic and dimensions of the tissue (for example, maintaining block and plot dimensions). The adjustment of the tissue should work as far as possible to make the desired connections into and through the site. Again the results are interrogated, looking at a range of issues involved in balancing local structure and the structure of the tissue.

Round 3: Inflection Again with a fresh site plan, the tissue is applied and, by cutting and/or redrawing, the tissue is transformed internally as necessary to fully fit and satisfy the aspirations for the site. In general this tends to involve modification of the plot pattern, which might be truncated, extended, stretched or skewed as well as allowing for a mix of types with individual elements substituted to achieve a specific aim. The aim at this stage is to end up with a fully resolved design without any gaps.

As shown in figure 9.25, the tissue study can be extended by using simple scaled block models to build up the third dimension of the tissue.

Figure 9.25
Image from a community workshop using the tissue study technique to explore different possible forms of development. Here the basic paper method is extended using simple wooden block models of houses to the appropriate scale.

APPRAISAL AND DESIGN

In site appraisals, tissues provide a means to quickly evaluate the potential of a site with a clear and realistic sense of the potential character of the development and its qualities as a place. A tissue-based appraisal helps establish development value and move from broad intentions to more detailed framework, generating a greater sense of detailed potential than purely numerical assessments – mute quantities such as average density – and taking into account the particularity and richness that contribute to value. Because of the inherent detail of tissue, the results are pragmatic, tangible and 'costable' and can easily be combined with spreadsheet valuation exercises.

An essential part of taking the approach beyond mechanical replication of a fixed pattern is the process of critical questioning or 'interrogation'. Putting a particular tissue in a particular place should prompt detailed investigation of the physical dimensions and relationships of the tissue, its relationship with the surroundings and the implications of these in terms of the tissue's characteristics in use (access, movement, density, capacities, parking, storage, play etc) as well as issues of control, servicing, perception and value.

COLLABORATION AND NEGOTIATION

A tissue-based approach makes design investigation transparent and accessible to non-professionals by using familiar examples. Participants can more clearly focus on achieving the aims and objectives of the design problem through familiarity and a collective interrogation of specific examples and following through the consequences of making specific transformations. The collaborative team can work more objectively because the 'authority' of the tissue as a source for design solutions is based not on the qualifications or 'genius' of any individual present but the fact of the tissue having been built and used.

EDUCATION

Within the educational context, tissues provide a quick and hands-on method of illustrating and teaching basic design principles. In order to get the full educational value from tissue studies, however, interrogation and critical questioning are of the utmost importance. The interrogation stage provides a platform and focus for dialogue, debate and understanding.

MASTERPLANNING AND REGENERATION: VILLA 31, BUENOS AIRES

Urban tissue and morphological principles can be applied in a more systematic way to the task of masterplanning and urban regeneration.

A fascinating example is a design research project undertaken by Marco Maretto et al for the regeneration of Villa 31, an informal settlement in Buenos Aires.[32] The aim of the project was to use urban morphological analysis and principles to first understand the structure, character and logic of the settlement and then suggest a regeneration proposal that retains the positive characteristics of the settlement. The approach is founded on the recognition that the informal settlement contains many successful design solutions that were generated by and meet the needs of the residents themselves, 'uncontaminated' by formal top-down controls.

The project involved the following elements:

- Analysis of the evolution of the principal residential building/plot types and their implications in forming the aggregates of urban tissue
- Analysis of the socio-morphological structure of the settlement in terms of route structure, polarities and tissues
- Development of proposals for regeneration and extension of the area

The study of the building types looks at the evolution of both the formal and informal types. What is striking is the strong cultural roots of the general idea of the house, leading to similarities between them. One expression of this is the fairly consistent shape and size of the plot (10 x 20m), despite the lack of any codified system of ownership or legal title, and a basic courtyard arrangement of buildings.

The key technical issues for Villa 31 at the level of the tissue are the lack of drainage, services and protection of common rights to light and air. The aim, however, was to address these issues within an overall structure that follows and makes use of the generative dynamics that have resulted in the overall socio-morphological structure of the area. The principal elements of the structure are:

- External poles (bus station, railway station and port)
- Primary and secondary through routes (matrix routes)

Figure 9.26
Image of streets in Villa
31, an informal settlement
on the periphery of
Buenos Aires, Argentina

Figure 9.27
Close view of a street
within Villa 31

(b)

- Commercial activity along the primary and secondary routes
- Access routes
- Nodal points of commercial activity at the junctions of Primary and Access routes
- Lanes (created by multiple occupancy of plots)
- Peripheral green spaces

The proposal takes these elements and their mutual relationships as the structural starting point for regeneration and extension. Existing poles and nodes are reinforced as locations for new services and public buildings. The pattern of a Primary route with commercial activity, Access routes with active nodal points and Lanes are used to structure the extension using the module of the typical local plot to dimension and build up the tissue. As set out in the proposal, the process for extending the area would involve setting out the routes and plots but leaving the construction of buildings to the individual.

THE BUILT ENVIRONMENT AS A DESIGN RESOURCE

The built environment is one of our most fundamental and long-standing technologies. As noted by Brian Arthur, successful innovation and the evolution of technology are predominantly achieved not by *de novo* invention but by the creative recombination of existing elements. Most 'pure' inventions fail. Re-purposing or combining

different elements that have been tested by continued use and reproduction is a safer bet than starting from scratch.

Taking this idea forward along with the principles of persistence and embodied types suggests that the most significant source of potential elements for innovation resides within the built environment itself. The built environment is a design resource – a library of mind tools.

One of the keys to finding and 'liberating' embodied types, patterns and associations for creative recombination is **abstraction:** selecting out patterns of relationships that we find in our perception of the built environment and using them as potential solutions – identifying assemblages of practices and components that are a means to fulfil some *current* human purpose.

Abstraction is the interpretation of a perceived example as a principle and is a necessary part of any reproduction, whatever the source of the idea. *Systematic* abstraction and recombination is facilitated by using the urban morphological concepts of:

- The association of aspects and elements
- The multi-level generic structure of built form
- The distinction of position, outline and internal structure as used to define generic and specific types of built form
- The process of formation

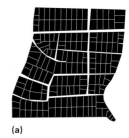

(a)

Figure 9.28-a Diagram of Villa 31 tissue. Note the tissue is complex and forms an articulated grid with plot series of single access plots fronting each side of the street spaces.

Figure 9. 28-b Analysis identifying the route structure, centres or poles and open spaces

(c)

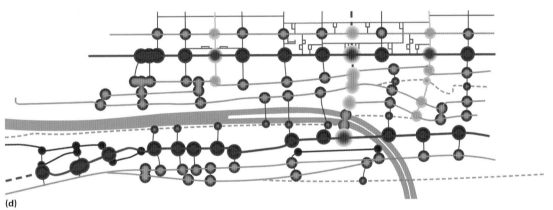

(d)

(e)

Figure 9. 28-c
Diagram of the project for
extending the settlement
using the structures
and configurations of
elements identified in
the analysis

Figure 9. 28-d
Abstracted diagram of
the structure of routes,
nodes and poles of both
the existing and
proposed areas

Figure 9. 28-e
Detail of the illustrative
plan for the projected
extension

These allow a combination of flexibility and precision in identifying specific relationships, configurations or patterns and the context in which they function. In principle, the abstracted patterns and assemblages might come from anywhere and may not necessarily correspond to conventional 'types'. One way or the other, *position* as an attribute is important because the full extent of an assemblage is not always clear. That is, what might be considered the 'context' could in practice be part of the assemblage as a functioning element. Public open spaces such as squares are a good example. An abstracted type defined only in terms of its size, shape and surrounding buildings might not function as expected within a new design because it also needs to be connected to particular types of route in a particular relative position within the settlement as a whole. To work as expected, the square needs to be in the right location in a network.

PLOT-BASED URBANISM

A very good example of using the built environment as a design resource by abstraction is the idea of plot-based urbanism as advocated by Anne Vernez Moudon in *Built for Change*,[33] Sergio Porta and Ombretta Romice in *Plot-Based Urbanism*[34] and Jonathan Tarbatt in *The Plot: Designing Diversity in the Built Environment*.[35] The principle also informed the Borneo Sporenburg Project in Amsterdam by landscape architects and urban designers West 8. In the Borneo example, the site was divided into individual plots with each plot designed by a different architect.

In terms of generic types of form, the central abstracted element is clearly the plot, in particular plots within a particular range of shape and size. Looking at examples, the abstracted 'assemblage' also includes the plot series and simple tissue as part of the generative idea. Implicit within the principle of plot-based urbanism is also the *process* generally referred to in North America as **platting**: the subdivision of land into parcels for sale to individuals who each develop their own plot.

THE CITY OF BATH MORPHOLOGICAL STUDY

The City of Bath Morphological Study[36] uses abstraction as a tool in seeking to balance the aims of maintaining the value of the city as a World Heritage Site and fostering economic growth. To that end, the study identified characteristic patterns, associations and configurations for key tissues in the city. Examples include node and landmark combinations, shared landmarks located on the boundaries between tissues, configurations of different types of plot series, axial compositions and tartan patterns of different types of street. The challenge was to select local patterns that could accommodate the economic realities of the property market, in particular the demand for large floor-plate buildings. The abstracted patterns proved to be a very effective tool for negotiations between the various interested parties.

AD HOC MODIFICATION AS A BASIS FOR DESIGN

A potential criticism of using the built environment as a design resource is that it is 'backward-looking'. As Brian Arthur emphasises in his discussion of recombination,[37] however, all innovation necessarily looks 'backward' for its component parts – the previously developed elements that are recombined to create something new – that works. A further refinement of this principle was articulated by Muratori and Caniggia and Maffei in setting out the typological process.[38] In brief, the innovation involves the small-scale, ad hoc modification of an existing type that becomes the basis for a new design (see figures 8.10 and 8.11). In general, the innumerable modifications are undertaken by individuals or small groups in order to adapt existing forms to new circumstances, needs and activities. In this respect recent modifications can be seen as a body of experimental types, anticipating future trends. Individual everyday acts of adaptation become a pool of creative innovation. Finding those potential new types is a matter of staying observant and being able to clearly articulate the modification as part of an integrated new design.

Finding design solutions in the existing built environment generated at a local level is also the basic principle behind the *Massive Small* initiative[39] with roots also in *A Pattern Language*.[40] What urban morphological concepts such as the typological process emphasise is that the generation of innovation and solutions is an ongoing process that is tied inextricably to the cultures that produce them. Any type has roots in the activities and cultural habits that generate the type. To successfully transplant a type, it is necessary to ensure there is a context that is sufficiently similar to the original for the transplant to succeed. The same principle applies with any borrowing of design ideas, whether new designs or models from the past or different cultures.

Figure 9.29
View of Borneo
Sporenburg,
masterplanned by
West 8, taking a plot-
based approach with
each plot designed by a
different team

The Medieval City

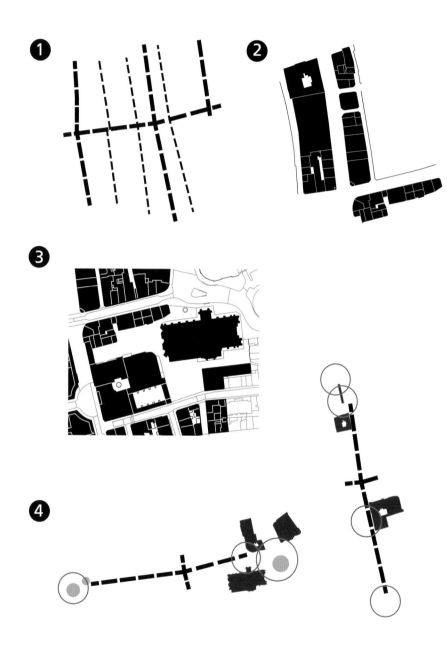

Figure 9.30
Diagrams from the Medieval City section of the City of Bath Morphological Study, identifying patterns, associations and combinations of elements as potential principles for future designs. Ideally the abstracted patterns are not used literally but interpreted and combined with new elements to allow change within a framework of continuity.

Medieval City
Design principles

1 Tartan grid with main streets and back lanes
2 Long, rectangular solid blocks with small, double-fronted plots and small, square blocks
3 Landmark buildings set in public open space
4 Axial composition with node at each end
5 Cross roads emphasised by nodes at the ends and at intermediate points
6 Shared landmark/node at edge of tissue
7 View of landmark/node in adjacent tissue
8 Well connected, secluded space
9 Street running along the line of the historical wall
10 Selected restriction of vehicular movement but through grid for pedestrians

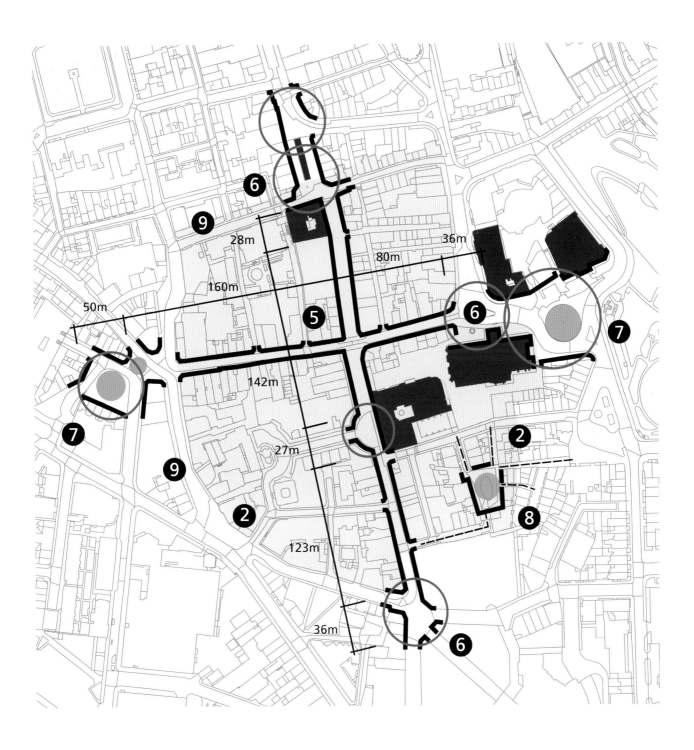

Kingsmead

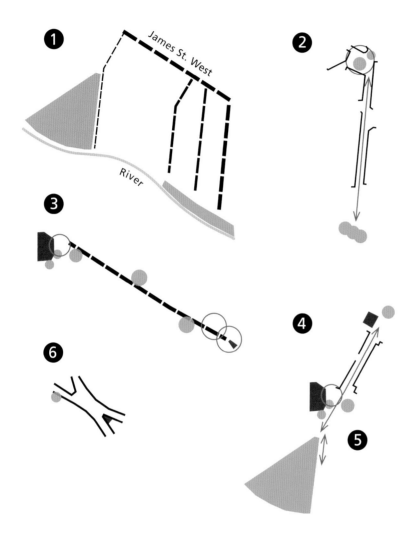

**Figure 9.31
Diagrams for the
Kingsmead section
of the City of Bath
Morphological Study.
The patterns and
configurations were
used in the context of
a workshop to explore
how to accommodate
current building types
such as large floor-plate
office buildings while
maintaining a sense
of 'Bathness'.**

**Kingsmead
Design principles**

1 Retention of historic routes
at more or less right angles
to the river allowing some
access and views to the
river corridor. Buildings run
parallel to the streets.

2 Axial composition with an
end node in an adjacent
tissue with views to the
river corridor closed
by trees.

3 Axial composition with node
and landmark combinations
at each end and trees at
points along the axis on
alternating sides.

4 Axial composition with
landmark building and tree
combinations at each end,
one including a node that
leads onto the park.

5 Landmark building, tree and
node combination on the
outside of a bend so visible
along two axes.

6 Double 'Y' shared nodal
space at the edge of the
tissue with good enclosure,
landmark building and tree.

7 Large green space opens
up toward river.

8 Green corridor along
the river.

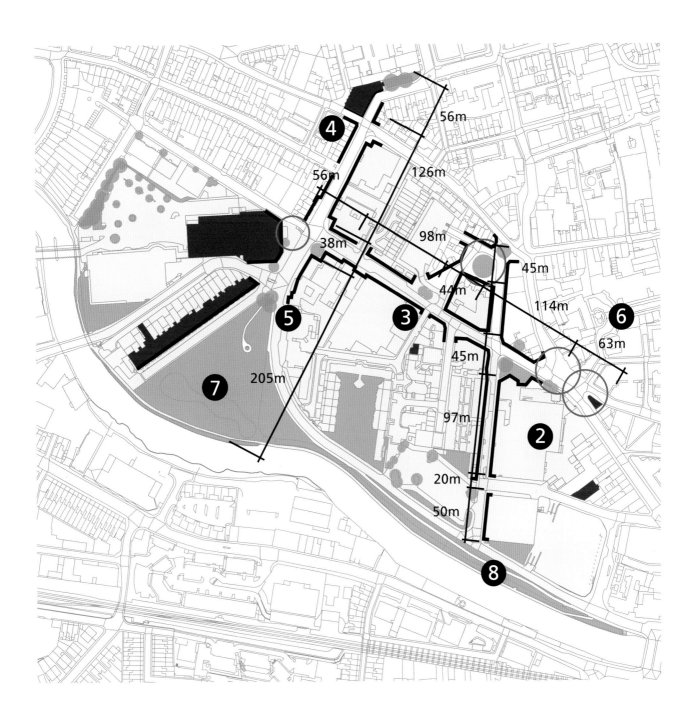

References

Possible forms: allometry, morphospace and combinatorics

1   George R McGhee, *Theoretical Morphology: The Concept and Its Applications*, Columbia University Press (New York), 1999. Print.

-   DM Raup and A Michelson, 'Theoretical Morphology of the Coiled Shell', *Science* 147 (1965): 1294–5. Print.

-   D'Arcy Wentworth Thompson, *On Growth and Form*, Cambridge University Press (Cambridge), 1917. Print.

2   Philip Steadman, *Architectural Morphology*, Pion (London), 1983. Print.

3   Leslie Martin and Lionel March, *Urban Space and Structures*, Cambridge University Press (Cambridge), 1975. Print.

-   See also Lionel March and Philip Steadman, *The Geometry of Environment*, RIBA Publications (London), 1971. Print.

4   Michael Batty, *The New Science of Cities*, MIT Press (Cambridge, MA), 2013. Print.

5   Elsa Arcaute et al, 'Constructing Cities, Deconstructing Scaling Laws', *Journal of The Royal Society Interface* 12.102 (2014): 20140745. Web.

6   Meta Berghauser Pont and Per Haupt, *Space, Density and Urban Form*, Technische Universiteit Delft, 2009. Web.

7   George R McGhee, *Theoretical Morphology*.

-   Philipp Mitteroecker and Simon M Huttegger, 'The Concept of Morphospaces in Evolutionary and Developmental Biology: Mathematics and Metaphors', *Biological Theory* 4.1 (2009): 54–67. Print.

-   Raup and Michelson, 'Theoretical Morphology', 1294–5. Print.

8   Philip Steadman, *Building Types and Built Forms*, Matador (Kibworth Beauchamp), 2014. Print.

9   Stephen Marshall, *Cities, Design and Evolution*, Routledge (London), 2008, pp 79–84. Print.

10 Philip Steadman, *Architectural Morphology*.

11 Stephen Marshall, *Cities, Design and Evolution*, pp 202–9.

Microclimate

12 Paul Osmond, 'An Enquiry into New Methodologies for Evaluating Sustainable Urban Form', unpublished PhD thesis, Faculty of the Built Environment, University of New South Wales, 2008. Print.

-   Paul Osmond, 'The Urban Structural Unit: Towards a Descriptive Framework to Support Urban Analysis and Planning', *Urban Morphology* 14.1 (2010): 5–20. Print.

Energy use

13 Philipp Rode, Christian Keim et al, *Cities and Energy: Urban Morphology and Heat Energy Demand*, LSE Cities, London School of Economics and European Institute for Energy Research (London and Karlsruhe), 2014. Web.

14 Philipp Rode, Christian Keim et al, *Cities and Energy*, pp 1–10.

15 Serge Salat, 'Energy Loads, CO_2 Emissions and Building Stocks: Morphologies, Typologies, Energy Systems and Behaviour', *Building Research and Information* 37/5–6 (2009): 598–609. Print.

16 Serge Salat, Françoise Labbé and Caroline Nowacki, *Cities and Forms: On Sustainable Urbanism*, Éditions Hermann (Paris), 2011. Print.

Acoustics

17 Yiying Hao, Jian Kang and Johannes D Krijnders, 'Integrated Effects of Urban Morphology on Birdsong Loudness and Visibility of Green Areas', *Landscape and Urban Planning* 137 (2013): 149–62. Print.

-   See also Jian Kang, 'On the Relationships between Urban Morphology, Noise Resistance and Soundscape', *Proceedings of the 40th Italian Annual Conference on Acoustics*, Euroregio, Merano, Italy, 2013. Print.

Historical significance and understanding: Urban Characterisation of Central Hereford

18 Nigel Baker, *A Characterisation of the Historic Townscape of Central Hereford*, Herefordshire Council (Hereford) and English Heritage, 2009. Print.

Social and cultural investigation: Ahmedabad

19 Marco Maretto and Nicola Scardigno, 'Muratorian Urban Morphology: The Walled City of Ahmedabad', *Urban Morphology* 20.1 (2016): 18–33. Print.

20 Jean Castex, Jean-Charles Depaule and Philippe Panerai, *Formes Urbaines: de L'îlot à la Barre*, Dunod (Paris), 1977. Print.

-   Jean Castex et al, *Urban Forms: The Death and Life of the Urban Block*, Architectural Press (Oxford), 2005. Print.

-   Marcel Roncayolo, *La Ville et ses Territoires*, Gallimard (Paris), 1997. Print.

21 Michael Conzen, *The Making of the American Landscape*, Unwin Hyman (Boston), 1990. Print.

-   Paul Erling Groth, *Living Downtown: The History of Residential Hotels in the United States*, University of California Press (Berkeley), 1994. Print.

-   John Brinckerhoff Jackson, *Discovering the Vernacular Landscape*, Yale University Press (New Haven, CT), 1984. Print.

Urban character and neighbourhoods: Brighton and Hove Urban Characterisation Study

22 Eline Hansen and Gill Thompson, *Brighton and Hove Urban Characterisation Study*, Brighton & Hove City Council (Brighton), 2009. Print.

23 Carys Swanwick and Land Use Consultants, *Landscape Character Assessment: Guidance for England and Scotland*, Countryside Agency and Scottish Natural Heritage (Cheltenham), 2002. Print.

Measures and qualitative evaluation: Morpho

24 Vítor Oliveira, 'Morpho: A Methodology for Assessing Urban Form', *Urban Morphology* 17.1 (2013): 21–33. Print.

-   Vítor Oliveira and Valério Medeiros, 'Morpho: Combining Morphological Measures', *Environment and Planning B: Planning and Design* (2015). Web. DOI: 10.1177/0265813515596529

25 Paul Osmond, 'An Enquiry into New Methodologies for Evaluating Sustainable Urban Form'.

-   Paul Osmond, 'The Urban Structural Unit', 5–20. Print.

Urban structure and development plans: the Anatomy of Sprawl

26 Brenda Case Scheer, 'The Anatomy of Sprawl', *Places* 14.2 (2001): 28–37. Print.

Route structure and development plans: North Northamptonshire Urban Structure Study

27 North Northamptonshire Joint Planning Unit, *Urban Structures Study*, North Northamptonshire Councils (Thrapston), 2015. Web.

Zoning plans and regulations: Rennes and Porto

28 Karl Kropf, 'Coding in the French Planning System: From Building Line to Morphological Zoning', *Urban Coding and Planning*, Stephen Marshall (ed), Routledge (London), 2011. Print.

- Karl Kropf, 'An Alternative Approach to Zoning in France', *European Planning Studies* 4.6 (1996): 127–40. Print.

29 Rennes: Plan Local d'Urbanisme
http://metropole.rennes.fr/politiques-publiques/transports-urbanisme-environnement/les-plans-locaux-d-urbanisme/consulter-le-plan-local-d-urbanisme-de-rennes/

30 Porto: Plano Diretor Municipal (PDM)
http://balcaovirtual.cm-porto.pt/PT/cidadaos/guiatematico/PlaneamentoOrdenamento/Plano%20Diretor%20Municipal%20(PDM)/PDM%20%E2%80%93%20Em%20vigor/Paginas/default.aspx

Tissue studies: appraisal, collaboration and education

31 N John Habraken, Henk Reyenga and Frans van der Werf, *The Methodical Formulation of Agreements in the Design of Urban Tissues*, Stichting Architecten Research (Eindhoven), 1973. Print.

- Richard Hayward, 'Talking Tissues', *Making Better Places*, Richard Hayward and Sue McGlynn (eds), Butterworth (Oxford), 1993. Print.

- Richard Hayward, 'The Use of Housing Tissues in Urban Design', *Urban Design Quarterly* 25 (1987): 4–6. Print.

- Stephen Kendall, 'Teaching with Tissues: Reflections and Observations', *Open House International* 9.4: 15–22. Print.

Masterplanning and regeneration: Villa 31, Buenos Aires

32 Marco Maretto, Anna Rita Amato and Gabriela Bandieri, *Morphological Analysis of the Informal City: The 'Villa 31' in Buenos Aires, Argentina*, Researches in Architecture and Urban Morphology (Parma), 2014. Web.

The built environment as a design resource

33 Anne Vernez Moudon, *Built for Change*, MIT Press (Cambridge, MA), 1986. Print.

34 Sergio Porta and Ombretta Romice, *Plot-Based Urbanism: Towards Time Consciousness in Place-Making*, Urban Design Studies Unit, University of Strathclyde, Department of Architecture (Glasgow), 2010. Web.

35 Jonathan Tarbatt, *The Plot: Designing Diversity in the Built Environment: A Manual for Architects and Urban Designers*, RIBA Publications (London), 2012. Print.

36 Karl Kropf, *The City of Bath Morphological Study*, Bath and North East Somerset Council (Bath), 2014. Web.

37 W Brian Arthur, *The Nature of Technology: What It Is and How It Evolves*, reprint edition, Free Press, 2011. Print.

38 Giancarlo Cataldi, *Saverio Muratori, Architetto (1910–1973): Il Pensiero e L'opera*, Alinea (Florence), 1984. Print.

- Gianfranco Caniggia and Gian Luigi Maffei, *Architectural Composition and Building Typology: Interpreting Basic Building*, Alinea (Florence), 2001. Print.

39 Kelvin Campbell, 'Make Massive Small Change', <http://www.massivesmall.com>, N.p., n.d. Web. Accessed 6 August 2016.

40 Christopher Alexander et al, *A Pattern Language: Towns, Buildings, Construction*, Oxford University Press (New York), 1977. Print.

Conclusion

A point made more or less in passing in the Introduction and Section 1 is that the built environment can be considered as a quasi-natural phenomenon. As a consequence, it was suggested the concepts and methods used to probe and investigate the built environment are not sensibly limited to those from only one or the other of the natural or cultural spheres. One could go further and reply that the distinction between the natural and the cultural is in any case misplaced. Humans are just one of many species that have emerged from an evolutionary process that we are beginning to see operates across a range of phenomena. One way or the other, the challenge is to select the concepts and methods that allow the common principles to show through and avoid naïve and overly specific analogies drawn from 'traditional' scientific disciplines on the one hand, and restrictive cultural paradigms on the other.

The further challenge presented by the normative impulse as discussed in the Introduction seems to reinforce the idea that we are dealing with something that defies containment in categories labelled natural or cultural. On the one hand, the normative impulse we cannot escape our human – animal – nature in the judgements and choices that we make about our own habitat. On the other hand, the results of those choices *in aggregate* are not like those of a singular intentional artefact such as a mural or a building. When we want to find out about the processes common to cities *in general*, we must necessarily take a comparative view of aggregate results.

As set out in the Introduction, the core concepts used in urban morphology in seeking to deal with these challenges are *process*, *type* and *hierarchy*, concepts also central to the now well-established principle of emergent behaviour and complex adaptive systems.[1] These concepts

are sufficiently abstract to avoid naïve analogies as are the general notions of *aspects of form* and *minimum elements*. At the same time, the specific definitions of the aspects of urban form and the specific definition of the minimum elements – surface, boundary and opening – pin down the particular phenomena of the built environment. As the principles of emergence, adaptive behaviour and evolution become both more generalised and articulated, we begin to move from analogy to the identification of different instances of the same principles.

But there are other respects in which the phenomena of the built environment seem to sit between the natural and the cultural. An emblematic case is the borrowing or importation of designs, building types and urban tissue from one cultural area to another. The channels through which such transfers occur are diverse, from colonial governments or immigrant populations to architectural journals. A central issue involved in importations is summed up by the half-joking advice given to undergraduate landscape architects, 'If you want to create a successful public square or piazza, import Italians'. The borrowing or importation is perhaps best seen as a *transplantation* – with all the associations that brings with it, such as 'systemic requirements'.

In this frame of mind we can ask, why do some types of built form such as the multi-storey, central service core apartment tower spread like weeds; some types persist beyond their apparent popularity such as suburban offices; and others seem to be nearing extinction such as courtyard housing? These are not just analogies but facts, facts that might be celebrated or lamented, but still facts.

However much physical built form is inert, it is only one aspect of the built environment. In other respects, *urban form* is living, as a viable habitat

– it lives so long as it successfully accommodates the lives of those who create it (or of those for whom it is created).

And the idea of urban form as 'living' can be as hard-headed as you choose. Urban form is part of a complex adaptive system. To be successful, forms must be adapted to meet existing needs and patterns of behaviour, fit into existing categories and expectations as well as ideals of urban life – and there are specific agents involved in specific processes that make the process work. As new needs, expectations and ideals arise, new forms will be created to meet them. If the processes also result in emergent phenomena, that does not mean that they adapt 'themselves' without specific mechanisms. So-called self-organisation is not a matter of metaphysics. All built form is made by people.

These reflections suggest that if there is going to be a 'science' of urban form, it is not going to look like traditional scientific disciplines. Nor will the 'histories' that come out of such investigations sit obviously in familiar genres of the cultural imaginary. And while we may have an inkling of where this might take us, it is not necessary, and perhaps even counterproductive, to have a fixed idea what 'it' should be. Rather, we need to work through the logic and implications of the existing framework of ideas and begin to fill in the spaces that are left empty. Some of those spaces have already become evident and, as suggested above, most involve more active *comparative study*.

Perhaps most pressing is the task of identifying and compiling common developmental regularities of urban form, in particular focusing on the internal transformations of urban tissue and the combinations of urban tissue in the process of polymorphogenetic accretion. The working hypothesis exemplified by the fringe belt concept is that there *are* common patterns and processes

across cultures but more needs to be done to test this hypothesis and put forward other specific patterns to be tested.

A related task is to elaborate and test the notions of *modularity* and *integration* – the interaction of cultural habits that results in the emergence, popularity and persistence of particular types of development. What are the mutually reinforcing habits and patterns of behaviour (integration) that lead to the reproduction and codification (modularity) of particular forms?

A further ongoing task is to look in more detail at the different approaches to urban morphology, in particular at their logic and specific focus, to understand if and how they fit together and might more actively complement one another. The rationale is simple enough: if the different approaches are investigating the same *thing* (urban form) and a multiple description provides more insight than a single viewpoint, we will benefit by understanding the specific relationships between the viewpoints.

Finally, having worked to slow down the normative impulse to get a clearer idea of the structure, formation and transformation of urban form, we need to explore the mechanisms for using the results so that they better serve our purposes when we let the impulse run.

References

1   See for example, Gregory Bateson, *Mind and Nature*, Bantam (New York), 1980; Douglas R Hofstadter, *Godel, Escher, Bach: An Eternal Golden Braid*, 20th anniversary edition, Penguin (London), 2000; Ilya Prigogine, *Order Out of Chaos: Man's New Dialogue with Nature*, Flamingo (London), 1993; Ian Stewart and Jack Cohen, *The Collapse of Chaos: Discovering Simplicity in a Complex World*, new edition, Penguin (London), 2000; Steven Johnson, *Emergence: The Connected Lives of Ants, Brains, Cities and Software*, new edition, Penguin (London), 2002.

Appendix: Sample Field Survey Record Sheet

[STUDY NAME]		[AREA/ELEMENT]		REFERENCE NO	SURVEYED BY:	DATE:
FIELD STUDY: SHEET 1		NAME:				

STREETS/SQUARES

PREDOMINANT TREE SPECIES	LIME		OAK		ASH		HORSE CHESTNUT		ORNAMENTAL FRUIT		OTHER
SURFACE MATERIALS	ASPHALT		CONCRETE			STONE			GRAVEL		OTHER
	PLAIN COLOURED TOP DRESSING		IN SITU SLAB PAVER SETT			SLAB PAVER SETT					

PLOTS

ACCESS	OPEN		ENCLOSED BUT ACCESSIBLE		TIME LIMITED ACCESS	ACTIVELY CONTROLLED		INACCESSIBLE		OTHER
FRONTAGE TREATMENT	BUILDING (NO SET-BACK)		WALL		FENCE	HEDGE/TREES		OPEN		OTHER
			BRICK STONE, ASHLAR DRY STONE		PICKET HIT AND MISS CLOSE BOARD METAL/WIRE CHAIN LINK	AGRICULTURAL/NATIVE ORNAMENTAL				
PLANTING TYPE	MIXED ORNAMENTAL		PARKLAND		TURFGRASS (PLAYING FIELDS)	URBAN FALLOW (MIXED ESCAPES AND NATIVES)		ARABLE		OTHER
PREDOMINANT TREE SPECIES	LIME		OAK		ASH	HORSE CHESTNUT		ORNAMENTAL FRUIT		OTHER

BUILDINGS

STOREY HEIGHT	1 STOREY		1 AND A HALF		2 STOREY		2 AND A HALF		3 STOREY		4 OR MORE
ORIENTATION OF ACCESS	FRONT			SIDE		REAR		ISOLATED		OTHER	
FACING MATERIALS	WALL		ROOF		OTHER						
	BRICK STONE TIMBER FRAME RENDER PROFILE METAL METAL/GLASS OTHER		TILE SLATE LEAD FELT/MEMBRANE CORRUGATED SHEET PROFILE METAL OTHER								
DETAILS/STYLE	VERNACULAR			AGRICULTURAL/INDUSTRIAL/SERVICE			HIGH STATUS/INSTITUTIONAL				
	MEDIEVAL/EARLY MODERN GEORGIAN VICTORIAN (GOTHIC, CLASSICAL) EARLY C20 MID-LATE C20 (HOUSE-BUILDER VERNACULAR)			MEDIEVAL/EARLY MODERN GEORGIAN VICTORIAN EARLY C20 MID-LATE C20			GOTHIC/TUDOR CLASSICAL VICTORIAN REVIVALS ARTS AND CRAFTS/HIGH STYLE VERNACULAR DECO MODERNIST				

ACTIVITIES

GENERAL	RESIDENTIAL		COMMERCIAL		INSTITUTIONAL		INDUSTRIAL	RECREATION/LEISURE		AGRICULTURAL		VACANT
			RETAIL OFFICE		PUBLIC PRIVATE		EXTRACTION PRODUCTION STORAGE UTILITY/SERVICE	ACTIVE/ORGANISED PASSIVE NATURAL		ARABLE PASTORAL HORTICULTURAL		
MOVEMENT	PEDESTRIAN		BICYCLE			MOTOR CAR/MOTOR CYCLE		GOODS VEHICLES		OTHER		
PARKING	ON STREET		INDIVIDUAL PLOT			GROUP, SMALL		GROUP, LARGE		OTHER		

[STUDY NAME]	[AREA/ELEMENT]		REFERENCE NO.	SURVEYED BY:	DATE:
FIELD STUDY: SHEET 2	NAME:				

VISUAL CHARACTER

LAND FORM		**PLANT COVER**		
PROMINENT	WITHIN THE FEATURE — LOCALLY — TOWN-WIDE	PROMINENT	WITHIN THE FEATURE — LOCALLY — TOWN-WIDE	
APPARENT		APPARENT		
INSIGNIFICANT		INSIGNIFICANT		

ACTIVITIES		**SPATIAL ENCLOSURE**		
PROMINENT	WITHIN THE FEATURE — LOCALLY — TOWN-WIDE	PROMINENT	INTIMATE — VAST	
APPARENT		APPARENT	HARD — SOFT	
INSIGNIFICANT		INSIGNIFICANT	CONTINUOUS — FRAGMENTED	

CROSSINGS/CENTRAL PLACES		**LANDMARKS**		
PROMINENT	WITHIN THE FEATURE — LOCALLY — TOWN-WIDE	PROMINENT	BUILDING/MONUMENT	WITHIN THE FEATURE — LOCALLY — TOWN-WIDE
APPARENT		APPARENT	NATURAL FEATURE	
INSIGNIFICANT		INSIGNIFICANT	ACTIVITY	

PATHS		**VIEWS**		
PROMINENT	WITHIN THE FEATURE — LOCALLY — TOWN-WIDE	PROMINENT	FILTERED	WITHIN THE FEATURE — LOCALLY — TOWN-WIDE
APPARENT		APPARENT	FRAMED	
INSIGNIFICANT		INSIGNIFICANT	OPEN	

EDGES			**NOTES**
PROMINENT	HARD — SOFT	WITHIN THE FEATURE — LOCALLY — TOWN-WIDE	
APPARENT	CONTINUOUS — FRAGMENTED		
INSIGNIFICANT			

CONDITION

ACTUAL ACTIVITIES	**CHANGE OF USE RELATIVE TO 'ORIGINAL INTENDED'**		EXTENT
	KIND		WIDESPREAD
			LOCALISED
			MINIMAL

PHYSICAL CHANGE		HIGHWAY	PLOT PATTERN	BOUNDARY	BUILDINGS	PLANTING
NOTES	EXTENT	MATERIALS	DIVIDED	ADDED	REPLACEMENT FEATURES	ADDITIONS
	WIDESPREAD				EXTENSIONS/	REMOVALS
		SIGNAGE	JOINED	REMOVED	ADDITIONS	REPLACEMENT
	LOCALISED				DEMOLITIONS	DISEASE-
	MINIMAL	FURNITURE	BACKLAND	REPLACED	REPLACEMENT	MANAGEMENT

CONTINUITY OF CHARACTER — SENSE OF CHARACTER OF AN AREA	**WITHIN AN AREA**	**AS PART OF SURROUNDINGS**
	INTACT — FRAGMENTED	INTACT — FRAGMENTED
CONNECTION — SENSE OF POSITION IN AND CONNECTION TO SETTLEMENT AS A WHOLE	**POSITION**	**CONNECTION**
	CENTRAL — PERIPHERAL	CONNECTED — ISOLATED

KEY FEATURES	

Further Reading

Typo-morphological approach

- Allain, Rémy, *Morphologie Urbaine. Géographie, Aménagement et Architecture de la Ville*, Armand Colin (Paris), 2004. Print.
- Aymonino, Carlo, et al, *La Città di Padova: Saggio Di Analisi Urbana*, Officina (Rome), 1970. Print.
- Caniggia, Gianfranco and Gian Luigi Maffei, *Architectural Composition and Building Typology: Interpreting Basic Buildings*, Alinea (Florence), 2001. Print.
- Castex, Jean, Patrick Céleste and Philippe Panerai, *Lecture d'une Ville: Versailles*, Éditions du Moniteur (Paris), 1980. Print.
- Castex, Jean et al, *Urban Forms: The Death and Life of the Urban Block*, Architectural Press (Oxford), 2005. Print.
- Cervellati, Pier Luigi, Roberto Scannavini and Carlo De Angelis, *La Nuova Cultura delle Città: La Salvaguardia dei Centri Storici, la Riappropriazione Sociale degli Organismi Urbani e l'Analisi dello Sviluppo Territoriale Nell'Esperienza di Bologna*, Edizioni scientifiche e tecniche Mondadori (Milan), 1977. Print.
- Chen, Fei and Kevin Thwaites, *Chinese Urban Design: The Typomorphological Approach*, Ashgate (Farnham), 2013. Print.
- Habraken, N John, *The Structure of the Ordinary*, MIT Press (Cambridge, MA), 1998. Print.
- Moudon, Anne Vernez, *Built for Change*, MIT Press (Cambridge, MA), 1986. Print.
- Muratori, Saverio, 'Studi per una Operante Storia Urbana di Venezia', *Palladio*, Istituto Poligrafico dello Stato (Rome), 1959. Print.
- Oliveira, Vítor, *Urban Morphology: An Introduction to the Study of the Physical Form of Cities*, Springer International Publishing (Cham), 2016. Print.
- Panerai, Philippe, Jean-Charles Depaule and Marcelle Demorgon, *Analyse Urbaine*, Éditions Parenthèses (Marseille), 1999. Print.
- Petruccioli, Attilio, *After Amnesia: Learning from the Islamic Mediterranean Urban Fabric*, Dipartimento di Ingegneria Civile e Architettura Politecnico di Bari (Bari), 2007. Print.
- Rossi, Aldo, *The Architecture of the City*, Diane Ghirardo and Joan Ockman (trs), MIT Press (Cambridge, MA), 1982. Print.
- Scheer, Brenda Case, *The Evolution of Urban Form: Typology for Planners and Architects*, American Planning Association (Chicago), 2010. Print.

Configurational approach

- Hillier, Bill, *Space Is the Machine*, Cambridge University Press (Cambridge), 1996. Print.
- Hillier, Bill and Julienne Hanson, *The Social Logic of Space*, Cambridge University Press (Cambridge), 1984. Print.
- March, Lionel and Philip Steadman, *The Geometry of Environment*, RIBA Publications (London), 1971. Print.
- Martin, Leslie and Lionel March, *Urban Space and Structures*, Cambridge University Press (Cambridge), 1975. Print.
- Marcus, L, 'Plot Syntax: A Configurational Approach to Urban Diversity', Proceedings of the 5th Space Syntax Symposium, Delft: N.p., 2005. Web.
- Ståhle, A, L Marcus, and A Karlström, 'Place Syntax: Geographic Accessibility with Axial Lines in GIS', Proceedings of the 5th Space Syntax Symposium, Delft: N.p., 2005. Web.
- Steadman, Philip, *Architectural Morphology*, Pion (London), 1983. Print.
- ———, *Building Types and Built Form*, Matador (Kibworth Beauchamp), 2014. Print.

Historico-geographical approach

- Aston, Michael and James Bond, *The Landscape of Towns*, Sutton Publishing (Gloucester), 1987. Print.

- Conzen, MRG, *Alnwick, Northumberland: A Study in Town Plan Analysis*, Institute of British Geographers (London), 1969. Print.
- ———, *Thinking About Urban Form: Papers on Urban Morphology, 1932–1998*, Michael Conzen (ed), Peter Lang (Oxford), 2004. Print.
- Larkham, Peter and Michael Conzen (eds), *Shapers of Urban Form: Explorations in Morphological Agency*, Routledge (London), 2014. Print.
- Larkham, PJ and JWR Whitehand (eds), *Urban Landscapes: International Perspectives*, Routledge (London; New York), 1992. Print.
- Sauer, Carl O, 'The Morphology of Landscape', *University of California Publications in Geography* 22 (1925): 19–53. Print.
- Schlüter, Otto, *Die Ziele der Geographie des Menschen*, Antrittsrede (Munich), 1906. Print.
- Slater, Terry, *The Built Form of Western Cities*, Leicester University Press (Leicester), 1990. Print.
- Vance, James E, *The Continuing City: Urban Morphology in Western Civilization*, Johns Hopkins University Press (Baltimore), 1990. Print.
- Whitehand, JWR, *The Changing Face of Cities: Study of Development Cycles and Urban Form*, Blackwell (Oxford), 1987. Print.

Spatial-analytical approach

- Batty, Michael, *Cities and Complexity: Understanding Cities with Cellular Automata, Agent-Based Models, and Fractals*, MIT Press (Cambridge, MA), 2007. Print.
- Christaller, Walter, *Central Places in Southern Germany*, Prentice Hall (New York), 1966. Print.
- Shevky, Eshref and Wendell Bell, *Social Area Analysis*, Stanford University Press (Palo Alto, CA), 1955. Print.
- Weber, Alfred, *Theory of the Location of Industries*, Carl J Friedrich (trs), University of Chicago Press (Chicago), 1909. Print.

- Wilson, Alan, *Entropy in Urban and Regional Modelling*, Pion (London), 1970. Print.
- ———, *The Science of Cities and Regions*, Springer Netherlands (Dordrecht), 2012. Print.

City image, townscape and patterns

- Alexander, Christopher, Sara Ishikawa, and Murray Silverstein, *A Pattern Language*, Oxford University Press (New York), 1977. Print.
- Cullen, Gordon, *Townscape*, Architectural Press (Oxford), 1961. Print.
- Lynch, Kevin, *The Image of the City*, MIT Press (Cambridge, MA), 1960. Print.
- McHarg, Ian L, *Design with Nature*, Doubleday/Natural History Press (Garden City, NY), 1969. Print.

Urban Ecology

- Adolphe, L, 'A Simplified Model of Urban Morphology: Application to an Analysis of the Environmental Performance of Cities', *Environment and Planning B: Planning and Design* 28, 183–200, 2001.
- Alberti, Marina, *Advances in Urban Ecology: Integrating Humans and Ecological Processes in Urban Ecosystems*, Springer Science & Business Media (Berlin), 2007. Print.
- Breuste, Jürgen, Hildegard Feldmann and Ogarit Uhlmann (eds), *Urban Ecology*, Springer Berlin Heidelberg (Berlin, Heidelberg), 1998. Print.
- Marcus, Lars and Johan Colding, 'Toward an Integrated Theory of Spatial Morphology and Resilient Urban Systems', *Ecology and Society* 19.4 (2014).
- Pauleit, S and F Duhme, 'Assessing the Metabolism of Urban Systems for Urban Planning', *Urban Ecology*, Jürgen Breuste, Hildegard Feldmann and Ogarit Uhlmann (eds), Springer Berlin Heidelberg (Berlin, Heidelberg), 1998. Print.

Illustration Credits

Fig. 0.5: public domain; **Fig. 0.6:** Reproduced under Creative Commons License Attribution 2.0 Generic (CC BY 2.0) from the Urban Redevelopment Division, Boston Housing Authority photographs in Boston Redevelopment Authority photographs, Collection 4010.001, City of Boston Archives, Boston; **Fig. 0.8:** Reproduced under Creative Commons Attribution-ShareAlike 3.0 Unported from Marc Planard http://creativecommons.org/licenses/by-sa/3.0.

Figs. 6.4 through 6.7: © Karl Kropf, all rights reserved, contours based on Terrain 50 data Ordnance Survey, Crown copyright 2013; **Fig. 6.9:** Historic maps courtesy of the Bath Record Office; **Fig. 6.11:** Historic maps courtesy of the Bath Record Office, overlay mapping Ordnance Survey, Crown copyright; **Figs. 6.12 and 6.13:** © Karl Kropf, all rights reserved, base mapping Ordnance Survey, Crown copyright and database rights, OS (licence number 100035655); **Figs. 6.15 and 6.16:** Land parcel information is subject to Crown copyright and is reproduced with the permission of Land Registry, mapping, Crown copyright and database rights, 2016, Ordnance Survey 100026316; **Fig. 6.18:** ©®Rennes Métropole (données PLU), 20/11/2014 http://metropole.rennes.fr/politiques-publiques/transports-urbanisme-amenagement/les-plans-locaux-d-urbanisme/consulter-le-plan-local-d-urbanisme-de-rennes/; **Figs. 6.23 through 6.25**: © Karl Kropf, all rights reserved, based on Ordnance Survey Meridian 2 data, Crown copyright and database rights 2010; **Figs. 6.29 through 6.36:** © Karl Kropf, all rights reserved, base mapping Ordnance Survey, Crown copyright and database rights, OS (licence number 100035655); **Fig. 6.40a**: © Karl Kropf, all rights reserved, base mapping Ordnance Survey, Crown copyright and database rights, 2016, OS (licence number 100035655); **Fig. 6.40d:** Image based on a research project supported by the Scientific and Technological Research Council, Scientific and Technological Research Projects Funding Program under award number 113K131; **Fig.**

6.41: © Karl Kropf, all rights reserved, base mapping Ordnance Survey, Crown copyright and database rights, OS (licence number 100035655); **Fig. 6.42:** N. Baker, Herefordshire Archaeology Report No. 266, Herefordshire Council 2010, base mapping Ordnance Survey, Crown copyright; **Fig. 6.43:** © Karl Kropf, all rights reserved, base mapping Ordnance Survey, Crown copyright and database rights, OS (licence number 100035655).

Fig. 7.2a: © Karl Kropf, all rights reserved, base mapping Ordnance Survey, Crown copyright and database rights, OS (licence number 100035655); **Figs. 7.5 through 7.7**: Reproduced by kind permission of Benjamin N. Vis, Leeds University, and Scott Hutson of the Pakbeh Regional Economy Program; boundary line type analysis by Benjamin N. Vis; base maps of Chunchucmil prepared by Scott Hutson as part of the Pakbeh Regional Ecology Program, directed by Bruce Dahlin; **Figs. 7.8 and 7.9:** © Karl Kropf, all rights reserved, base mapping Ordnance Survey, Crown copyright and database rights, OS (licence number 100035655); **Fig. 7.10**: Courtesy of Dr. Jon Cooper, Oxford Brookes University; **Fig. 7.11:** Courtesy of Dr. Jon Cooper, Oxford Brookes University and Su Mei-Lin.

Fig. 8.4: © Karl Kropf, all rights reserved, base mapping Ordnance Survey, Crown copyright and database rights, OS (licence number 100035655); **Fig. 8.5:** Reproduced by kind permission of Karin Schwabe Meneguetti, as first published in *Urban Morphology* 19, no. 1; **Fig. 8.6:** © Karl Kropf, all rights reserved, base mapping Ordnance Survey, Crown copyright and database rights, OS (licence number 100035655); **Fig. 8.9:** Provided courtesy of Yones Changalvaiee; **Fig. 8.14:** © Karl Kropf, all rights reserved, base mapping Ordnance Survey, Crown copyright and database rights, OS (licence number 100035655).

Fig. 9.6: Reproduced by kind permission of Paul Osmond, Faculty of Built Environment, University of New South Wales, Australia; **Fig. 9.7 and Table 9.1:** From Rode, Keim et al, *Cities and Energy*; **Fig. 9.8:** Building level accessibility metrics produced by Pete Ferguson using

igraph package for R v1.0.1 (GPU license), based on Ordnance Survey Mastermap Topography and ITN data, Crown copyright Ordnance Survey 2015; **Fig. 9.9:** N. Baker, Herefordshire Archaeology Report No. 266, Herefordshire Council 2010, base mapping Ordnance Survey, Crown copyright; **Fig. 9.10:** Courtesy of Marco Maretto, R.A.M.-Researches in Architecture and Urban Morphology (www.r-a-m.it); **Figs. 9.11 through 9.13:** From the Brighton and Hove Urban Characterisation Study produced by Gill Thompson and Eline Hansen for Brighton and Hove City Council; **Figs. 9.14 and 9.15**: Drawings by Vitor Oliveira, Teresa Heitor and Joao Pinelo, reproduced by kind permission; **Figs. 9.16 through 9.19:** By kind permission of Brenda Case Scheer; **Fig. 9.20:** By kind permission of the North Northamptonshire Joint Planning Unit; **Figs. 9.21 and 9.22:** ©®Rennes Métropole (données PLU), 20/11/2014 http://metropole.rennes.fr/politiques-publiques/transports-urbanisme-amenagement/les-plans-locaux-d-urbanisme/consulter-le-plan-local-d-urbanisme-de-rennes/; **Figs. 9.23 and 9.24:** Courtesy of Plano Diretor Municipal, Câmara Municipal do Porto Praça General Humberto Delgado 4049-001 Porto http://sigweb.cm-porto.pt/mipwebportal/; **Figs. 9.26 through 9.28:** Courtesy of Marco Maretto, R.A.M.-Researches in Architecture and Urban Morphology (www.r-a-m.it); **Fig. 9.29:** Photograph by Taz, reproduced under the Creative Commons Attribution 2.0 Generic (CC BY 2.0) https://creativecommons.org/licenses/by/2.0/; **Figs. 9.30 and 9.31:** © Karl Kropf, all rights reserved, base mapping Ordnance Survey, Crown copyright and database rights, OS (licence number 100035655).

Index